URBAN DEVELOPMENT DEBATES IN THE NEW MILLENNIUM

Studies in Revisited Theories and Redefined Praxes

Volume – I

Edited by

K.R. GUPTA

With an Introduction by

PRASENJIT MAITI

ATLANTIC

PUBLISHERS & DISTRIBUTORS

Published by
ATLANTIC PUBLISHERS AND DISTRIBUTORS
B-2, Vishal Enclave, Opp. Rajouri Garden, New Delhi-110027
Phones : 25413460, 25429987, 25466842

Sales Office
7/22, Ansari Road, Darya Ganj, New Delhi-110002
Phones : 23273880, 23275880, 23280451
Fax : 91-11-23285873
web : www.atlanticbooks.com
e-mail : info@atlanticbooks.com

ISBN 81-269-0389-9 (Vol. I)
ISBN 81-269-0392-9 (Set)

Printed in India at
Nice Printing Press, Delhi

Preface

The multi-volume book *Urban Development Debates in the New Millennium* includes papers on urban development issues and concerns by leading academicians and by practitioners from all over the world. The focus is on theories and practices for the attainment of sustainable urban development. Experiences of a large number of countries have been collected at one place and, consequently, the book covers a wide spectrum of issues relating to basic urban amenities such as water supply and sanitation services, solid waste management, sewerage and drainage, domestic electricity connections, transport and telecommunication networks, access to primary healthcare and basic literacy resources, common property resources, law and order maintenance, markets, means of livelihood, housing facilities etc.

I will feel amply rewarded if these Volumes provoke fresh debates and generate new ideas about sustainable urban development with minimum social tensions.

The book would be found highly useful by town planners, municipal administrators, NGOs working in the field of urban development and common readers interested in urban problems and policies. It will be equally valuable for policy makers as well as students, researchers and teachers of urban economics, urban sociology, urban geography and public administration.

I thank all the contributors to these Volumes for their refreshingly original and insightful papers.

My sincere thanks are also due to Dr. Prasenjit Maiti for helping me in the preparing these Volumes.

K.R. GUPTA

Contents

Urban Development Debates in the New Millennium: An Introduction

PRASENJIT MAITI
pmaiti@vsnl.com
Member, Resettlement Plan Implementation Working Group,
Kolkata Environmental Improvement Project.

> An initial social assessment is required for every development project in order to identify the people who may be beneficially and adversely affected by the project. It should assess the stage of development of various subgroups and their needs, demands and absorptive capacity. It should also identify the institutions to be involved in the project and assess their capacities. The ISA should identify the key social dimensional aspects (such as involuntary resettlement, indigenous peoples, poverty reduction and women in development) that need to be addressed under the project.[1]

This collection of essays by academics and practitioners from around the world underscores issues and concerns of sustainable urban development[2] and best practices in terms of theory as well as praxes. Contributors have made an attempt to critically reconcile the hypothetical with the applied in order to arrive at innovative solutions for urban good governance in the context of steady proliferation of habitats and conurbations worldwide. Their papers more often than not transcend regional specifics to address the common agenda of urban development debates as informed by assorted modernization perspectives in the 21st century.

When this volume was planned [December 2003] in consultation with the editor/publisher it was decided that our call for papers would be flexible enough to accommodate social scientists, urban planners, development consultants, non-profit professionals as well as regulatory policymakers so that theories [old and new] and multicultural praxes might be reflected in a uniform manner in their papers based on empirical research and field-level insights. This subsequently entailed a difficult academic exercise on our part when an incipient—but problematic—rationale began to emerge from different context-bound voices and situation-specific experiences.

This was, however, anticipated because the narratives of development theory often tend to ramble along with the deterministic chaos of praxes that ordinarily precede any agenda of proposed physical work/engineering designs based on the norms of participatory development.[3] Collective choice theory plays an important role at this juncture: so does neoinstitutional theory that explores the dynamics of equations between actors [primary stakeholders/project affected persons] and their institutions.

Any agenda of urban development—whether approved or not by secondary stakeholders—is necessarily defined by the praxes of choice on the part of beneficiaries on the one hand and the regime of theoretical discourse [that is in reality an exercise in choice among options] as maneuvered or manipulated by donor and funding agencies, NGOs, CSOs, local-level advocacy and/or activist groups and different tiers of government down to the level of the municipal administration.[4]

Such a structure of decision-making based on feedback networks decides the politics of development from above while sociability at the grass-roots—so far as the popular understanding and acceptance of the developmental philosophy and welfarist vision of urban development projects are concerned—generally emerges at a subsequent stage of the project cycle as a manufactured [following Noam Chomsky] version of consent appropriated in terms of political correctitude.

This is especially true in the developing/underdeveloped South where postcolonial LDCs are often inconvenienced by inadequate levels of regime-building and depleted stocks of social capital.[5] Major urban development projects in such a context may run the risk of disjointed planning and uneven implementation due to lack of updated theoretical knowledge, imperfect participatory monitoring and evaluation of the progress of physical work [on the part of primary as well as secondary stakeholders] and incorrect collective choice exercises that do not serve utilitarian purposes. Innovative institutional mechanisms may be designed to resolve such problems: water user groups, public-private participation, core committees/representative groups and grievance redress cells at the community-level are examples of mechanisms widely utilized by practitioners in order to tackle angularities that arise from a hiatus between theory and praxes.[6]

LDCs may be typecast by political systems where logic and rhetoric are yet to reconcile skewed issues of human development because the level playing field required for such diverse exercises [plus their implications] is not readily available. The stakeholder versus beneficiary debate assumes new meanings so far as the objectives of urban development debates are concerned. One such priority area of most urban good governance/best practices programmes is to downsize superfluous bureaucracy so that non-merit expenditures ["free rider costs"] are reduced and service delivery mechanisms made efficacious. Compulsions of the politics of everyday life, however, may inform radically different public policy choices. See Table 1 in this connection.

TABLE 1: Social Impact Assessment Variables[7]

PROJECT/POLICY STAGE				
Project/Policy Setting	Planning/Policy Development	Construction/ Implementation	Operation & Maintenance	Equity of minority groups
Project affected persons	Perceptions of risk, health and safety	Influx of temporary workers	Trust in political and social institutions	Alteration in size of local government
Distribution of power/ authority	Formation of attitudes towards the project	Change in community infrastructure	Change in income characteristics	Change in employment

This entails that human entitlements with regard to basic urban amenities such as water supply and sanitation services, solid waste management, sewerage and drainage, domestic electricity connections, transport and telecommunication networks, access to primary healthcare and basic literacy resources, common property resources, law and order maintenance, markets, sources of livelihood, housing facilities and conservation of nature—as informed by the exercise of choice—should be facilitated by urban development policies so that capacities of primary stakeholders are built in the process.[8]

Urban development strategies more often than not emerge from conflict resolution and collective choice dynamics *i.e.*, there is generally a method that underpins dislocations and conflicts that attend the inception phases of developmental projects in metropolitan cities. This is to be ordinarily expected, however, as cities generally share complex histories, cultural baggages and collective memories that are multiple and not always amenable to unilinear project interventions. Development is not extrinsic like politics imposed from the above to impact on end-users of limited resources. Actors who will interface with their own ground-level institutional arrangements/mechanisms during the project cycle/interventions should be catalyzed to facilitate social capital that coheres organic ethos of community existence.

Deriving lessons from project interventions is imperative. Urban development is often made complicated by political overtones and culture root paradigms that may not work in tandem with the project's rationale and objectives/outputs. This necessitates reassessing community-level needs and perceptions in order to minimize dislocations with regard to implementation of physical work, poverty alleviation programmes and awareness-generation activities.

It necessarily follows, therefore, that Stakeholders Consultation Process has steadily emerged as the mantra of the new millennium so far as urban development strategies are concerned. SCP is development of the community, for the community and [if practicable] by the community that involves primary stakeholders in [1] needs assessment exercises, [2] resource and benefit mapping, [3] planning for community-level needs and [4] Participatory Monitoring & Evaluation of progress of physical work to expand networks of social capital at the community-level.[9]

SCP relates to crisis management [tactical] and sustainable development [strategic] approaches utilizing different time-frames and priorities for the purpose of resource and benefit mapping underpinned by "an authoritative allocation of values" *i.e.* who gets what, when, how, where and why.

Participation is an interactive process whereby primary stakeholders take part in the decision-making process either in a direct manner or via CBOs/NGOs. Community development events and awareness-generation campaigns are generally strategized to streamline project-related interventions and facilitate dialogues between primary and secondary stakeholders. Such programmes serve to build empathy at the community-level and facilitate dialogic rather than pedagogic terms of discourse at the project implementation, monitoring and evaluation levels. Community mobilization and participation activities are not an end but a means to secure rapport-building that may ensure acceptance of development interventions on the part of project affected persons.

Primary stakeholders may be suitably empowered to sustain developmental impacts of the project *i.e.* their entitlements should be converted into capacities [following Amartya Sen]. This will ensure that project interventions and their benefits sustain over a considerable period of time and motivate future development and further popular initiatives at the grassroots level where communities have been made capable to make critical decisions affecting the quality of their everyday life. Axes of civic participation and/or preparedness should be identified in order to plan NGO/CBO/CSO interventions in consultation with local-level resource persons and/or key informants. Interventions should be scientifically implemented and underpinned by a definitive plan of action. This is despite the fact that development generally emerges out of flux and can seldom be planned in a rigid manner. Field-level lessons [and insights], therefore, should be utilized to coordinate between theory and praxes.

NOTES

1. "The ISA should be undertaken as early as possible in the project cycle and preferably by the time of fact-finding for a project preparation

technical assistance." <http://www.adb.org/Documents/Policies/Involuntary_Resettlement/reset400.asp>

2. "Sustainable development is defined as a pattern of social and structured economic transformations [*i.e.* development], which optimizes the economic and societal benefits available in the present, without jeopardizing the likely potential for similar benefits in the future. A primary goal of sustainable development is to achieve a reasonable and equitably distributed level of economic well-being that can be perpetuated continually for many human generations." <http://sdnp.delhi.nic.in/>
3. "Participation of the stakeholders create conditions for consensus and potential conflict resolution; people's participation not only make programmes and policies more acceptable, they make them cost-effective and enhance ownership; and the stakeholders, once brought into a participatory mode, undertake significant follow-up activities on their own accord and enhance social mobilization. These are key contributions to sustainable development." <http://www.ecouncil.ac.cr/rio/national/reports/asia/bangladesh/ban4.htm>
4. No development project can result in complete alienation of the rights, customary and legal, of people through payment of a one-time compensation or facilitated relocation. On the contrary, the process must result in the creation of new rights that will render people direct beneficiaries of the development project. <http://www.eldis.org/static/DOC7649.htm>
5. "Social capital refers to the institutions, relationships, and norms that shape the quality and quantity of a society's social interactions. Increasing evidence shows that social cohesion is critical for societies to prosper economically and for development to be sustainable. Social capital is not just the sum of the institutions, which underpin a society—it is the glue that holds them together." <http://www.worldbank.org/poverty/scapital/whatsc.htm>
6. Development tends to pose an occasional problem for LDCs—state nations that are yet to cohere [in most cases] stable political systems underpinned by norms of good governance, transparency and public accountability.
7. See Guidelines and Principles for Social Impact Assessment prepared by the Interorganizational Committee [United States Department of Commerce, National Oceanic and Atmospheric Administration & National Marine Fisheries Service] May 1994 in this regard. <http://www.nmfs.noaa.gov/sfa/social_impact_guide.htm>
8. "The contemporary view of capacity-building goes beyond the conventional perception of training. The central concerns of environmental management—to manage change, to resolve conflict, to manage institutional pluralism, to enhance coordination, to foster communication, and to ensure that data and information are shared—require a broad and holistic view of capacity development. This

definition covers both institutional and community-based capacity-building." <http://nrm.massey.ac.nz/changelinks/capacity. html>

9. See Prasenjit Maiti, "Silenced Rivers", in this connection. Trust indicates a system of values; a system of values implies social mores; and social mores are themselves an important institution. So trust can, and often does, lead to the sustenance of institutions. [This article was written in *Seminar* (2001) on the landmark grass-roots resistance movement of indigenous peoples—*Narmada Bachao Andolan* (Save the River Narmada Movement)—in Western India.] <http://www.india-seminar.com/2001/498/498%20comment.htm>

1

Municipal Administration in India: Retrospect and Prospect

M.R. BIJU
mrbijueditor@yahoo.com
Editor, *South Asian Journal of Socio-Political Studies* and Faculty Member,
Post Graduate & Research Department of Political Science,
Sree Narayana College, University of Kerala, India.

According to the 1991 census, out of the country's total population of nearly 84.5 crores, slightly less than 22 crores people dwell in urban areas. This means that India is getting urbanized very rapidly. In 1901 merely 11 per cent of India's population was living in urban areas. The 1941 census, the first of its kind in the country made an alarming disclosure that the country was in for massive urbanization in years immediately ahead. In 1951, more than 17 per cent of the population was found living in the cities and towns. The 1991 census further reveals that more than 25 per cent of the population was urban. The census reports also disclose that there are 23 cities with more than one million people and 300 cities with population over 1,00,000. Rapid urbanization is not a feature of India alone. But it is the case of almost all developing countries. Latin American countries have as much as 40 per cent of the population living in urban areas. The following tables illustrate the rural and urban scenario in an in-depth manner.

TABLE 1: Rural and Urban Population in India

Year	1901	1911	1921	1931	1941	1951	1961	1971	1981	1991
Urban	11	10.40	11.2	12	13.9	17.3	18	19.9	23.24	25.72
Rural	89	89.60	88.8	88	86.1	82.7	82	80.1	76.27	74.28

TABLE 2: Forms of Urban Government

	In 1968	In 1971	In 1987	In 1990
Municipal	30	34	73	73
Municipal Councils	1473	1493	1745	1770
Notified Area Committees	115	202	—	717
Town area Committees	385	385	—	229
Cantonment Boards	59	58	62	62

Professor S.R. Maheswari (1997) has rightly pointed out four major trends in the urbanization of India. According to him, the rapid pace of urbanization in India is the most striking feature of the population scenario in India. The urban trend would became clearly marked in the seventies and it was expected that this trend would become more conspicuous in the coming years because of the conspicuous emphasis laid on industrialization during the Fifth, Sixth and Seventh Five-year Plans. This did not happen in the period 1981-91. What is conveyed is that the tempo of urbanization since 1981 has somewhat slowed down. Yet another trend in urbanization is the accelerated growth of population in cities especially in mega cities. India at present is witnessing more of metropolisation than urbanization. Another remarkable feature of urban development as disclosed by the 1991 census was that as much as one-third of the new towns are the constituent towns of the latter. Largest cities have seen the emergence of outgrowths around them and these outgrowths are mostly inhabitant by people who daily commute to the core cities for livelihood.

HISTORICAL SETTING: DEVELOPMENT OF MUNICIPAL GOVERNMENT IN INDIA

The first statutory enactment relating to municipal administration in India is section 158 of the Charter Act, 1793, which established Municipal Corporation in the three presidency towns. This enactment authorized the appointment of Justices of Peace and to levy and collect taxes on houses and lands for the provision of sanitary services. During 1793 to 1842 no attempt was made to establish municipal boards in the district towns.

Although there were no statutory municipal bodies, there were voluntary associations in all the provinces. In the Punjab, the Board of Administrators established the *Chowkidari* Police System in all towns and villages in 1840. In Madras also there were voluntary associations for the purpose of local improvement. In Bengal the experiment was tried at Jessore. It was a successful one and later the same was extended to Assam. In Assam, there were voluntary associations in several places.

But attempts were made for the introduction of statutory municipal boards. The first small beginnings of municipal action in the province is to be found in the introduction of Act 26 of 1850. The Act of 1850 determined the composition, powers and functions of the municipal boards. It would consist of the Magistrate and such number of commissioners as were necessary. It would be autonomous and the government would exercise limited control over it. The Act permitted the levy of town duties but it was left to the people themselves to decide, in every instance, which mode of taxation they would prefer.

The provincial government circulated the Act among the district officers with a request whether it could be introduced in their districts. At the same time the district officers were warned to be very careful to inform themselves accurately of the real sentiments of the people in respect of the proposed measure and should the general feelings be in its favour, would explain whether it was the wish of the inhabitants that the Act should be brought into force in their town for all purposes specified in the Act or shall be applicable in part only and in the later case to which objects it should be restricted.

Most of the district officers reported that the people of the towns were against the introduction of the Act. When it was introduced in some towns there were disturbances and military had to be called for to maintain law and order.

The major reasons for the failure of the Municipal Act of 1850 were—firstly, the dislike of the people to be ruled or interfered with by those of their own body who were not in the employ of the government. Secondly, there was notorious suspicion and apathy of the people in regard to everything like improvements suggested for the promotion of common welfare; the absence of public spirit and mutual sympathy; the universal practice of looking up to the government for all amendments in their condition. Third, sufficient provision was not made in the Act to enable the Executive officer to act with vigor. Fourth, the board was authorized to determine the persons and property to be taxed and the mode and the amount of taxation to be levied. Finally, the board was also authorized to make regulation relating to conservancy. As a consequence, the Act worked according to local conditions.

The government was convinced that as long as the introduction of the Act of 1850 depended upon the general consent of the people, all attempts for the provision of municipal services would meet with failure. Therefore, the provincial governments recommended in 1855, that the Act should be amended and its voluntary basis should be abrogated. The Town Improvement Act, 1865, was enacted.

The Town Improvement Bill 1864 contemplated compulsory taxation to defray the cost of police administration, while taxation for other services would be voluntary. The Select Committee on the Bill, however, decided that taxation should be compulsory for all municipal services. Provision was, therefore, made in the Act for compulsory taxation not only for place but also for other services. The Act also contemplated the payment of a grant of 25 per cent of municipal expenditure to the municipal boards. The intention in making the grant was to indicate to the municipal councils that the government was not shifting the entire expenditure on police to the municipal councils.

The Resolution of 1864

In the meanwhile the Government of India issued its Resolution on the Administration of Police and incidentally on municipal government. The main principles laid down by the Resolution were that the cost of police, maintained expressly for the service of any city or town should, as far as practicable, be defrayed by its inhabitants; that the inhabitants should raise funds required for this and other municipal purposes; that this transfer of charge of the municipal police from Imperial to local funds should take place as soon as possible. The

Government of India also pointed out that inequality between the taxation of the rural and town population did not exist under the previous native governments.

Lord Mayo's Reforms

In the meanwhile, the financial position of the Government of India deteriorated. Prior to 1833, all the provincial governments were separated clocks with separate mainsprings, working according to their lights. In that year, the superintendence, direction and control of the whole of the civil and military government of all territories and their revenues were vested in the Government of India. An imperial system of government was inevitably followed by an imperial system of finance. Except in the cases of cess levied principally for local purposes, the provincial governments were absolutely dependent on the central government for everything. Such a system of financial arrangement produced disastrous consequences. First, the provincial governments were not responsible for augmenting their revenues. On the expenditure side, the Government of India miserably failed to control the provincial governments because, it was at a distance and, therefore, lacked knowledge of local circumstances and of local needs, which were essential for the successful control of provincial finance. But the existence of a common purse with an unknown depth encouraged the provincial governments to secure for themselves the largest possible share of general funds. In these circumstances, deficits, in the imperial budget were inevitable. Between the years 1834 to 1860 as many as ten years had deficit budgets. It was also the case during the period 1860 to 1870.

Apart from financial chaos, there was only administrative chaos. In 1870, there were various and confusing systems of municipal government with several independent statutes. To consolidate the old laws, a bill was introduced in 1871. But it was vetoed by the Governor-General in Council on the ground, that the measure would increase municipal taxation, which was unnecessary and inexpedient, and that it made the expenditure on education obligatory.

In 1876 another Act consolidating the existing municipal law was passed and it was adopted by some provinces. Under this Act, the urban local authorities were divided into four, the first and second grade municipal board, unions and stations.

Lord Ripon's Reforms

In 1881, the Government of India issued a Resolution containing the principles for the revision of the Agreement, then in force, for the administration of the provincial services and to establish the decentralized system of finance on uniform basis. It was then explained that intimately connected with the decentralization of finance was the development of local self-government. Although considerable progress was made in regard to the development of local self-government institutions, services which were admirably suited for local self-government institutions, services which were imposed on the inhabitants of the town for the maintenance of police over which they had no control.

In 1882, the Government of India issued another Resolution on the same subject, which gave an important position to Lord Ripon in the history of local self-government. Lord Ripon is deservedly known as the Father of Modern Local Self-Government in India. To him, goes the credit for giving more prominence to the idea of more local taxes for the services, which was the dominant feature in the preceding years. The keynote of the resolution is that local self-government should be made an instrument of political and popular education even at the risk of a temporary period of administrative inefficiency. He, therefore, laid down certain principles. Firstly, the provincial government should maintain and extend in every district, where intelligent and non-official agency could be found, a network of local authorities, charged with definite duties and entrusted with definite funds. Secondly, the jurisdiction of the local bodies should be so limited in areas so as to secure both local knowledge and local interest on the part of each member. Thirdly, the Chief executive officer of the district or of the division should not be the chairman of the local authority. Fourthly, non-officials should act, wherever possible as Chairman of the local authorities and the non-officials Chairman should be elected as far as possible.

The result of Ripon Resolution was the enactment of Municipal Act by the various provincial Legislatures. The Madras

District Municipalities Act and the Bengal Municipal Act were enacted in 1884. But the Acts did not embody all the principles enunciated by Ripon. The Preamble to the Acts made reference to self-government but it is said that the Act was brought into existence to make better provision for the organization and administrator of the district municipalities in the province, and to promote public health, comfort and convenience of the inhabitants of the municipal areas.

Decentralization Commission

The next landmark in the history of municipal administration is the publication of the report on the Royal Commission on Decentralization. The most important of its were firstly, the relaxation of governmental control over the local authorities in regard to the preparation and approval of budgets, control over the local authorities, and the delegation of functions to committees. Further, the finances of the local authorities should be based on sound foundations.

The other recommendations of the Commission were, first, outside the presidency towns, there should be three different forms of municipal government. Larger cities with one lakh population should have a special form of government with a full-time paid executive officer, towns of moderate size should have the ordinary forms of government and the semi-urban areas, a town panchayat.

Secondly, the government accepted the recommendation of the Commission that the municipal boards should be relieved of their financial responsibilities in connection with the maintenance of police, famine and such other services.

Thirdly, the Commission recommended that the municipal boards should control the services which they maintain from their own resources. If the government desired to control any service, it should be provincialised.

Fourthly, the government did not accept the recommendation of the Commission that the municipal board should be relieved of the veterinary charges on the ground that the veterinary assistants were employed solely for municipal works.

Resolution of 1914

In 1914, the position was that besides municipal corporations, there were different types of municipal authorities, municipal boards, stations, town committees and unions throughout the country.

A new approach to municipal government was imperative. Therefore, the Government of India issued a resolution in 1914, suggesting certain reforms. Firstly, small towns should be governed by a separate statute. The Chairman and the Vice-Chairman of the town committees should, in the first instance, be appointed but provision should be made for election of the Chairman, the Vice-Chairman and the members of the committees.

Second, Municipal Acts laid down certain conditions for the formation of municipal boards, namely that the total population of the area should not be less than 5000 and the density of population should not be less than 1000 per sq mile, and that three-fourths of the adult population should be non-agriculturists.

Third, the Resolution said, ordinarily the Chairman should be elected and he should be a non-official. A substantial number of members should be elected.

If local conditions warrant, the government should have the power to nominate the Chairman, and certain number of members.

Fourth, provision should be made for penalizing corrupt practices at elections.

Fifth, persons who were deeply indebted should not be the Chairman or the Vice-Chairman or Secretary of the board.

Sixth, gratuity or pension would be paid to the families of the municipal employees who die while in service.

Seventh, legal practitioners who were also members of the board should not be permitted to appear against the board, because as members of the board they might obtain valuable information and use it against the board.

Thus, the resolution of 1914, which tried to give effect to the recommendations of the Royal Commission on Decentralisation, was a tame affair. It was old wine in new bottle. Real stimulus had to come from some other source. It did come and effectively also, with the publication of the Report on the Indian Constitutional Reforms, popularly known as the Montague-Chelmsford Report. The First World War had aroused new emotions, new ambitions and new ideas among the people of the country. The demand for Home Rule and *swaraj* became more and more insistent and irresistible. The British government found it absolutely necessary to take steps for the introduction of responsible form of government. It was in pursuance of this policy the Joint Report was drawn up. The Report contained the formula that there should be, as far as possible, complete popular control in local bodies and the largest possible independence for them from outside control.

Resolution of 1918

The principal points of the resolution are, firstly, elective majorities in all the local boards, nomination being retained to secure the representation of the minorities. Secondly a fairly wide franchise; thirdly, elected Chairman as far as possible; fourthly, full liberty to impose or alter taxation within the limits laid down by law; fifthly, full control over their funds; sixthly, a free hand to frame their own budgets; seventhly, elimination of outside control over their establishments and finally, freedom in several other directions.

After Independence

Even after the attainment of Independence, the conditions of the local self-government remained without any radical change. The reason for this primarily lay in the neglected status according to the urban government in India, by the centre till 1989. The municipal bodies did not have adequate financial resources at their disposal to carry out their tasks. They did not have any assured existence as they could be suspended at will for indefinite periods. This meant that election to urban bodies could not be held within a specified time limit in case of super session. There was no regularity in the holding of elections. Nor was the relationship between the controlling state government and municipal bodies put on a firm footing. This was particularly the case in respect of functions and taxation powers of the urban bodies. These weaknesses were very well-known and from time to time a suggestion was made to remedy them by enshrining urban government in the Constitution itself through an amendment. This, indeed, has been a long-standing demand in the field of municipal reform. But the Central government began to show interest in this direction only since 1989. The rejuvenation of grass-roots government became the concern of the Rajiv Gandhi government since 1989. The Rajiv Gandhi government set the ball rolling by holding wide-ranging consultations with the elected members of the municipalities. Three regional *sammelans* (conferences) were held at Bangalore, Cuttack and Delhi during June 1989. Earlier, there was a seminar of Municipal Officers. Separate discussions were held with Chief Ministers. The theme of an appropriate constitutional amendment to provide a constitutional base to municipal government was discussed in the Consultative Committee of Parliament relating to the Ministry of Urban Development. On the basis of these long discussions, the Rajiv Gandhi government introduced the Constitution (Sixty-Fifth Amendment) Bill in parliament in August 1989. The Bill was passed by the Lok Sabha but not by the upper house and thus it introduced a revised Bill, namely the Constitution (Seventy-Fourth Amendment) Bill 1990 incorporating the provisions relating to panchayats (rural local government) as well as municipalities. This was done in September 1990. The Bill, however, lapsed on account of the dissolution of the then Lok Sabha.

THE 74TH INSTITUTIONAL AMENDMENT ACT 1992

The Congress government headed by P.V. Narasimha Rao came to power in 1991, drafted the constitutional (74th Amendment) Bill, 1991 pertaining to municipalities and introduced in the Lok Sabha in September 1991. It was passed by the Lok Sabha in December 1992 and by the Rajya Sabha the same month. Following the ratification by more than half the state Assemblies, it received the assent of the President on 20 April 1993 and is known as the operative since April 1993 introduces a new part namely Part IX-A in the Constitution which deals with matters relating to urban government.

Composition of Municipalities

There are various forms of urban local bodies existing at present in India. These are municipal corporations, municipalities, and town area committees. Notified Area Committees and Cantonments, which are directly under the Union Ministry of Defence.

Municipal councils are constituted in smaller urban areas while for the larger urban areas municipal corporations are constituted. Demographic and other conditions which are determining factors for constituting a particular type of municipality differ a great deal from one state to another. It has, therefore, been left to the state governments to decide which specific type of municipality will be constituted for each urban area.

As far as the composition of the municipality is concerned all seats shall be filled by direct election. The territorial constituencies in a municipal area for the purpose of elections shall be divided into wards. Each seat shall represent a ward in the municipality. Besides the seats filled by direct election, some seats may be filled by nomination of persons having special knowledge or experience in municipal administration. For this purpose the state law may specify the conditions and procedure for nomination of such persons. But the persons so nominated will not have the right to vote.

Reservation for SCs and STs

The constitution Amendment clearly provide for reservation of seats for SC/ST in the Municipalities on the basis of population. Further, one-third of the total seats reserved for SC/ST shall be reserved for women belonging to corresponding reserved seats of SC/ST. Thus women from SC/ST shall have reservation from their reserved seats. This is a unique provision and it would have been more happy position if the Constitution amendment makers should have thought it to extend this provision to the election of Legislative assemblies and seats of Members of Parliament. The pending Constitution (81st Amendment) Bill, 1996 may be a step in the right direction.

Reservation for Women

As cited above, though there is no reservation of seats for women at State Legislature or at Parliament level, the Constitution Amendment Act, 1992 has clearly laid down the reservation of one-third of total number of seats in all municipalities to be reserved for women. It is not known to what extent this amendment will be welcomed and will serve the purpose but in local bodies, where the political parties have been found by the people that they are more interested in Politics rather than civic administration and services for the people, it is hoped that reservation for women may deliver better goods. Provided that they are given better understanding and training and suitable candidates from the nearest relatives of the politicians in power without seeing the suitability of the candidates for the local services. It is also noteworthy that not less than one-third of the seats of the Chairpersons in the urban local bodies shall be reserved for women. This amendment will be radical in the history provided it is well accepted by social and political organizations. The efforts shall have to be made sincerely to find out the suitable candidates and support them without too much of politics. In the urban bodies the office of Chairpersons shall be reserved for SC/ST and women in such a manner as state may by Law provide.

Ward Committees and Other Committees

Under the present system, each municipality is divided into wards. In smaller and medium sized municipalities, the average population per ward varies from 1500-6000. In larger cities, however average ward size may be fairly large ranging from 30,000 to even 2 lakhs. This has led to a situation where the common citizen does not have ready access to his elected representative. The need to reduce the distance between the electorate and the elected and to provide for increased participation of the people in the urban local bodies has been recognised. Hence, provision has been made for the constitution of ward committees in all municipalities.

The composition, the territorial jurisdiction and the manner in which the seats to ward committees shall be filled have been left to the state Legislature to specify by law.

Barring the ward committee, there are some other committees for urban local bodies viz., standing committees, zonal committees etc. The Chairperson of such committees will have representation and voting rights in the municipality concerned.

Duration of the Urban Bodies

Mandatory provisions under Article 342-E and 243-U have been made that every municipality will continue, unless it is dissolved, the five years from the date of holding the first meeting. But there is no provision of any extension of period of five years and elections shall have to be made before the expiry of the period. In case of dissolution if municipalities elections shall have to be made within six months from the date of dissolution, it would have been better if the provision should have been on the lines of Gujarat Act that in case of unavoidable circumstances like riots, natural calamities like floods, extension of term can be given instead of recourse to dissolution as per present amendment.

Finance Commission to Review Financial Position

It is a most welcome provision in Article 342(1), that Finance Commission shall be constituted by the Governor of the state within one year from the commencement of the 74th Amendment Act, and thereafter, the expiry of every five years. The greatest difficulties for the local bodies regarding their financial resources may accordingly be solved. Only time will tell to what extent this has solved the problem.

The Finance Commission shall review the financial position of the municipalities and make recommendations to the Governor who shall place it before the state Legislature. The recommendations of the Commission will cover the following aspects:

1. distribution between state government and municipalities of the net proceeds of the taxes, duties, tolls and fees to be levied by the state;
2. allocation of taxes, duties, tolls and fees to be assigned or appropriated by the municipalities;
3. determination of taxes, duties, tolls and fees to be assigned or appropriated by the municipalities;
4. grants-in-aid to municipalities from the Consolidated Fund of the state; and
5. measures needed to improve the financial position of the municipalities.

The state Governor would be free to refer any other matter to the Finance Commission as he may deem fit in the nearest of sound financial management of the municipalities. The Finance Commission shall determine its procedure and it shall have such powers as are necessary for it to perform its functions and which the state Legislature may, by law confer on it. In other words, the Commission will be free to determine its own procedure within the framework of powers as may be provided by the state law. It will be mandatory for the Governor to lay before the state Legislature every recommendation made by the Finance Commission together with the explanatory memorandum on the action taken on such recommendations.

State Election Commission

Each state and Union Territory will have to constitute a state Election Commission. The superintendence, direction and control of the preparation of the electoral rolls for and the conduct of all elections to the municipalities shall be vested in it. The Commission will be headed by the state Election Commissioner appointed by the Governor of the state. The Governor may determine the rules governing the conditions of service and tenure of office of the Commissioner. The Commissioner cannot be removed from office except in a manner similar to and on ground to those by which a judge of the High Court can be removed from his office. The conditions of service cannot be varied to his disadvantage after his appointment.

Addition of the Eleventh Schedule

Under Article 342-G regarding powers, authority and responsibility of the local bodies with respect to the preparation of plans for economic development and social justice and implementation of such plans and schemes has to be entrusted to them including the matters listed in the Eleventh Schedule and the Schedule is also added to the Constitution of India.

Dissolution and Disqualification

The state government may decide to dissolve a municipality before expiration of its usual term of five years. However, before taking any decision on such dissolution, the state government would have to give the municipality a reasonable opportunity for being heard. If a municipality is dissolved before the expiry of five years, the election for constituting a new municipality would have to be completed within a period of six months from the date of dissolution. This would mean that the municipality could remain dissolved for a maximum period of six months only.

Disqualification for being a member of the municipality has been prescribed on the lines of disqualification prescribed for being an MLA. The minimum age for being chosen as a member of a municipality has been laid down as 21 years.

Powers and Functions of the Municipalities

The municipalities would be empowered with such powers and responsibilities as may be necessary to enable them to function as effective institutions of self-government. An illustrative list of functions that may be entrusted to the municipalities has been incorporated in the 12th Schedule of the Constitution. This gives an idea of functions that may be entrusted to the municipalities, and the state Legislatures would be free to choose from the following list or add to this list while stipulating the functions to be performed by municipalities. The list is given under:

1. Urban planning including town planning.
2. Regulation of land use and construction of building.
3. Planning for economic and social developments.
4. Roads and bridges.
5. Water supply for domestic, industrial and commercial purposes.
6. Public health, sanitation, conservancy and solid waste management.
7. Fire services.
8. Urban forestry, protection of the environment and promotion of ecological aspects.
9. Safeguarding the interests of the weak sections of the society including the handicapped and the mentally retarded.
10. Slum improvement and upgradation.
11. Urban poverty alleviation.

12. Provision for urban amenities and facilities such as parks, gardens, and playgrounds.
13. Promotion of cultural, educational and aesthetic aspects.
14. Burials and burial grounds, cremation ghats/grounds and electric crematoria.
15. Cattle pounds, prevention of cruelty to animals.
16. Vital statistics including registration of births and deaths.
17. Public amenities including street lighting, parking lots, bus stops and public conveniences.
18. Regulation of slaughter houses and tanneries.

Taxes and Finances of Municipalities

It has been left to the Legislature of a state to specify by law matters relating to imposition of taxes. Such law may specify:

1. Taxes, duties, fees etc., which could be levied and collected by the municipalities as per the procedure to be laid down in the state law.
2. Taxes, duties, fees etc., which could be levied and collected by the state government and a share passed on to the municipalities.
3. Grants-in-aid that would be given to the municipalities from the state.
4. Constitution of funds for crediting and withdrawal of money by the municipality.

Committee for District Planning

The Committee for District Planning has also been given constitutional status *vide* Article 243-Z in the 74th constitutional Amendment and it provides that there shall be statutory District Planning Committee to constitutional Amendment and it provides that there shall be statutory District Planning Committee to consolidate the plans prepared by the municipalities in the district and to prepare draft development plan for the district as a whole. The composition and filling of seats to the District Planning Committee shall be as per law made by the state legislature but as provided in Article 243-ZD, not less than four-fifth of the total number of seats of the committee shall be elected by and from amongst the elected members of the panchayats and municipalities in the district in proportions of the ratio between population of the rural area and urban area of the district. The manner in which the chairpersons of such committee should be chosen and functions relating to district-to-district planning shall be decided by law by state legislature.

The district planning committee in preparing the draft development plan shall have regard to:

1. Matters of committee interest between the panchayat and the municipalities including spatial planning.
2. Sharing of water and other physical natural resources.
3. Integrated development of infrastructure and environment conservation.
4. Extent and type of available resources, whether financial or otherwise.

Committee for Metro Planning

In Article 243-ZE, a provision has been made that there shall be a committee in every metropolitan area (with a population of 10 lakhs or above) to prepare draft development plans for the metropolitan areas as a whole and composition and other details will be worked out by the state legislature, but two-thirds members shall be elected from among the elected members of the municipalities and chairpersons of the panchayats in the metropolitan area in proportion to the population of municipalities and chairpersons of the panchayats in the metropolitan area in proportion to the population of municipal and panchayat areas.

Bar to Interference by Courts in Electoral Matters

Articles 243-O and 243-ZG provide that no election in panchayat or municipality shall be called in question except by election petition presented to such authority and in such a manner as is decided by the Act of state Legislature. It is also provided that validity of any law relating to its limitation of constituency or allotment of seats, such constituencies in respect of panchayats and municipalities shall not be called for in question in any court.

NATIONAL SEMINAR ON THE ROLE OF WOMEN IN URBAN LOCAL BODIES

A national Seminar on Role of Women in Urban Location Bodies in the context of the Seventy-Fourth Amendment Act, 1992 was organized by the Ministry of Urban Affairs and Employment, Government of India in 1997. The Seminar had twin objectives of reviewing the implementation of the Seventy-Fourth Amendment in states and discussion the role that women Mayors, Chairpersons and Councillors could play in promoting the cause of responsive and responsible local self-government and safeguarding the interest of the urban poor, weaker sections, women and children as envisaged in the 74th Amendment. This was viewed with a perspective of urban planning and development.

The Seminar included two sessions (1) Emerging Bodies and (2) Capacity Building for women in Municipal Governance.

Major Recommendations of the Seminar

The participants in the seminar had deliberated on various aspects of the implementation of the Constitution (74th Amendment) Act, 1992 and the challenges faced by the women Mayors, Chairpersons and Councillors in discharging their new responsibilities. They called a "*Shevolution*" in which women should not only be represented in the formal political structures adequately, they should also be included in the decision-making process at all level in equal partnership with their male counterparts.

The following recommendations emerged during discussions and debates in the national seminar:

1. The women Mayors, Chairpersons and Councillors should not only address the key civic issues of the provision of infrastructure and services, they should also act as the voice of the poor and disadvantaged sections who remain left out from the mainstream of development process. They should play a key role in sensitizing the municipal bodies to the problems of the masses and ensuring transparency in municipal administration and accountability to the electorate. They should also be instrumental in reorienting municipal administration and accountability to the

electorate. They should also be instrumental in reorienting municipal budgets to support civic activities such as immunization of children, pre-school and primary education, primary and preventive health care, education of the girl child, economic empowerment of women, general audit etc. They should mobilise mass support against of women, child abuse, prostitution etc. Their areas of concern should include all the facets of civic life, including problems of security, health hazards, food, fuel, shelter, employment and civic amenities.

2. Each municipal corporation, municipal council and a nagar panchayat should have a special committee on women and child development and there should be earmarked municipal funds for specific women and child development activities in cities and towns. The funds provided by the Ministry of Women and Child Development may be made available to the municipalities for the implementation of action programmes as worked out by the women and child development should converge at the municipal level.
3. Ward committees may be constituted in all the municipal corporations and municipalities so that they can act like gram sabha and would be the link points with the voters. The women Mayors, Chairpersons and Councillors may actively associate themselves with the Ward Committees, either directly or indirectly. They may exercise necessary vigilance over the provision and delivery of civil services at the ward level and within the municipality.
4. The provisions of District and Metropolitan Planning Committees are mandatory. However many states are yet to implement these constitutional provisions. These committees are meant to provide a critical decision-making role to elected municipal councillors and panchayat representatives in matters relating to regional and urban planning. The Government of India is required to take up the matter with the state governments for the speedy constitution of the District and Metropolitan Planning Committees.

5. In the absence of financial autonomy and adequate municipal resources, it has been difficult for the newly elected representatives to fulfil the aspirations of the people who elected them after the municipal bodies were revived. It was resolved that the Government of India may take up with the state governments regarding empowering the municipalities and adequate taxing powers and grants-in-aid so as to enable them to discharge their constitutional obligations effectively.
6. The Municipal Mayors, Chairpersons and Councillors observed that although municipal elections have been held throughout the states of the country, real empowerment of women in the municipalities have not taken place in many states. They resolved that Government of India local bodies with adequate tax resources and inter-governmental grants and both administrative and financial autonomy and also clearly define the role of bureaucrats versus elected representatives.
7. Some states have not only reserved one-third of seats for women in municipal council, they have also reserved one-third of the posts of Mayors and Chairpersons for women. It was resolved to request the state governments which have not reserved seats of Chairpersons in local bodies to make necessary reservations.
8. Women's Resource Centres may be stabilized at the municipal and district levels to provide the all-round assistance to women including raising awareness regarding their rights and role in political structures and society.
9. A group of mayors and municipal chairpersons may be constituted for reviewing and monitoring the implementation of the Constitution (74th Amendment) Act in the states with a view to ushering in strong grass-roots level local self-government and ensuring the empowerment of women. This group may be serviced by an agency nominated by the Ministry of Urban Affairs and Employment which may provide

financial support to a few selected state governments for organizing regional meets to discuss inter-state problems and suggest action programmes for the Government of India and the state governments.

10. The Ministry of Urban Affairs and Employment may organise periodic study tours and promote exchange visits to enable the elected representatives to have the first hand knowledge of innovative practices adopted by selected states and municipalities.

11. The Government of India and state governments may organise regular orientation programmes for the newly elected mayors and chairpersons covering aspects such as municipal laws, administrative practices, municipal taxation, user charges and inter-governmental grants, mechanism to mobilize internal resource setting up of priorities for provision of services, minimization of cost of administration and tax collection, maximization of benefits to the public, performance measurement, cross subsidisation for the poor and weaker sections through appropriate pricing policies, proper interface mechanisms between bureaucrats, elected representatives, public, state government, privatization of civil services, public-private partnership, market liberalization etc. Capacity building programmes for female councillors cannot be and should not be same across the board. Such programmes should be rather need-based and offered by applying the means test.

12. To make the functioning of female councillor effective in municipal bodies and eliminating the gender gap and bias, especially in attitudes training programmes for both male and female councillors should be organised together. Appropriate human resource development strategies should be designed and adopted accordingly.

13. Neighbourhood groups and community development societies of women should be entrusted with the task of identifying the priorities for women and children and implementing poverty alleviation programmes

so that the municipalities may play the role of facilitators.

14. The status of mayors and municipal chairpersons in the protocol needs to be clearly defined. The Ministry of Urban Affairs and Employment should take-up the matters with the Union Home Ministry and the State Governments.

Women in Urban Local Bodies

The population of women in the country constitutes nearly 50 per cent of the total population. In spite of such enormous population, the women do not have the adequate representation in the urban local bodies. To involve the women's participation in the development and in the decision-making process, the role of women assumes importance in urban local bodies. The 74th Constitution Amendment Act, 1992 has specified the reservation of seats for women in the municipalities and other urban local bodies. It spells out that not less than one-third of the total number of seats to be filled by direct election in every municipality shall be reserved for women and such seats may be allotted by rotation to different constituencies in a municipality.

The one-third reservation for women has been considered as partnership contribution in the field of development and decision-making in urban local bodies as a vital instrument of democratic decentralization for planning and administration. It has been a fact that the women community has been neglected and their representatives can effectively monitor and administer the schemes like health, education and family planning.

The women representatives as mayors, chairpersons and councillors will contribute significantly in the context of 12th Schedule, Article 243-W of Constitution 74th Amendment Act with reference to:

1. Planning for economic and social development
2. Water supply for domestic industrial and commercial purposes
3. Public health, sanitation, conservancy and solid waste management

4. Urban forestry protection of environment and promotion of ecological aspects
5. Safeguarding the interests of the weaker sections of society including the handicapped and mentally retarded
6. Slum improvement and upgradation
7. Urban poverty alleviation programme
8. Provision for urban amenities and facilities such as parks, gardens and playgrounds
9. Promotion of cultural, educational and aesthetic aspects, and
10. Public amenities including street lighting, parking lots, bus stops and public conveniences.

As mayors, chairpersons and councillors women would be enable to exercise in local self-government, their administrative, executive and political power in managing efficiently and effectively the management of urban local bodies. Thus the women can play a significant role in the development and policy-making decision in the functioning of urban bodies.

With the appropriate organizational constitutes of urban local bodies, functions of women mayors, chairpersons and councillors would enable the effective delivery of the civil amenities. The central and state governments have to strengthen the financial and administrative support system to urban local bodies. The adequate financial powers have to be provided to urban local bodies to mobilise its tax resources for providing the necessary basic amenities like water and electricity supply, sanitation, garbage disposal, education, primary health centres and transport facilities in a comprehensive and efficient management.

In the context it would be meaningful and appropriate to add a few suggestions and recommendations, put forwarded by B.S. Vasihnar, IAS (Retd.) to revitalize the urban local self-Government in India.

Primarily, the 74th Constitutional Amendment Act, 1992 is a milestone in the history of the local governance of the country but steps should be taken to implement the same in letter and spirit, by all concerned and Central Government should appoint a monitoring committee.

Secondly, as already envisaged by Balwant Rai Mehta Committee Report on Panchayati Raj all the three-tier PPIs should be real local self-government bodies for planning development and local administration. Duplication in the form of rural development agencies or district planning boards etc. should have been avoided and abolished.

Thirdly, like in Gujarat there should be a state panchayat/ municipality council under the State Act in every state and all the presidents of district panchayats representatives of urban local bodies, representative of state legislative assembly should be members of such council, with the state ministry for local government as its Chairman. Such statutory state level council is most useful for proper co-ordination between local bodies and state government. It will facilitate proper supervision and implementation of various schemes and development programmes.

Fourthly, like in Gujarat there should be a Social Justice Committee for every panchayat comprising of majority members belonging to SC-ST-OBC and endowed with special powers and funds in proportion to the population of such class from the panchayat/municipalities budgets to ensure justice to weaker sections of society.

Fifthly, with the increased number of seats reserved for women, special efforts are required to encourage women to become members of panchayats/municipal bodies and special training programme will be necessary to enable them to play their role effectively and efficiently.

Sixthly, as rightly observed by Sardar Patel, giving more powers and functions to the local bodies without adequate financial resources is dressing like a dead woman. Central and state governments should provide adequate financial support to the local bodies.

Lastly, the need and importance of training of officers and members cannot be overlooked or underestimated. Central and state governments should also take necessary steps for this programme.

REFERENCES

A. Avasthi (ed.), *Municipal Administration in India* [Agra: Lakshmi Narain Agarwal, 1972].

A. Robson William, *Great Cities of the World* [London: George Allen & Unwin, 1954].

B.K. Batra, "Role of Women in Urban Local Bodies", *Employment News*, Vol. XXII, No. 13, 28 June 1997.

Chand Gyar, *Local Government Personnel System* [New York, 1966].

Committee on Public Undertakings (Third Lok Sabha): Eighth Report on Township and Factory Building of Public Undertakings [New Delhi: Lok Sabha Secretariat, 1965].

Decentralisation for National and Local Development [New York: United Nations, 1962].

R.B. Dass, *Deliberative and Executive Wings in Local Government* [Calcutta: Oxford & IBH Publishing Company, 1968].

Report of the Rural Urban Relationship Committee, Vol. 1 [New Delhi: Ministry of Health and Family Planning, Government of India, 1966].

Report of the Urban Local Self-Government Committee [Bhopal: Government of Madhya Pradesh, 1959].

S.R. Maheswari, *Local Government in India* [Agra: Lakshmi Narain Agarwal, 1997].

Ursula Hicks, *Development from Below* [Oxford: Clarendon Press, 1961].

V. Venkata Rao and Niru Hazarika, *Local Self-Government in India* [New Delhi: S. Chand & Company, 1966].

2

The Urban Poor Versus Housing Sources

CARLOS R. HERNÁNDEZ-VELASCO
0205896H@student.gla.ac.uk
Ph.D. Scholar in Urban Studies, University of Glasgow, Scotland, United Kingdom.

ABSTRACT

The delivery of housing for the poor is essential in rapid urbanisation settings, especially in those which have become leading industrial and services poles attracting flows of migration in many developing countries. This is the case of a number of Mexican cities where rapid urban growth and pressure for land and housing provision exist. This paper analyses the four sources of home production—*self-produced, government programmes, commercial financial institutions, and NGOs and microfinance institutions*—suggested by UN-HABITAT (2001), and the efficiency of its delivery to the poor, who despite the lack of financial assistance of any sort obtain housing by implementing their own mechanisms, usually referred to as *informal*. A summary of a more extensive review of such housing sources is presented by which relevant factors are taken into consideration to understand exclusive housing practices that affect the poorer groups, especially in Mexico.

Introduction

In developing countries, formal market design excludes the poor from access to housing. To obtain shelter, the poor create their own *mechanisms*, usually referred to as informal. Some areas, usually unsuitable both physically and legally for housing, represent their alternative spaces, where shelter is progressively built. Informal settlements are found in many cities and represent a major concern for local governments and international organisations (Thomas 1999: 1). One of the main problems faced by the poor is that existing formal financial institutions do not provide them with banking and financial products (Thomas 1999: 114-15). If financial assistance were more effectively allocated, the poor will thus further its own housing consolidation process quicker and cities will improve in their cohesive social-spatial integration accordingly. By assisting the poor, the course of legal home provision, and hence consolidation and infrastructure delivery will arguably be quicker.

Currently, informal financial schemes are not only directed towards income-generating activities for survival and maintenance, but also by easing the access to land and shelter. According to the UN-HABITAT report (2001), four mechanisms of housing provision are identified as supposedly to be the sources of sheltering the poor. Though, in each one of these housing sources—*self-produced, government programmes, commercial financial institutions, and NGOs and microfinance institutions*—represent advantages and disadvantages for the poor. This paper analyses the role of the poor when participate in each of the above mentioned mechanisms of housing delivery. The research is centred on the case of Mexican housing delivery schemes where author's research is taking place.

The Housing Delivery Chain for the Urban Poor

A booming population growth, whether due to new household formation or migration flows, represents a major challenge for the developing countries. Few cities have absorbed this growth through the production systems of the physical fabric of the city in absolute or relative terms. In Latin America, many cities have increased their attractiveness for many: to obtain a job may represent an opportunity for individuals coming from surrounding areas. Newcomers arrive in cities in search for better life quality and earn one's living. People, however, have few opportunities to obtain a job paying sufficient to satisfy their family needs; for them, the reality is different. Locals and newcomers participate in an employment race where jobs are those of the low-waged type.* Lack of sufficient family income derives on the need to be finally inserted into informal employment either to have an extra or as the only source of income for many. Thus, housing represents a key challenge for the poor as formal market barriers remain: credits are not granted for those working outside the formal sector and for earners within the lowest wage scale, and without pointing collateral. These restrictions represent insurmountable barriers for the poor. Informal housing remains as a better alternative for them.

The following section review how the poor, within all their limited possibilities, cope with the need to access housing and how through the four sources of housing suggested by UN-HABITAT (2001: [79]) present different scenarios to overcome shelter provision:

1. self-produced housing,
2. housing programmes sponsored by the government,
3. housing financed by commercial institutions, and
4. NGOs and microfinance institutions' housing-related programmes.

First source of housing: Self-produced housing

The urban poor manage to shelter themselves after a period of time by saving money from their own earnings and borrowing from relatives or informal moneylenders. By implementing their own financial mechanisms, the poor confront the barriers to access formal housing and financial support to acquire their assets. It is recognised that the poor invest more in low-cost housing than private or public bodies (UN-HABITAT 2001: [79]). Large populations exceed the capacity of housing markets and the poor do not represent effective demand for formal financial institutions. Informal land and housing markets emerge as the only solution for most of the people who acquire land by invading unused areas, buying peasants' parcels, constructing via stages to reduce costs (*i.e.*

* For example, many multinational companies are established in Latin America and provide employment to assembling parts and electronic components, clothes, cars, and so on. Labour required is non-skilled. High levels of personnel rotation exist due to working conditions and low salaries.

starting with a shanty to be gradually replaced by permanent materials), and adding rooms according to dwellers' possibilities. The construction process is uneven and depends on the capacity of the household to buy materials and time to build their own home.

A number of years may pass in order to have a finished well-built house (Hardoy 1985: [62]-66). For instance, Baross (1998: 71) reports a period of time between 8 to 15 years. Resources are scarce to invest in housing and it is especially difficult to extend this investment towards community services (*i.e.* water supply, sewage, electricity, and so on). This fact may delay consolidation for few more years, not only of the house, but also of the community. Baross (1998) considers that a *consolidation stage is reached when the settlement is totally built, it is densified, it has been provided with basic services, and schools, shops, and workshops have been established* (Baross 1998: 73). With resources more effectively allocated beyond that of advice and capacity training (given at the most in self-help housing schemes supported by governments), the poor would shorten the time of such a long process of consolidation.

A constant problem for informals is their complex relationship with local authorities, especially with those in charge of urban control. However, governments have modified their attitude towards informality in the last decades. From a negative to a more relaxed attitude and judgment, the officials' attitude has changed but slowly and with great difficulty (De Soto 1989). During the 60s and 70s, the official discourse was aggressive and negative; as Gilbert (1997: 97) reports, the policy was basically to *eliminate* any dwelling or squatter area in order to *keep order* in urban patterns. Nevertheless, this approach changed; residents started to present some potential advantages for governments, their programmes, and candidates (Warnock 1995: 31). The urban poor became the supporting foundation of many *weak* governments, who were unable to satisfy and fulfil social demands of their own supporters once power was retained or gained (Hardoy 1985: 89, 96). Thus, the officials silently accepted populated informal areas and the pressure on its provision was somehow alleviated (Hardoy 1985: 103-05).

Irregularity abounds resulting in continuing negotiations to expel or legalise the *occupation*. Social polarisation and lack of waged opportunities for the majority of the population prevail (De Soto 1989: 56). This concern has been taken into account by governments in the last decades by trying to deliver their *constitutional* mandate of providing shelter to citizens. But the reality is different: urban poverty belts, creation of informal settlements, lack of adequate services and infrastructure, and health and security concerns all proliferate (Gilbert 1994, 1997; Datta 2001; De Soto: 1989; Drakakis-Smith 2000; Ferguson 1999; Hart 1973; Hardoy 1985; Hernández 1999; Hinderink 1999; Jiménez 2000; Lea 1996; Sethuraman 1981; Thomas 1999; van Lindert 1999). However, there is still a missing point though: *the legal delivery systems produce a completed housing unit that is not affordable by most of the poor, supposedly the targeted group.* A small part of the population—those with formal and sufficient income—has access to credit, but the majority is deprived by not being able to provide sufficient income or collateral. Informal housing stands as their option despite great difficulties to achieve further stages of individual and community consolidation.

Second source of housing: Housing programmes sponsored by the government

High levels of dependency, vulnerability, inflation, currency's devaluation, low-waged type employment, high cost of goods, and an increasing impoverishment of the majorities have represented important constraints to deliver social programmes in the developing countries. Thus, economic resources are insufficient. Government's inability to invest on social programmes impacts on the provision of affordable housing, basic services, and infrastructure, especially for the poor. The attachment to *imported* living standards and economic models has represented the mismatch between costs of living and people's income. As a consequence, the poorest of the poor hardly satisfy their family needs.

Mexico is not an exception in this trend. A bottleneck is found since access to jobs is relatively easy—though of the low-waged type—, while obtaining housing is not that accessible (Gilbert 1994: [57]-64; Hernández 1999: 69). The factors, which may explain this situation, include cycles in the national economy and state policy. From a relatively stable economy during the 1960s and 1970s, the following decades were characterised by economic recession and salaries decline; for instance, in the 1990s, in real terms, it declined by 3.8% (OIT 2000). If employment and salaries are meant to be referential parameters, one needs to declare that people in Mexico work, but salaries have lost value. For example, in April 2003, the minimum official wage in the country was only £2.52 per day (or $41.53 Mexican pesos) (INEGI 2003). In March of the same year, 30% of the working force in a sample of 47 urban centres earned less than 2 minimum wages, or £5.04 per day, and almost half, less than 5 minimum wages, or £12.60 per day. These wages help explain the struggle to satisfy people's basic needs, including housing. Better salaries elsewhere may represent a reason for people to leave their place of residence and many times, the country.

Housing markets face a brick wall; the poòr have no access to the market since they are unable to meet the minimum requirements to obtain financing. On the other hand, the markets have been unable to diminish the existing housing deficit, estimated as 4.2 million of units for the period 2001-2006 (SEDESOL 2001: 69). The main formal housing workers' funds—INFONAVIT for formal workers and FOVISSSTE for federal government workers—in Mexico have been unable to provide sufficient credit to their own affiliates (See Table 1).

TABLE 1: The main housing funds as providers of finance for workers' housing in Mexico

Programme	Potential market	Own Market attended		Own Market unattended	
		Percentage	Total	Percentage	Total
INFONAVIT	11,624,141	9.72%	1,129,866	**90.28%**	10,494,275
FOVISSSTE	1,948,438	27.35%	532,897	**72.65%**	1,415,541

Sources

INFONAVIT http://www.infonavit.gob.mx

FOVISSSTE http://www.issste.gob.mx/fovissste/mpPBen.htm

Note: Potential market refers to the own affiliates contributing to each housing fund.

Other agencies and organisations also participate in the housing provision, resulting in a small contribution to reduce the deficit (See Table 2). The housing shortage prevails and more action needs to be taken in the following years.

TABLE 2: Formal organisations participating in the delivery of housing in Mexico
(Figures in number of credits)

Agency or Housing Organisation	1995	1996	1997	1998	1999	2000	TOTAL	Market Partici-pation %
INFONAVIT	96,745	103,184	99,231	108,035	198,950	250,110	**856,255**	35.177
Self-Help Sedesol	280,011	323,801	241,211	0	0	0	**845,023**	34.715
FOVI	35,662	25,318	46,688	56,952	59,118	46,704	**270,442**	11.110
Others	35,669	10,130	71,538	35,914	21,193	38,152	**212,596**	8.734
FOVISSSTE	32,469	28,731	23,241	16,712	18,007	22,508	**141,668**	5.820
FONHAPO	26,281	18,666	14,826	5,523	6,446	6,716	**78,458**	3.223
Banks	17,503	2,317	4,588	3,500	764	996	**29,668**	1.218
Total	**526,335**	**514,143**	**503,320**	**228,634**	**306,477**	**367,186**	**2,434,110**	**100.000**

Others include BANOBRAS, VIVAh, CFE and PEMEXy FOVIMI-ISSFAM.

Source: *Cómo está el Sector Vivienda* in <www.sedesol.gob.mx/comision/comision.htm>

Banks barely participate in financing low-cost housing as they are focused on higher-income earners. INFONAVIT and SEDESOL (housing-related programmes administered by the Social Development Ministry) remain as the main housing funds. From Table 2, listed agencies are focused on those working in the formal sector and with certain levels of income and stability in their jobs. SEDESOL is the only agency which provided support to the very poor by implementing self-help plans. Policies have changed in this agency and this sort of approach is not longer applied. More housing programmes are needed but not only for those working formally who have potential sources of financing, but for those informally working and inserted in the lowest salary scale.

Third source of housing: Commercial institutions

Commercial financial institutions provide finance programmes to potential homebuyers. Invariably, banks operate in the income principle and demand collateral for loans, which exclude the very poor since requirements cannot be fulfilled. Mexican banks have to struggle hard to simply *survive* in the last decades characterised by economic crisis, companies' bankruptcies and inefficiencies. The government has tried to amend erroneous policies by encouraging housing markets in different ways. First, as Lea (1996: 88) describes, in the 1960s and 1970s strategies were directed to channel funds to housing by imposing mandatory payroll deductions and mandatory lending ratios for housing. These policies, the inflation of early 1980s, and fixed mortgages rate caused major fiscal deficits and losses. In 1984, a more successful policy was implemented when the dual-index mortgage (*DIM*) was introduced. Nationalised banks in the 1980s were privatised in 1991-1992, when all the 18 banks were sold to private investors as attempts to liberalise internal credit (Lea 1996: 90; Mayer 2001: 325). During a short *stable* period of 1991-1994, credits were widely given to public. However, the currency's devaluation in December 1994 devastated the economy and the financial system. The exchange rate fell from $1US for 3 pesos, to 6 pesos in 1995, to 10 pesos in 1999, to 11 pesos in 2003. The banks had been over-priced, legal reserves were reduced, and the new bankers were totally inexperienced to manage this situation (Mayer 2001: 327). Interest rates increased, the purchasing power was reduced, and people were incapable for repaying mortgages (Mayer 2001: 327-28). Confidence in the banking system from both creditors and bankers has not been recovered.

Under these circumstances, resources for financing housing in the country were unavailable over the last decade. Banks needed to secure the repayment of credits by imposing many restrictions on borrowers. These requirements still apply nowadays. For example, as for BANAMEX, the biggest bank in the country, the minimum income required to obtain a credit for housing is of about 16.5 minimum wages or £1,250 a month; the interest rate is fixed at 16.45%, and the repayment period of at least 15 years (BANAMEX: 2002). In the case of BITAL, the third biggest bank, the minimum income is 6.5 minimum wages or £468 a month, a 16.9% interest rate, for up to 75% of financing of the value of the house, and up to 15 years to repay (BITAL: 2002). In a country, where 75% of the population earn less than 5 minimum wages a month, bank schemes for mortgages are not accessible to the middle classes, let alone to the poor.

In the late 1990s, new private financial organisations—called *SOFOLES, Sociedades Financieras de Objeto Limitado*—were authorised. The objective of SOFOLES is to finance projects related to plan, buy, develop or build, and administrate any type of personal property and real estate, directed to specific sectors without access to credit by the established financial intermediaries (CONDUSEF: 2002). SOFOLES act as intermediaries of the Central Bank Housing Fund and direct the resources to borrowers. Their responsibility is to select the borrowers to guarantee returns. Therefore, requirements are strict. SOFOLES eligibility for mortgages presents similarities to those parameters required by the banks. For example, a *SOFOL* called *HIRCASA* do not grant credit to those earning one minimum wage, while, those earning two minimum wages are required to make repayments equalling 44.5% of their income (HIRCASA: 2002). In the case of *Terras Hipotecarias*, the income required to obtain any credit equals 10 times the minimum wage (Terras Hipotecarias: 2002). Generally, loan periods are from 20 to 30 years, at fixed interest rates of about 12%; the mortgage covers only 90% of the house value, and borrowers require having an income at least 4 times higher than the monthly repayments (SOFOLES 2002). Under these circumstances, it is clear that SOFOLES are not designed to assist those having low incomes. SOFOLES and banks are not the options for the poor.

Fourth source of housing: Microfinance institutions and NGOs

The last decades have witnessed an increasing participation of microfinance institutions and NGOs. These organisations have traditionally focused their efforts on helping people to overcome poverty by implementing income-generating schemes (UN-HABITAT 2001: 81).

Microfinance is defined as

> *...mechanisms which offer opportunities to people to save very small amounts, not usually handled by finance institutions and offer small loans, usually for the purchase*

of inputs to small-scale enterprises (UN-HABITAT 2002: 11).

These programmes have proved successful in many countries, such those implemented by the *Grameen Bank* in Bangladesh, which have been extensively replicated elsewhere, including Latin America (Conde 2000: 46; Stauffenberg 2002: 20; SDINET 2003; UN-HABITAT 2001: 81, 84). A shift occurred in terms of microfinance in the last years; NGOs initially participated in these schemes, but then formal institutions took over the leadership by the late 1990s by increasing their portfolio by 23% in 2001 (Stauffenberg 2002: 19). Other approaches have been followed by including other micro credit programmes related to housing, focused on land tenure arrangements, sanitation provision, and credit for sheltering the poor (UN-HABITAT 2001: 84). In the latter, HABITAT (2001) reports that there are two basic strategies to finance it through micro credits:

1. by extending micro credits schemes into housing, and
2. by addressing urban poverty based on the encouragement of savings and loans (UN-HABITAT 2001: 81).

The first strategy is based on the ease the lack of access to formal financial services by providing them through micro credits organisations. The second scheme is to enhance resources directly into housing. In either case, micro credits may represent a new option for those lacking access to traditional financial markets, as Khandker notes:

> *...microfinance matters a lot for the very poor borrowers and also for the local economy. In particular, microfinance programmes matter a lot to the poor in raising per capita consumption, mainly on non-food, as was as household non-land asset* (Khandker 2003: 21).

Thus, micro credits may play an increasing role in housing finance. In the near future dwellings must be considered not just as a *house* but also as a place for income generation. Unfortunately, literature related to these types of programmes focused on housing was not found in Mexico. Micro credit schemes are directed towards income generating activities but not for housing so far. As experimented elsewhere, these schemes have proved effective and more research is recommended to prove feasibility to implementing in Mexico in the near future as a way to alleviate housing needs.

Conclusion

As explained, Latin American cities have experienced tremendous growth and have surprisingly achieved large and consolidated neighbourhoods through informal mechanisms. This does not mean, however, that the processes have been acceptable in a modern society as they unquestionably represent a severe cost in the individuals who have struggled long and hard, and also on the city which must construct infrastructure around their efforts. Commercial institutions and official housing programmes have not solved the problem of its delivery to poor basically because requirements (*i.e.* formal employment and collateral) and construction standards (*i.e.* delivery of complete unit) represent constrains for the poor to access to housing through these schemes. Self-produced housing may represent a more flexible way to acquire housing but it takes a long period of time and represents difficult living conditions for residents in the meantime.

Therefore, the main concern remains as finding options to improve the process of home production at a cost within the grasp of the majority of the poorer population. Clearly, this entails a review of how, by whom, and from whom, the financial resources available to the sectors are articulated. The vast debate about how microfinance might be tapped into by the relating poor is also important, especially in terms of to where it might be more efficiently applied in the housing delivery chain. Microfinance is basically the instrument that incorporates the poor into a savings culture and banking services by recognising that they have savings capacity if the institutional structures and facilities are provided (Conde 2000: 28). Microfinance responds to the specific needs of the poor by mobilising resources according to their capacity and demand. From an extensive literature, though, the impact on the housing delivery chain of implementing small-scale financial assistance directed to the poor, remains only partially answered. The reason for this is that this approach (*i.e.* microfinance) has been usually implemented as a strategy to alleviate poverty, rather than to satisfy housing needs. This reasoning is a matter of a more extended research to translate them into housing programmes. If microfinance succeeds in productive activities for the poor, it is argued that it may work also regarding housing-related programmes. The extension of these programmes towards housing is a subject that may also help overcome the burden of poverty since housing represents many times the income-generating place for the poor. Microfinance for housing is suggested by many as *an effective approach to the housing finance problem* (Conde 2000: [43]-51; Grameen 2003; UN-HABITAT 2001: 4).

Finally, in Mexico, housing may be essential to develop productive activities (*i.e.* small shops, sewing workshops, babysitting, and extra income generation via renting one or more room). The poor are wealth-generating agents despite the prejudices towards the *informality* in which they may generally be involved. Physical consolidation may be achieved through the recognition of the diversity of capabilities, the levels, and the ways of participation of a heterogeneous population. More inclusive policies towards the home delivery mechanisms should result in further research of non-traditional housing finance schemes, and micro credits may represent an option as proved elsewhere. The poor must be recognised as creditworthy and reliable individuals. Effective financial support provided at the precise stage of the housing delivery chain will quicken housing consolidation.

REFERENCES

BANAMEX (2002). *Banamex.com Simulador de Crédito Hipotecario.* http://www.banamex.com/esp/servicios/cgi_reg/hipot.cgi

Baross, P. (1998). "Secuenciando el Desarrollo del Suelo: Las Implicaciones en el Precio del Crecimiento de Asentamientos Legales e Ilegales" in *Análisis del Suelo Urbano,* (Comp.). Jiménez, E. Aguascalientes: Instituto Cultural de Aguascalientes.

BITAL (2002). *Grupo Financiero Bital-Habital.* http://www.dsrefw03.bital.com.mx/aptrix/bitalinternetpub.nsf/Content/Habital_C

Castells, M. and Portes, A. (1989). "World Underneath: The Origins, Dynamics, and Effects of the Informal Economy" in *The Informal Economy: Studies in Advanced and Less Developed Countries.* Castells, M. *et al.* (eds.). Baltimore: The John Hopkins UP.

Conde, C. (2000). *¿Pueden Ahorrar los Pobres? ONG y Proyectos Gubernamentales en México*. Zinacantepec: El Colegio Mexiquense, La Colmena Milenaria.

CONDUSEF (2002). *Cuadros Comparativos.* http://www.condusef.gob.mx/informacion_sobre/sofoles/sofoles.htm

Datta, K. and Jones, G. (2001). "Housing and Finance in Developing Countries: Invisible Issues on Research and Policy Agendas" in *Journal of Habitat International* 25 (2001): 333-57. www.elsevier.com/locate/habitatint, Pergamon.

De Soto, H. (1989). *The Other Path: The Invisible Revolution in the Third World.* London: Tauris and Co. Ltd.

Drakakis-Smith, D. (2000). *Third World Cities.* London: Routledge.

Ferguson, B. (1999). "Micro-Finance of Housing: A Key to Housing the Low or Moderate-Income Majority?" in *Journal of Environment and Urbanisation.* 11 No. 1, 186-99.

FOVI (2002). *FOVI Banco de México.* http://www.fovi.gob.mx

FOVISSSTE (2002). *FOVISSSTE.* http://www.issste.gob.mx/fovissste/mpPBen.htm

Gilbert, A. (1997). "Squatters and Shanties: the Typical Latin American Housing Solution?" in *The Diversity of Development: Essays in Honour of Jan Kleinpenning.* Pp.: [190]-201. Naerssen, T. *et al.* (eds.). The Netherlands: Van Gorcum.

—— (1994). *The Latin American City.* Nottingham: Russell Press.

Gómez, J. *et al.* (1998). *El Desarrollo Histórico de la Vivienda en Aguascalientes.* Aguascalientes: Talleres de Impresión y Diseño.

GRAMEEN BANK (2003). *Grameen-Banking for the Poor* http://www.grameen-info.org

Hart, K. (1973). "Informal Income Opportunities and Urban Employment in Ghana" in *Journal of Modern African Studies* 11, 61-89.

Hardoy, J. and Satterthwaite, D. (1985). *Squatter Citizen: Life in the Urban Third World.* London: Earthscan.

Hernández, C. (1999). "Irregular Settlements in Mexico, 1999-2000: Ejido Lands in Aguascalientes, Mexico." *Dissertation.* Montreal, McGill University.

Hinderink, J. (1999). "Small Towns, Big Dreams?" in *The Diversity of Development: Essays in Honour of Jan Kleinpenning.* 1997: [180]-89. Naerssen, T. *et al.* (eds.). The Netherlands: Van Gorcum.

HIRCASA (2002). *Hir Casa.* http://www.hircasa.com/1b.html

INEGI (2002). *Encuesta Nacional de Empleo.* http://www.inegi.gob.mx/difusion/espanol/fiest.html

INFONAVIT (2002). *INFONAVIT.* http://www.infonavit.gob.mx

Iracheta, A. and M. Smolka (eds.) (2000). *Los Pobres de la Ciudad y la Tierra.* Zinacantepec: El Colegio Mexiquense, Lincoln Institute of Land Policy.

Jiménez, E. (2000). *El Principio de la Irregularidad: Mercado del Suelo para Vivienda en Aguascalientes, 1975-1998.* Guadalajara: Universidad de Guadalajara Press.

Khandker, S. (2003). "Micro-finance and Poverty: Evidence Using Panel Data from Bangladesh", in World Bank Policy Research Working Paper 2945, January 2003.

Krantz, L. (1991). *Peasant Differentiation and Development: The Case of a Mexican Ejido.* Montevideo: Edinor.

Lanzetta, M. *et al.* (1989). "The Articulation of Formal and Informal Sector in the Economy of Bogotá, Colombia" in *The Informal Economy: Studies in Advanced and Less Developed Countries.* Castells, M. *et al.* (eds.). Baltimore: The John Hopkins University Press.

Lea, M. and Bernstein, S. (1996). "Housing Finance in an Inflationary Economy: The Experience of Mexico" in *Journal of Housing Economics* 5 Article 0005, 87-104.

Lee, T. (1993). "Creating an Enabling Environment for Housing: Recent Reforms in Mexico" in *Journal of Housing Policy Debate.* 4 Issue 2, 239-49.

Lowder, S. (1993). "The Limitations of Planned Land Development for Low-Income Housing in Third World Cities" in *Journal of Urban Studies* 30 No. 7, 1241-55.

Mayer, J. and Woodside K. (2001). "Crises of Confidence: Attitudes of the Domestic Bankers Towards the Credit Problem in Mexico" in *Bulletin of Latin American Research,* Vol. 20, No. 3, 325-41. Oxford: Blackwell Publishers.

Morduch, J. (1999). "The Microfinance Promise", in *Journal of Economic Literature,* Vol. 36, Issue 24 (Dec. 1999): 1569-1614. http:/uk.jstor.org.

OIT (2000). *International Labour Organisation Report.* http://www.conasami.gob.mx/indice

Satterthwaite, D. (2002). *Coping with Rapid Urban Growth* in RICS Leading Edge Series. London: RICS.

SEDESOL (2001). *Programa Nacional de Desarrollo Urbano y de Ordenación del Territorio 2001-2006.* Mexico: SEDESOL. http://www.sedesol.gob.mx/sesuryvi/desurb/pnduot.htm

—— (2003). *Cómo está el Sector Vivienda.* http://www.sedesol.gob.mx/comision/comision.htm

Sethuraman, S. (1981). "The Role of the Urban Informal Sector" in *The Urban Informal Sector in Developing Countries: Employment, Poverty and Environment.* Sethuraman, S. (ed.). Geneva: International Labour Office.

SIDNET (2003). *Shack/Slum Dwellers International.* "Saver's Network 'Tres Fronteras'". http://www/sdinet.org/Colombo.htm

Smith, S. and Wied-Nebbeling, S. (1986). *The Shadow Economy in Britain and Germany.* London: George Over Ltd.

Stauffenberg, Damian von (2002). "Trend in Latin American Microfinance", in the *Microbanking Bulletin*, November 2002.

Tanzi, V. (1982). "Underground Economy and Tax Evasion in the United States: Estimates and Implications" in *The Underground Economy in the United States and Abroad*. Tanzi, V. (ed.). Toronto: Lexington Books.

Terras Hipotecarias (2002). *Bienvenidos a Terras Hipotecarias S.A de C.V.S.F.L.* http://www.terras.com.mx/compre_su_casa.htm

Thomas, J. (1992). "Informal Economic Activity" in *LSE Handbooks in Economics*. Hertfordshire: Harvester Wheatsheaf.

—— (1999). *Surviving in the City: The Urban Informal Sector in Latin America* in Critical Studies on Latin America Series. London: Pluto.

UN, ECLAC. (2001). *A Territorial Perspective: Towards the Consolidation of Human Settlements in Latin America and the Caribbean*. Santiago: United Nations Press.

UN-HABITAT (2001). *Cities in a Globalising World: Global Report on Human Settlements 2001*. London: Earthscan.

—— (2002). *Financing Adequate Shelter for All: Addressing the Housing Finance Problem in Developing Countries*. Nairobi: UN.

Van Lindert, P. (1999). "Housing Strategies of the Urban Poor in Latin America" in *The Diversity of Development: Essays in Honour of Jan Kleinpenning*. 1997: [202]-13. Naerssen, T. *et al.* (eds.). The Netherlands: Van Gorcum.

Varley, A. (1998). "Decentralisation or Fragmentation? Reflections on Urban Land Market Reform in Mexico". Paper delivered at the workshop on "Comparative Policy Perspectives on Urban Land Market Reform in Latin America, Southern Africa and Eastern Europe". Lincoln Institute of Land Policy, July 7-9, 1998, Personal file sent by the author.

Warnock, J. (1995). *The Other Mexico: The North American Triangle Completed.* Montreal: Black Rose Books.

World Bank (2002). *Mexico Urban Development: A Contribution to a National Urban Strategy*. Vol. I. http://www.wds.worldbank.org/servlet/WDSContentServer/WDSP/IB/2002/09/06/000094946_02081904011340/Rendered/PDF/multi0page.pdf

Yunus, M. (2003). "Expanding Microcredit Outreach to Reach the Millennium Development Goal—Some Issues for Attention". Paper presented at the International Seminar on Attacking Poverty with Micro credit, organised by PKSF in Dhaka, January 8-9, 2003. http://www.grameen-info.org/bank/ExpandingMicrocredit.html.

3

Strategies for Reducing Vehicular Pollution: A Case for Emission-Based Vehicle Taxes

PRAGYA JASWAL
pragyaj@teri.res.in
Research Associate, The Energy and Resources Institute <www.teriin.org> [New Delhi, India]

KAUSHIK DEB
kdeb@teri.res.in
Research Associate, TERI.

It has been universally recognized that improved transport systems are essential for accelerated economic growth. Transportation in the urban context assumes even greater significance as large agglomerations are seen as the vertices of continued economic growth. The productive efficiency of urban agglomerations will be maintained only if mobility requirements in cities are fully met. However, this productive efficiency in urban India is now threatened due to the increasing number of vehicles causing congestion and, thus, slower speeds on roads. Obviously, transportation infrastructure could be the primary bottleneck in the unimpeded growth of the country. Thus, it is important that the existing transportation infrastructure is utilized optimally. This would imply that the pricing policies in the transport sector reflect not just the cost of providing mobility services, but also incorporate the external costs that emerge from the transport sector.

This sector has become one of the major contributors to the total emission loading, with substantial health implications. In order to develop an environment-friendly transport system, it is essential that the costs imposed by the transport sector on the environment be taken into account in the provision of transport services. This chapter analyses some market-based instruments for reducing vehicular pollution.

International experience

The international experience in the use of MBIs for environmental regulation in the transport sector reveals that most of these target either fuel consumption, vehicle price, or travel demand itself (Table 1).

TABLE 1: International experience in environmentally motivated fiscal policies

Instrument	Developing countries	Developed countries
Price differential between leaded and unleaded gasoline	Hungary, Mexico, the Philippines, Portugal, Taiwan, and Thailand	Australia, Britain, Denmark, Finland, Germany, Luxembourg, Netherlands, New Zealand, Norway, Sweden, and Switzerland
Price differential between ultra-low sulphur diesel and ordinary diesel		The UK and Sweden
Vehicle taxes based on emissions	South Korea	Austria, Belgium, Britain, British Columbia, Germany, Japan, the Netherlands and Sweden
Taxes on non-catalytic converter cars	Greece	Finland and Sweden
Higher tax on diesel cars		Germany
Annual road tax differentiated by vintage		Germany
Emissions trading	Chile	
Tax on lead acid battery		British Columbia and the US
Congestion pricing	Chile	Norway

Source: Pandey, Bharadwaj [2000] and Gupta [1999].

Until the late 1980s, taxation of motor vehicles and motor fuels focused primarily on raising revenue. Since the early 1990s, many countries have implemented coordinated fiscal and environmental policies aimed at reducing vehicular emissions.

Economic instruments for mitigating transport emissions

The application of economic instruments in the transport sector is recognized to be more complex than in other sectors due to the mobile nature of the source of emissions. Thus, it is not possible to tailor emissions to local conditions. As a result, emission norms based on desired air quality in dense areas may impose a disproportionately higher cost on less dense areas. Also, as vehicles have to be where people are, relocation is not a viable strategy. Thirdly, the number of polluters is substantially more than stationary sources—for instance, in India there are about 35 million vehicles registered. Consequently, enforcement is significantly more difficult and expensive. Finally, as mentioned earlier, emissions from the urban transport sector are rapidly growing and attention is increasingly being focused on abatement strategies in this sector.

The optimal design of strategies in the transport sector to control emissions in the transport sector would have to consider the number of agents to be regulated as also the change in the emission patterns over the lifetime of the vehicles. The economic instruments could then be applied either at the point of manufacture or at the point of usage.

In India, though the government has used economic instruments to regulate the economic and social behaviour of people for a long time, their potential has not been utilized in the environment regulation policies. Also, policy decisions in the transport sector are not driven by environmental considerations. As discussed earlier, environmental regulation in the transport sector has seldom used MBIs (market-based instruments).

There are however, various fiscal instruments in the union as well as the state government budgets that influence the emission loading from the transport sector. These include the central sales tax, the customs duty, and excise duty, which are in the purview of the central government, and the sales tax in the budgets of state governments. Also allocations for various activities and government instrumentalities, like the STUs (state transport undertakings) impact the environment. Finally, there are other instruments also available such as depreciation allowance and R&D (research and development) allowances to the manufacturers to encourage a shift towards the production of less polluting vehicles.

Suggested interventions

In this section, a framework for modifications in the existing tax structure of vehicles to be based on the emissions of the vehicles is suggested. The guiding principle in this strategy is to adjust the existing structure of the sales tax, excise duty, and the special excise duty levied on vehicles, so as to reflect the total emissions loading of a vehicle within a particular mode. However, adjustments in the tax structure should be made keeping in view the rationalization of the tax regime as described in the earlier section. The following interventions are therefore suggested:

1. Lower taxes on less polluting vehicles
2. Raise taxes on more polluting vehicles
3. Adjust taxes in accordance with rationalization of taxes

In order to achieve these, vehicles should be placed in a particular tax bracket depending upon their level of contribution to pollution. For instance, if there are three categories of emission norms—high polluting, medium polluting, and low polluting—then the vehicles which are in the low polluting category should be placed in the lowest tax bracket, vehicles which are in the medium polluting category should be placed in the intermediate tax bracket and the high polluting category vehicles should be placed in the highest tax bracket.

An analysis was undertaken to demonstrate the design of this strategy. Based on the emissions during the entire lifetime of a vehicle, an ordinal ranking was established for the vehicles within each mode. Similarly, based on the tax liability for each vehicle, an ordinal ranking was established for vehicles within each mode. The environmental ranking was then compared with the tax ranking of the vehicles. Then adjustments in the tax structure were suggested so as to achieve rankings in the tax liability, similar to those in the emission loading within each mode. Thus, taxes on the more polluting technology within each mode were raised, while those on the less polluting were lowered. However, adjustments in the tax structure were made keeping in view the rationalization of the tax regime.

Emission ranking

To estimate emission rankings, the aggregate emissions for each vehicle during its lifetime were estimated based on the emission factors (obtained from TERI 2000), daily utilization of vehicles (ENCON 1987), and average life of the vehicles (Bose 1998). To aggregate the emissions of different pollutants for each vehicle, the level of environmental severity for each pollutant was established. This was approximated using the toxicity weights and the degree to which each pollutant exceeds or is less than its NAAQS (national ambient air quality standard). In the absence of appropriate toxicity weights of different pollutants for the Indian context, the toxicity weights suggested in a World Bank report (Wijetilleke, and Karunaratne 1995) were used. Also the NAAQS were compared with the annual average ambient air quality reported at ITO, a busy traffic intersection in Delhi, to establish the degree to which a pollutant exceeds or falls short of the standards. The index so calculated thus also reflects the desirability to reduce pollutants in the city so as to achieve the legislated ambient air quality standards. Only those pollutants that are currently regulated in the automobile sector were considered—HC, CO, NO_x, and RSPM (respirable suspended particulate matter). The detailed estimation procedure for the Emissions Severity Index is given in the Table 2.

TABLE 2: Emission Severity Index of the pollutants

Pollutant	Annual average ambient air quality (1998) μg/m³	NAAQS (μg/m³)	Degree in excess of desirable standards	Toxicity weights	Emission Severity Index
	(1)	(2)	(3)=(1)/(2)	(4)	(3)*(4)
CO	5450.00	2000.00	2.73	0.04	0.11
HC[a]			0.94	1.80	1.70
No_x	63.00	60.00	1.05	4.70	4.94
RSPM	210.08	60.00	3.50	2.30	8.05

* Since there are no NAAQS (National Ambient Air Quality Standard) for HC (hydrocarbon), though it is one of the regulated pollutants in the automobile sector, the degree to which it exceeds its desirable standard was approximated using the NAAQS for CO and the proportion of the total emissions loading of CO and HC estimated in Bose [2000].

Source: MoEF [2000], Wijetilleke and Karunaratne [1995].

Each vehicle was ranked according to its emissions within its mode. For this, the total lifetime emissions of each vehicle and each fuel was compared within the same mode and ranked accordingly. For instance, within private cars, gasoline cars have the highest emissions, followed by diesel cars. The least emission levels are for CNG cars. Accordingly, the gasoline car was given a rank of one, the diesel car is ranked second, and the CNG car is at number three. The emission levels and the environmental rankings are given in Table 3.

TABLE 3: The lifetime toxicity emissions (tonnes) and environmental rankings

Category	Total life emissions (tonnes)	Environmental ranking
Two-wheelers		
Two-stroke	0.54	1
Four-stroke	0.29	2
Three-wheelers		
Gasoline	4.14	1
CNG (compressed natural gas)	2.41	2
Private cars		
Gasoline	0.85	1
Diesel	0.75	2
CNG	0.72	3
Taxis		
Gasoline	2.01	1
Diesel	1.76	2
CNG	1.69	3
Buses		
Diesel	140.24	1
CNG	55.74	2

Tax ranking

The tax ranking for vehicles in each mode was calculated in a manner similar to the emission ranking. The first step was estimating the tax liability of each vehicle. This was arrived at by taking into account the sales tax, excise duty and special excise duty as described in the earlier section. The tax liability of the vehicle was then compared within the mode and ranked accordingly. For instance, in private cars, diesel cars having the highest tax liability were given the first rank, followed by CNG cars, which ranked second. Gasoline cars, with the least tax liability, were given the third rank. The mode-wise tax ranking of vehicles is given in Table 4.

TABLE 4: The existing tax structure

Category	Tax liability (Rs.)	Tax ranking
Two-wheelers		
Two-stroke	5,669	2
Four-stroke	7,700	1
Three-wheelers		
Gasoline	15,507	2
CNG	25,344	1
Private cars		
Gasoline	82,337	3
Diesel	134,063	1
CNG	113,090	2
Taxis		
Gasoline	91,983	1
Diesel	84,192	2
CNG	80,484	3
Buses		
Diesel	209,249	2
CNG	354,655	1

Optimizing the tax structure

The optimum tax rate for each vehicle in a given mode was then calculated such that the proposed sales tax, excise duty, and special excise duty structure reflected the environmental ranking. This was done by adjusting the existing tax levels within the existing tax slabs so as to achieve a ranking similar to the environmental ranking. The principle that followed is that within each mode, the proposed sales tax for the vehicle with the highest environmental ranking is 20%; for the next on the ranking, it is 8%; and for the vehicle with the lowest ranking, it is 0%. Similarly, for modes that were less polluting, the special excise duty is proposed to be reduced to 0%. The rankings and the adjusted tax structure are shown in Table 5.

TABLE 5: Proposed changes in tax structure for vehicles

Category	Environmental Rank	Proposed			Tax rank (pre-adjust)	Rank
		Sales tax (%)	Excise tax (%)	Special excise duty (%)		
Two-wheelers						
Two-stroke	1	20	16	0	2	1
Four-stroke	2	0	16	0	1	2
Three-wheelers						
Gasoline	1	20	16	0	2	1
CNG	2	0	16	0	1	2
Private cars						
Gasoline	1	20	16	16	3	1
Diesel	3	8	16	0	1	3
CNG	2	0	16	0	2	2
Taxis						
Gasoline	1	20	16	0	1	1
Diesel	3	8	16	0	2	3
CNG	2	0	16	0	3	2
Buses						
Diesel	1	20	16	0	2	1
CNG	2	0	16	0	1	2

Next steps

It is evident that strong policy interventions need to be initiated to curb the growth of transport energy demand and emissions. The proposal in this paper, however, must form a part of an integrated effort to provide an efficient and environmentally sound transport system for urban India. The goal of sustaining mobility must be linked with goals of fostering economic development, enhancing the environment, reducing energy consumption, promoting transportation-friendly development patterns, and encouraging fair and equitable access to residents of different socio-economic groups. In this regard, different forms of transport must be seen as parts of an integrated and interdependent whole.

The simultaneous pursuit of these goals would call for strategies to bring about the desired changes in a time-bound manner, based on prioritized issues in the short, medium, and long term. Nevertheless, the gains from adjusting the tax structure to reflect the environmental impacts of transport activities, as suggested above, should have an impact.

REFERENCES

Bose, R.K. 1998. "Automotive energy use and emissions control: a simulation model to analyze transport strategies for Indian metropolises." *Energy Policy* 26(13): 1001-16.

—— [September] 2000. *Urban transport, energy and environment: a case of Delhi* [New Delhi: Tata Energy Research Institute].

Carbajo, José. 1992. Regulations and Economic Incentives to Reduce Automotive Air Pollution. The Science of Total Environment.

ENCON, 1987. *Estimation of total road transport freight and passenger movement in India.* New Delhi: Engineering Consultants Private Limited.

Eskeland, Gunnar S. [December] 1992. "Attacking Air Pollution in Mexico City". *Finance and Development,* Vol. 29, No. 4.

Gupta, S. 1999. Country environment review—India: Policy measures for sustainable development. Discussion Paper [Asian Development Bank].

HM Customs and Excise [November] 2000. *Using the tax system to encourage cleaner fuels: The experience of ultra low sulphur diesel.* UK Government.

May, Anthony D. [June] 1991. "Demand Management: An Overview". *Australian Road Research,* Vol. 21, No. 2.

Ministry of Environment and Forests [2000]. Air Quality Status and Trends in India [New Delhi: Central Pollution Control Board].

Orski, C. Kenneth. [April] 1992. "Congestion Pricing: Promise and Limitations", *Transportation Quarterly,* Vol. 46, No. 2.

Pandey, R. and G. Bhardwaj [March 2000]. *Economic policy instruments for controlling vehicular air pollution* [New Delhi: National Institute of Public Finance and Policy].

Wijetilleke, L. and S.A.R. Karunaratne [1995]. "Air Quality management: Considerations for developing countries" [Washington DC: The World Bank]. Technical Paper No. 278 [Energy Series].

URLs

http://www.cbec.gov.in

http://www.delhisalestax.com

http://www.lta.gov.sg

http://www.westport.com

4

Urban Transport Solutions to Mitigate Emissions: Strategies for India

PRAGYA JASWAL

pragyaj@teri.res.in

Research Associate, The Energy and Resources Institute <www.teriin.org> [New Delhi, India].

The transport sector is one of the most important arteries of the economy. It provides access to goods and people and is essential for economic and social development. However, this sector has become one of the major contributors to the total emission loading. This is especially the case in developing countries which are experiencing rapid population growth and urbanization. It had been estimated that in 2000, out of the 28 megacities in the world, 22 would be in the developing countries. India is a rapidly growing country with the second largest urban population in the world and characterized by rapid urbanization. It has three mega cities with a population of over 12 million, ten metropolitan cities with a population ranging between 2.1 million to 5.4 million and 27 cities with a million plus population. The metropolitan cities of the country, namely Delhi, Mumbai, Chennai and Kolkata have experienced much higher rates of population and urbanization growth as compared to the rest of the country. The growth in essential services and infrastructure facilities in the urban areas of India has, however not kept pace with the continuing high rate of urbanisation. As a result of the high rate of growth of population in these urban areas and inadequacy of infrastructure facilities, a number of people and businesses have shifted their base to surrounding areas, leading to spatial expansion of the urban area. This in turn has led to substantial increase in work, education and leisure related trips.

As a result of all these factors namely demographic, economic, spatial growth of the urban agglomerates and increase in mobility rates, there has been substantial increase in the travel demand in the country. The transport demand for the last 10 years has grown at the rate of 10% per annum. In almost all urban centres, the public transport systems have failed to meet the rising travel demand. In most of the cases, the bus fleets of the city transport authorities have not grown much over the past years. Moreover, most of the existing fleets are in a very poor condition. Thus, with the public transport system in most of the urban areas lacking in terms of adequacy, efficiency, accessibility and reliability, the personal modes of transport (scooters, motor cycles and cars/jeeps) cater to a large portion of the travel demand. For instance, Delhi, the capital city of India has the largest number of registered vehicles in the country. The growth of vehicles has been exponential. The dominance of personalised modes of transport has been a characteristic feature of this growth. Personal vehicles (two wheelers and car/jeeps) comprise more than 85% of the total registered vehicles in the city today. The share of registered buses, which cater to substantial portion of passenger travel, demand (around 50%) is a paltry 1%.

The Problem

While the growing vehicle fleets are burdening the cities and the environment, there has not been a commensurate increase in the road space in the city and as a result there are significant traffic problems. During the last decade, motor vehicle ownership in India, including two wheelers, had grown at 15 per cent per year in the metropolitan cities. But the streets in most Indian cities are not capable of catering to the needs imposed by such large vehicle fleets, as they occupy less than 10% of the urban land area. The rapid increase in the vehicle traffic, inadequate public transport, the existing inefficient land use pattern, inadequate traffic management and the resultant travel pattern together have lead to congestion on the most of the urban roads. The peak hour speeds in the central areas in many of the major cities have been reduced to 5-10 km an hour. The reduced speeds in turn lead to increased fuel consumption, further adding to the emissions loading. The problem is aggravated by the poor fuel quality, the poor condition of the existing vehicle fleet, and inefficient vehicle technology.

Various studies on the concentration of various pollutants in the ambient air have revealed that the contribution of auto exhaust to carbon monoxide, nitrogen oxide and particulate matter are fairly high. For most of the cities, suspended particulate matter (SPM) levels exceed the national standards.

A matter of concern is that even though the vehicle ownership rates are much lower in India as compared to the developed countries, the traffic congestion and resultant air pollution is very severe. In the urban areas, private passenger vehicles are in high demand and the car ownership is growing rapidly at over 10 per cent per annum. Hence the congestion and the consequent pollution problems are likely to become more severe in the future. Thus these mega cities are posing unprecedented challenges for traffic and transport authorities.

Strategies for controlling pollution from the transport sector

There are two basic approaches for reducing vehicular emissions: one is restraining vehicle demand and use and the other is through technology-based strategies. The first option aims at reducing the total number of kilometres travelled by either limiting/discouraging the ownership of vehicles or by discouraging their excessive use. The latter aims to reduce emissions per vehicle kilometre travelled by encouraging use of improved vehicle technologies. These strategies require active government interventions and aggressive measures. Theoretically, the first best solution for reducing vehicular emissions is an emission tax. However, such a tax is difficult to administer and monitor. A more practical strategy would be to use a mixed set of instruments, which are dictated by either command or control, and/or the market based principle. Also, the kind of instrument that is used is important. As against the command and control approach, market based instruments (MBIs), such as input-output taxes, differential tax rates, and user fees have been used extensively, use market and price mechanisms to promote adoption of environment friendly practices. Command and control policies do not in anyway provide dynamic incentives for technological innovation and diffusion.

In India, the approach has been to use command and control measures for environmental regulation. Greater emphasis has been laid on setting standards and promoting specific technologies by mandating their usage. Emission control strategies in this sector, however, do not employ MBI for pollution control. Judicial activism has been responsible to a large extent for the substantial progress that has been made in several issues relating to minimizing of vehicular pollution. Also, policy decisions in the transport sector are not driven by environmental considerations.

Options available to India

India can draw lessons from the experiences of various countries, which have successfully used a number of instruments to deal with congestion and pollution problems. India can also improve the efficiency of its pollution control strategies. One thing that must be kept in mind is that there cannot be a single solution to pollution problems posed by the transport sector. The best approach would be to have a combination of strategies. Also, given the vast differentials in the characteristics of different cities across the country, these strategies need to be city specific.

Given below is a set of strategies that can be used for transport authorities of a city like New Delhi:

Taxation: Taxes constitute a significant percentage of the final price of a vehicle or fuel. In India, taxation is used only as a revenue-generating source. However, in a number of countries taxation has been used as an instrument to discourage or encourage the use of a particular item. Taxation of fuels and vehicles can be used to restrict vehicle ownership and also to promote improved technology. There are a variety of taxes available in the Union as well as the State Government budgets that can influence the emission loading from the transport sector. These include the customs duty and excise duty, which are in the purview of the Central Government, and sales tax in the budgets of State Governments.

Taxing motor vehicles: In a number of countries taxes on motor vehicles have been used in the environment regulation policies. Vehicle taxation based on the potential emissions loading from a vehicle in its entire life span has been very popular. Most countries in the European Union have imposed such levies on vehicles that do not comply with the EU recommended standards. A number of countries subsidize the purchase of low emission vehicles. In Japan, for instance, tax deductions are provided at purchase of battery operated vehicles and alternate fuel vehicles. In a number of countries taxation has also been used to restrain ownership of vehicles. In Hong Kong and Japan, taxation has been used to make the ownership of vehicles more expensive and has been successful in reducing the private vehicle fleets. In India, taxation of motor vehicles is not based on environmental considerations. Moreover, in case of private vehicles only a one-time tax is charged at the time of purchase of the vehicles. The taxation scheme for motor vehicles can be designed in a manner that reflects the environmental characteristics of the vehicle. This would take into account the polluter pays principle, whereby the vehicle owners are made to pay for polluting the environment. A differential taxation system can be adopted, whereby a vehicle which is environmentally "more dirty", *i.e.* which pollutes more, should be taxed more. The Government can promote low emission vehicles by taxing them at lower rates. Also, apart from the initial purchase tax, an annual tax based on the environmental performance of vehicles should be collected. This can be used to discourage the more polluting vehicles from operating. Since the emission intensity of older vehicles, other things remaining same, is likely to be more, some specific measures are required to discourage use of older vehicles. Incentives can be given to encourage higher fleet turnover rate. For example, waiving off certain taxes for replacing the older vehicles.

Taxation of fuels: Across the world, various incentives are being given to promote alternate and cleaner conventional fuels. For instance in London, tax incentives were given to the refineries to encourage them to shift to producing diesel with 50-10 ppm of sulphur. A number of countries have used differential taxation regime to promote the use of alternative fuels like CNG and LPG. For instance, in Argentina, the country with the largest Natural gas vehicle population, the initial policies to encourage CNG included a differential of over 65% between gas and liquid fuel prices. Further, fuel taxes have also been used to contain and reduce usage of private vehicles. In Seoul, for example, effective restraint of vehicles was achieved primarily with very high gasoline prices. In India, historically taxes have formed a very significant percentage of the gasoline price, so as to cross-subsidize other petroleum products, including diesel. The oil and gas sector in India was completely regulated till 1991 under the Administered Pricing Mechanism (APM). In April 2002, the APM was completely dismantled and the prices of petroleum products (except for kerosene and domestic LPG) are now market determined. However, the gasoline continues to subsidize kerosene and domestic LPG. A cess of Rs. 6 per litre has been imposed on gasoline. Also, the excise duty on CNG has been raised to 16% from the initial zero level duty. The high level of taxes on gasoline can continue and can be used as a restraint measure on the usage of private vehicles. At the same time, the Government can give tax incentives to the refineries so as to improve the quality of the conventional fuels. The taxation of motor fuels, as suggested for motor vehicles, can also be based on the environmental characteristics of the fuels.

Improvement in the public transport system: The measures to restrict private vehicles ownership and usage should be necessarily accompanied by measures to make the public transport system more reliable and efficient. This is because, in the absence of any improvement in the public transport system, the above measures would find it difficult to attain their objectives. If they are successful in restraining the vehicle usage, then it would further burden the already stressed public transport network and would lead to reduction in the overall efficiency of the economy. In Brazil, the city of Curitiba has developed a non-subsidized, private owned public transport system. The mass transportation system has grown to utilize varying types of bus services that cater to the needs of passengers within the metropolitan areas and surrounding municipalities. Buses efficiently serve the entire city with a hierarchy of routes, including feeder routes and some dedicated routes. 75% of the commuters use this system during the weekdays. In India, the share of public transport in catering to the travel demand is quite high. However, this share is fast declining. There is a need to improve the efficiency, frequency, and reliability of bus system. Since the majority of trips are work related, the segment of the travel catered to by private vehicles can be targeted to shift to public transport. In particular, the two-wheeler users can be targeted. Fortunately, people who use two-wheelers are willing to shift to mass modes if they are conveniently provided. For this it is necessary to augment the capacity of the public transport system. Also, premium services such as express buses and air-conditioned buses need to be provided to wean away the four-wheeler segment. Further, it is essential to provide easy access to public transport if it is to be accepted by those who have other choices.

Traffic management and restraint measures: There are various measures available for improving the traffic flow in the cities. These include measures to restrain traffic by either controlling the physical number of vehicles or by use of instruments like congestion charges and through improved traffic management. For instance, by an "odds and evens" system[1] and by restricting the number of personal vehicles in congested areas.[2] In Singapore, access fees for the central business districts have been levied to reduce the congestion during peak hours. Congestion charges in Singapore are enforced as part of an elaborate Area Licensing Scheme (ALS). In this regime, a number of congested corridors in the city have been identified where a charge is payable by every vehicle. Electronic Road Pricing (ERP) is simply an electronic ALS. It is designed to automate the road pricing system.

The traffic flow in various cities of India can be improved by grade separation, scientific designs of bus stops, flexi-laning to allow flexibility in road capacity during the peak hours, and synchronization of traffic lights, restricting the hours during which large commercial vehicles may enter city limits (usually to night hours), and constructing bypasses to divert highway traffic whose destination is elsewhere.

There is a dire need to address the problems posed by the growing motorization and making the transport system more sustainable and environment friendly. It is essential for the transport authorities of the country to take some fast action in controlling the vehicular demand and mitigating the adverse impact that the increasing vehicular fleet has on the environment. The above-mentioned strategies are some of the strategies that can be pursued by the transport authorities of the country.

NOTES

1. The odd/even number plate system prohibits the use of private vehicles one day a week, as has been done in Mexico City since November 1989 mainly because of its air pollution problem (Carbajo 1992).
2. Aside from public transport, government and residents' vehicles, private vehicles are forbidden to enter a cordon surrounding central Milan, Italy, during the day between 7:30 a.m. and 4:30 p.m. (Orski 1992).

5

Economic Development in the 21st Century Metropolis: The Transnational Growth Machine

ANDREW KIRBY

Andrew.Kirby@asu.edu

Professor of Social & Behavioral Sciences, Arizona State University, Phoenix, United States of America and Editor, *Cities: An International Journal of Urban Policy and Planning*.

ABSTRACT

The paper explores some of the ways in which the processes of urban economic development have begun to change in the new Century. Globalization has encouraged new processes of large-scale economic development, which can be traced in both the rapidly growing cities of the US and the evolving economies. This convergence is a manifestation of privatized planning and development, which has the capacity to produce different city forms in the future.

Introduction

This chapter addresses two topics. The first involves laying out some general principles through which to approach the process of contemporary economic development, as it is commonly understood, in the context of urban growth. The second goal of the chapter will be to illustrate this argument via reference to two brief examples of metropolitan development from very different political-economic settings. Through these cases, we will see some convergence of urban development trends in different parts of the world at the start of the 21st Century.

Economic development and the growth machine

The 20th Century was an episode of intense urban development. When it began, the United States, to take one instance, was a rural nation; now it is an urban one, with a majority of the population living in its cities. The same is true at the global scale, insofar as the close of the Century saw the world's rural/urban balance shift from the former to the latter for the first time (UNCHS, 2001).

The particular political economic form that we have known throughout much of the 20th Century has been identified as the growth machine. This term is typically employed to describe the processes of city building via civic boosterism, a convergence of economic and political interests in the process of attracting investment capital to a particular location. As those with capital have always had investment options, and labour too is mobile, we have historically seen competition between cities for both investment and skilled workers. Once the process of attraction has begun—a function of geography, subsidies in the form of infrastructure and tax breaks, and a variety of other factors ranging from climate to political stability, then the growth machine perpetuates itself, as the demand for goods and services establishes a cycle of economic demand and consumption (Jonas and Wilson, 1999).

The principles of boosterism have not disappeared, for there are still examples of economic managers who see the development process as one of assembling specific attributes in order to attract labour and capital to a city. For instance, the recent debate about the importance of attracting an urban 'creative class' (which at times seems little more than a mechanistic device for recruiting a gay population, with large disposable incomes and a demand for certain high order goods and services) seems a somewhat bizarre throwback to this position (Florida, 2002).

After the urban growth machine?

As we have made the transition to the millennium, it is appropriate to question whether this familiar form of urban economic development remains important, not least as the most rapid rates of growth are concentrated now in the evolving economies. Indeed, we find that the growth machine has not passed away, precisely because of its continued importance throughout those parts of the world where economic development and urbanization converge. There, good research shows that the booster model persists, with city managers working to build cities and to bring corporations to their cities as a result of tax breaks, infrastructural provision, labour attributes and so forth (Urban, 2002, Wu, 2001). It is worthwhile to note that a significant proportion of this development involves explicitly foreign investment and global expertise in terms of design and construction, which is a break from the past.

It is important, too, to address the differences in the manner in which growth is being pursued, organized and financed. For instance, the *Economist* recently carried an advertisement with the tag line "CIDCO—we make cities" (*Economist*, 2002). The summary information was even more intriguing: "close to Mumbai, India's vibrant commercial capital, a new city will emerge. The Special Economic Zone—Navi Mumbai (New Bombay) will be a city with just commerce on its mind. It's a city that can be yours—to build, to plan, to market, to own." Cities devoted exclusively to making a profit are not new (in the United States, we find Commerce City and City of Industry, for example), but the notion of creating such a city so explicitly through the marketplace seems to go one long step further, as does the suggestion that once a corporation has built the city, then it owns it. As the advertisement emphasizes, "even at a time of unusual products, the offer of a city is admittedly rather out of the ordinary."

CIDCO is the City & Industrial Development Corporation of Maharashtra, which will maintain only a minority stake in the new special economic zone (SEZ). The latter will occupy over 4,000 hectares and is expected to provide employment eventually for over 150,000 people. The advertisement requested expressions of interest from corporations that have participated in the construction of at least one infrastructure project worth in excess of $20 million and that have a tangible net worth of at least $50 million [see also www.navimumbaisez.com].

The way that the SEZ is described is informative and is, consequently, quoted at length: "The SEZ-Navi Mumbai. A city with the advantages Mumbai never had. [It] will occupy a distinctly favoured position. It will function as a duty-free enclave. A 'delineated territory' with hassle-free administration, enjoying a host of special concessions from the Government of India. The SEZ will be a city inspired by Shenzen and Jebel Ali. It will be exempt from all taxes, levies, charges and customs and excise duties on the import of capital goods, raw materials and spares. It will enjoy a corporate tax holiday until 2010 [...]. Offshore banking units operate freely here. While the SEZ will be insulated from the domestic tariff area, it will have unrestricted access to it."

The advertisement concludes, "full autonomy will be granted for development. The allocation and pricing of land, facilities and services will be left to the [joint venture]. It's your city, it's your decision!"

There is a significant difference between this proposed entity and its neighbour Mumbai (O'Hare, 1998), and between this development process and the more traditional growth machine. Based on the Shenzen model, the EZ concept can be enormously profitable, as it allows foreign direct investment (FDI) to occur without the restrictions of corporations having to deal with multiple ministries and endless layers of bureaucracy. As CIDCO points out, Shenzen was responsible for $45 billion trade in 1998, which exceeded all of India's exports in that year. Latecomers, such as India, are now competing with China and Dubai, and must offer larger incentives. This will include restrictive labour legislation; for instance, all employees will be held to the same standards that currently bind utility workers, removing the possibility of taking industrial action. Note, then, that the traditional growth machine, drawing on municipal largesse, is being replaced by subsidies from regional and national government, and the stakes are, in consequence, higher.

Despite the new emphasis upon FDI, some aspects of the past are, though, still in evidence; for instance, governments are providing infrastructure at the taxpayer's expense, and at a higher level of provision than has been offered before. Critics of the traditional growth machine have emphasized the subordination of the public sphere to the needs of the private sector, and the placing of costs on the taxpayer, who may be paying subsidies long after the corporations in question have moved on. Should an evolving economy be keen to allow its cities to be offshore holdings of foreign corporations? This will remain a joint development, despite the gushing claims that "It's your city, it's your decision!" but the danger signals are clear. The proud claim, that the entire site will be surrounded by a high fence, brings back memories of colonial enterprises from an even earlier Century, with echoes of the East India Company, although at least there is no talk of corporate armies and navies in this Century. The equally enthusiastic choice of accountancy firm Arthur Andersen to lead up the investment process pointed (albeit with perfect hindsight), to precisely the wrong kind of model for a country like India, which has had some success with the creation of a domestic software industry via government incentives and especially the provision of a sophisticated educational system. Andersen is now associated with a different kind of capitalism, marked as rapacious at the least, criminal at worst.

As the Navi Mumbai advertisement concludes, "it is only appropriate that a tale of two cities should be accompanied by great expectations." The question is, of course, whose expectations are to be met? Those who work in the SEZ, whose labour will be governed by restrictive contracts; the state and local governments, who will expect returns on their expenditure on infrastructure; or the offshore investors? Ideally, everyone's expectations can be met, but if we stay with the Dickensian theme of the advertisement, we also remember the first line of his story; another bonanza of Enron-style offshore development might be an opportunity for investors, a disappointment for residents and workers, which is the best of times, and yet the worst of times.

Summary

The above example begins to point, then, to the emerging differences between the old and new growth machine models. In the 20th Century case, boosterism was a form of managerial entrepreneurialism, a means to bring capital and skills to a nascent urban area. In the 21st Century, it is much more likely that growth is planned to bring the urban area into being, or to enlarge it rapidly and significantly, and is designed consequently at a much more sweeping scale. A particularly important component of the difference is the role of the construction, real estate and property sector, which is increasingly operating at both the national and the transnational scale. What was once a geographically focused sector of booms and busts is now spearheaded by large corporations with an international portfolio, capable of building cities (or, as seen in Iraq, repairing nations damaged by war, or as seen in Turkey, by natural catastrophe). These corporations are most visible for their involvement in large-scale urban development projects (see Swyngedouw et al., 2002).

This question of scale is a quite important point of difference between the older and newer forms of growth machine. Indeed, because of this shift to large projects, much economic development is now above and beyond the management of specific municipalities, as already noted. Many large projects are also planned privately (Kirby, 2002). They touch down in specific localities but may have little to do with the traditional attributes of those localities, such as vibrant city centres or low crime rates. They transcend traditional urban growth issues insofar as their sheer scale distorts traditional ways of thinking about city planning and development. By constructing integrated residential, commercial and even industrial campuses, the global construction industry operates in a parallel world of private development and governance. Norms of public and private space, taxation and governance become rewritten by these new developments.

Perhaps most interesting is the manner in which homes, stores or industrial campuses become building blocks with design features that reorient different forms of individual behaviour. The integration of commercial, residential and service spaces via private planning undermines traditional notions of the spatial separation of land-uses, based on bid rent competition. This is a process that is also facilitated by changes in the way in which consumers think about intra-urban travel. As the quantitative importance of the journey-to-work diminishes in many cities, it is the overall profile of non-work trips that assumes greater importance; consequently, more importance is being placed on travel to larger malls and recreational spaces with a greater volume of opportunities for the consumer.

It should be pointed that while these privatized spaces—notably gated communities and shopping malls—have been seen in the 20th Century as a measure of American capitalism and consumption practices, it is now clear that they represent a new international style, somewhat like the international airport, that is being reproduced globally. For some, this simply argues for an imitative process of consumption, but this would discount the manner in which contemporary capitalism is adept at creating things that are attractive to consumers in specific political, economic and cultural settings. Gated communities are important for security purposes in some such contexts, such as Indonesia (see Leisch, 2002), but they are also ways to enhance the status and thus the cost of a residential development (Kirby, 2003). The same is true of the shopping mall, which offers advantages to the consumer and brings about a revolution in consumption practices simply because it is a perfected device that creates consumers and offers them experiences that they cannot replicate elsewhere (Hannigan, 1998).

That is not to say, of course, that these changes are without social importance or social risk. Privatized spaces distract the resident from traditional forms of citizenship and recast social organization toward privatized relations. This means essentially that typical forms of municipal governance are further hollowed out because the traditional forms of patronage have been dissipated within the growth consensus. Local politics is now reoriented towards broader issues [peace, the environment] or smaller issues [neighbourhood governance and the environment, or NIMBYism and the environment: Kirby, 2003].

Thinking about the city: which city?

All of these changes have long-term implications for the city itself, but also for its analysis. Efforts to construct integrated models of the city throughout the 20th Century have all revolved around patterns; this is true both of the original work done in Chicago and subsequently in Los Angeles, extending back as far as Banham's study (1971). The very fact that efforts to construct "postmodern urbanism" have begun with attempts to dismantle the ecological blueprint indicates just how pervasive such patterns remain [Dear, 2002]. But these are 20th Century concerns. The 21st Century city is indeed a city of fragments, but its patterning is perhaps the least interesting aspect of its development.

I have developed these insights both deductively and inductively through observation of Phoenix over the past decade. This is one of the fastest growing metropolitan areas in the US, and has now attracted over 3 million inhabitants. Yet it has few of the characteristics that one might expect from a city of such a size, and possesses none of the attributes of a city with global pretensions: it was described as an 'anticity' back in the 1980s, and that remains a provocative description today (Luckingham, 1989). It exists as a city in two parts; one of the past, built upon federal largesse, and of the present, which possesses a decidedly libertarian cast. The part that is privately developed is relatively prosperous (though by no means universally affluent), while the older city plays by the old growth machine rules, busily trying to attract sports teams and build downtown sports complexes. It is a metropolis that contains both a private city and a public city. And interestingly, the latter is losing ground, manifested most obviously by the recent decision of the Phoenix Cardinals (a local sports team) to relocate themselves away from the city core to a vast, new, purpose built, edge city, sports and retailing complex. This is consistent with the kinds of growth and change already indicated, particularly its newer privatized forms, such as planned housing communities; the emergence of integrated planned retail and commercial developments, and the nexus of research and industrial development.

It should be stressed that the goal of this necessarily brief chapter is naturally not to create some new urban orthodoxy of the 'Phoenix school' variety, but rather to draw some broad inferences about the changing intersection of urban and economic development processes in the new Century. In its interplay of public and private forms, the chapter does not place itself so far from other interpretations of the city (*e.g.* Dear, 1996), although it is different for a number of reasons. It does not ground itself in the post-modern need to view the contemporary city in terms that are at once dystopic, apocalyptic and whimsical (Davis, 2002). Little is served by identifying privatized spaces as theme parks; these are serious commercial developments with only a very thin popular cultural veneer. Little is gained by dismissing contemporary housing developments as rich white enclaves, when the data indicate that these are more complex social entities (Kirby, 2003). When all is said and done, the claims of postmodern urbanism have offered us remarkably little in our goal of understanding contemporary metropolitan development.

Conclusions

The goal of this chapter has been to conjecture about the trajectory of urban growth in new Century. In its broadest contours, this is of course still a recognizable political economic form, where public and private forces intersect. But in its details is noteworthy. The global organization of investment and construction is generating a convergence of form and function, with massive developments appearing throughout the world. These are different from what has gone before, in scale but also in terms of the importance of foreign investment, an international style and privatized planning and governance. As the Navi Mumbai case suggests, the beneficiaries of such developments may be far from the site of construction and development. Consequently, the new political economic form of the 21st Century has been identified as a transnational growth machine, with new rules and demanding a new research agenda.

REFERENCES

Banham, R. *The Four Ecologies of Los Angeles* [Harmondsworth: Penguin, 1971].

Dear, M. "In the city, time becomes visible" [76-105] in Scott, A. and E. Soja (eds.), *The City* [Berkeley: University of California Press: 1996].

Davis, M. *Dead Cities* [New York: New Press, 2002].

Dear, M.J. *Postmodern Urbanism* [Newbury Park: Sage, 2002].

Economist 8291 [2002] "A tale of two cities", 21.

Florida, R. *The Rise of the Creative Class* [New York: Basic Books, 2002].

Jonas A. and D. Wilson, *The Urban Growth Machine* [Albany, SUNY Press, 1999].

Kirby, A. "Globalization and growth in the new American city" [paper presented to the Societat Catalana de Geografica (2002)] (in press).

——. "Building walls, building communities?" [paper presented to the 2nd Annual International Conference in Social Science, Hawaii (2003)].

Leisch, H. "Gated communities in Indonesia", *Cities* 19(5) 241-50 [2002].

Luckingham, B. *Phoenix: the history of a Southwestern Metropolis* [Tucson: University of Arizona Press, 1989].

O'Hare, G. Abbott, D. and M. Barke, "A review of slum housing policies in Mumbai", *Cities* 15(4) 269-84 [1998].

Swyngedouw, E. "Neoliberal urbanization in Europe: large scale urban development projects and the new urban policy" [195-229] in Brenner, N. and N. Theodore (eds.), *Spaces of Neoliberalism* [Malden, MA: Blackwell, 2002].

UNCHS, *Cities in a globalizing world* [London: Earthscan, 2001].

Urban, F. "Small town, big website?" *Cities* 19(1) 49-60 [2002].

Wu, F. "Place promotion in Shanghai, PRC" *Cities* 17(5) 349-63 [2001].

6

The City, Globalisation and Social Transformation: A View from Liverpool

RONALDO MUNCK

R.P.Munck@liv.ac.uk

Professor of Political Sociology at the University of Liverpool and Director of the Globalisation and Social Exclusion Unit <www.gseu.org.uk> in the United Kingdom.

RUTH MELVILLE

ruth1@liv.ac.uk

Research Director at the Department of Sociology, Social Policy and Social Work at the University of Liverpool.

The city has long been a privileged site for critical social enquiry given its undisputed centrality for human life in the modern era. More recently, there has been a surge of interest in the postmodern city, the exemplar being usually Los Angeles. We also hear much of the 'global city'—the New Yorks, Londons and Tokyos of the world—linked together through the flows of finance. Yet somewhere like Liverpool—arguably neither postmodern or global—is studied mainly in relation to its social problems and the perennial schemes for urban regeneration it has been subjected to over recent decades. This volume seeks to redress the balance by making Liverpool its focus but with a purpose that is firmly comparative and general. This introductory chapter sets the scene for the various contributions by re-examining the postmodern global city thesis, surveying the various attempts at regenerating cities like Liverpool, exploring the diverse connections between the local and the global in the city, studying various forms of (re)presenting the city discursively, and, last but not least critically examining attempts and prospects for transforming the city.

The Postmodern Global City

Peter Hall, in his influential study *The World Cities*, argued some time ago that 'there are certain great cities, in which a disproportionate share of the world's most important business is conducted' (Hall, 1966: 7). These world cities are the seats of national government, crucial nodes in the flow of trade and finance and cultural powerhouses. With globalisation—a qualitative advance of economic internationalisation since the mid-1980s—the importance of these global cities has, if anything, increased. In the new dynamic international system we call globalisation, the great cities play a pivotal role in its variable configuration. As Saskia Sassen shows in *The Global City*, 'a combination of spatial dispersion and global integration has created a new strategic role for major cities' (Sassen, 1991: 3). This includes, pre-eminently, being a command point in the organisation and reproduction of the global economic system, a key location for finance, which has now replaced manufacturing as the leading economic sector, and a major site for the production and consumption of the goods, services and innovations being produced by the new capitalism.

In the literature on the city and globalisation we can detect two broad positions, albeit ones that might be complementary. On the one hand, Manuel Castells tends to emphasise how the power of the global city is mobilised *through* the networks of globalisation (Castells, 1996: 410). Emphasis is placed on the global focus more than on the city as a site of globalisation. For Saskia Sassen, on the other hand, 'place is central to many of the circuits through which economic globalisation is constituted' (Sassen, 1999: 171). By placing the city (as place) at the centre of the process of economic globalisation we reconceptualise the city and globalisation debates. What Sassen's analysis leads to are three central propositions:

1. While globalisation leads to dispersal and flows, it is also embedded in the global city where its central functions of management and co-ordination are organised.
2. Globalisation does not just 'happen', nor does the 'magic hand' of the market just run it; rather the

network of global cities designs, manages and services the new global economy.

3. The new global economy as a highly networked system requires a network of global cities which compete but which also create a division of functions to provide the necessary infrastructure and resources. (Sassen, personal communication)

Against the 'globalisers' who argue that place no longer matters, Sassen thus places globalisation firmly within the mega-cities that are one of the crucial spatial and social manifestations of the globalisation processes. For Sassen, 'Global cities become the sites of immense concentrations of economic power, while cities that were once major manufacturing centres suffer inordinate declines' (Sassen, 1994: 210). The winners in this process are able to agglomerate the necessary resources and skills in these central locations (or nodes) that service and reproduce the new globalised economy. So, globalisation is not 'out there' but in the corridors of power (and the mean streets) of New York as a new geography of centres and margins is shaped. For Manuel Castells the emphasis is on the flows he sees as characteristic of what he calls the new 'network society' (Castells, 1996). For Castells,

> The global city is not a place, but a process. A process by which centres of production and consumption of advanced services, and their ancillary local societies, are connected in a global network, while simultaneously downplaying the linkages with their hinterlands on the basis of information flows. (Castells, 1996: 386)

The power of the mega-city is mobilised precisely through the global networks it is part of, and it is the resources flowing through these that empower certain groups in the New Yorks of the world. It does not seem impossible, however, to work with an understanding of the city as part of this 'space of flows' but also with a critical political economy of the city focused on power struggles within its social and spatial boundaries.

At this point it may be useful to explain why the city and globalisation debates might be pertinent to somewhere like

Liverpool, which is not a London or even a sub-regional urban centre such as Manchester. Castells explains the process clearly:

> The global city phenomenon cannot be reduced to a few urban cores at the top of an hierarchy. It is a *process* that connects advanced services, producer centres, and markets in a global network [...]. Inside each country, the networking architecture reproduces itself into regional and local centres, so that the *whole system* becomes interconnected at the global level. (Castells, 1996: 380)

The scale and the intensity of connections may vary but all parts of the world system are interconnected. Globalisation has led to a new regionalisation and, for many commentators, a new localism. Being connected does not imply a simple interdependence, because the process is uneven and the 1970s dependency analysis may still have purchase. What are interdependent are the relations between the global, regional and local logics. What we are saying—against any 'out there-in here' analysis of globalisation as counterposed to the local, conceived of as fixed and traditional—is that globalisation takes shape in particular locales.

If we take a broad historic sweep we can also see how Liverpool always/already was a global city in a different way or in a different time. In his popular history of Liverpool, Tony Lane refers to its inhabitants' sense of superiority at the turn of the last century: 'The swagger derived from an inherited collage of beliefs celebrating the significance of a complete seaport economy at the heart of the largest global empire of the modern epoch' (Lane, 1997: 131). The 'triangular trade' between Europe, Africa and America (manufactured goods for slaves, slaves for raw materials) that helped build British hegemony had Liverpool as a key player. Liverpool's global connections created its docks, banks and factories but also its identity as an early global city. As Cameron and Crooke put it, 'Liverpool was not just the economic capital of the slave trade, it was also its political capital' (Cameron and Crooke, 1992: 24). Later, Liverpool became a key staging post for Irish emigration to America and a major recipient of Irish emigrants itself. Liverpool was thus always turned outwards to the Irish

Sea and beyond to the Atlantic, symbolising its overseas connections and their precedence over any organic connections with the rest of Britain.

But, as with marriages, what led to Liverpool's early success would also lead to its decline from the mid-twentieth century onwards. Following the decline of the transatlantic trade after the inter-war heyday, there was a spate of manufacturing activity in Liverpool, but by the time that had come to fruition it was the era of de-industrialisation. Tony Lane refers appositely to 'an inescapable chain of accelerating external economic forces' (Lane, 1997: 134) hitting Liverpool. The social dislocation caused by these external economic factors can be gauged by the decline of the city's inhabitants from 870,000 just before the Second World War to 440,000 by the time of the 2001 Census. If the rise of Liverpool during the eighteenth century was prodigious, its decline since the mid-twentieth century is equally dramatic. While slavery and colonialism helped make Liverpool, it is the global connection which helped unmake it, as Richard Meegan explains: 'Liverpool's recent decline is similarly set within a new global economic and political context and a newly emerging web of global relationships: the evolution of a new international division of labour [...] and the making of a "new Europe"' (Meegan, 1995: 84). In this way, Liverpool can be seen to be a post-colonial city as much as any metropolis of the so-called Third World.

While Liverpool may be a post-industrial city it is not readily associated with postmodernism. For Ed Soja, Los Angeles epitomises the decentred, decentralised metropolis characterised by post-Fordist working relations and a postmodern cultural setting typical of the flexible (even disorganised) capital accumulation regime of the future (Soja, 1989). The urban social structure is a fragmented quilt or mosaic of different social groups and cultures. This postmodern urban landscape is eclectic and celebrates difference and polyvocalism. There is a belief that 'Every single American city that *is* growing, is growing in the fashion of Los Angeles' (Garreau, 1991: 3). While for some, Los Angeles symbolises the American Dream, for others it is the American Nightmare (Davis, 1990), characterised by repression and poor conditions for its 'non-white' majority population. While Jonathan Raban had famously foreseen the postmodern city as a 'soft city'—'the city goes soft, it awaits the imprint of an identity [...] it invites you to remake it, to consolidate it into a shape you can live in' (Raban, 1974: 11)—for Mike Davis, Los Angeles represents, perhaps more realistically 'the hard edge of postmodernity' (Davis, 1992: 155).

Even if we accept the ideal of a decentralised, pluralist and innovative postmodern society, there are problems in applying the concept to a city such as Liverpool. In what way can a 'dirty old town' in the de-industrialised north of England be described as postmodern? Certainly, Liverpool—in spite of its much-vaunted 'nightlife'—seems hardly a city of fun and pleasure for the majority of its inhabitants. Take, for example, shopping—on which postmodern urban theorists wax lyrical in relation to North American shopping malls—and examine the practices of a citizen in one of the outlying north of England urban estates. Thus one study of Manchester, while not seeking 'to deny the presence in these cities of the kinds of casual and even pleasurable shopping described in so much of the contemporary writing...on the postmodern city' (Taylor, Evans and Fraser, 1996: 156) goes to show the prevalence of a more 'subsistence' bargain-hunting mode of shopping for most. Or, as a resident of Speke (an outlying estate) put it in our Rowntree study of Liverpool, 'If you want to buy shoes for your kids you've got to drag them into town [...] and they start playing up as soon as you get there [...] McDonald's, that's the first thing they say [...]. You go into town to get something specific and you end up coming home without what you wanted, and the kids with a "Happy Meal"' (Andersen et al., 1999: 22).

Postmodern urbanism operates with a conception of a radical break with the past. The new globalised postmodern city is seen as a homogeneous intervention that somehow flattens history and culture. The local/social is seen to dissolve under the influence of the global/economic. Ian Taylor, Karen Evans and Penny Fraser, in their study of two 'not-postmodern' cities (Manchester and Sheffield), argue against this interpretation, that 'the current regeneration of old industrial cities (at least in the north of England) actually reworks and re-represents the facts of local identity and difference, and therefore, importantly, preserves and symbolises these identities, albeit in a modified fashion by comparison with the custom and practice of the modernist period' (Taylor, Evans and Fraser, 1996: 35). It is local structures of feeling that shape and set the parameters of the post-industrial (but not necessarily postmodern) city. There is no *tabula rasa* in relation to local history, culture and class struggle. Our study of two neighbourhoods in Liverpool (Andersen et al., 1999) showed how even in the same city its history and community were 'lived' in very different ways and thus the prospects for regeneration and for community development varied considerably.

If Liverpool was in the past 'a complete seaport economy' (Lane, 1997: 131), it could today be seen as a 'decentred' city, and in this sense postmodern. The port and its global role is no longer a unifying focus and nor is manufacturing. The attempt to have a culture-led regeneration has not been as successful as in Glasgow, for example. In short, Liverpool is still characterised by what it was rather than having reinvented itself. We cannot envisage the same totalising gaze Engels developed for Manchester in *The Condition of the Working Class in England* (Engels, 1969) being articulated for Liverpool today. This big modernist picture is no longer possible. What Liverpool is, or might be, is necessarily fluid and even the boundaries of the debate are fuzzy. The language to describe this transition to a new city will also need to be fluid, open and non-necessitarian. The debates on regenerating the city do not generally accept this interpretation and on the contrary, they seek to impose a unifying logic—regeneration—on a social and spatial world that has become decentred and thus post-structuralist. What this might mean for its citizens we examine in subsequent sections.

The Local in the Global

What the last section has shown, above all else, is the importance of the local in the new global order. Michael Porter, guru of the competitive 'global class' city, recognises that competitive advantage 'is created and sustained through a highly localised process' (Porter, 1999: 19). It is to the complexity of this localised process and world that we now turn. Our knowledge of globalisation has not kept pace with the globalisation of knowledge (Appadurai, 1999) and our categories of analysis tend to be a bit crude. For example, in response to globalisation many critics have argued for reasserting the power of the local (*e.g.* Cox, ed., 1997). This has a certain attraction in that it is seen to 'bring people back in' to the workerless story or meta-narrative of globalisation. But ultimately, it seems simply to assert a militant place-based particularism against the evils of an abstract 'globalisation as demonisation.' Liverpool has already suffered the consequences in the 1980s, under the Militant administration of the city, of a conception of politics based on 'us against the world,' in this case the evils of Thatcherism, which were never going to be defeated by one (declining) city. The local/global connections must be conceived in a more subtle way if they are to serve as a basis for a strategy of social transformation.

It is common now in the globalisation literature to see reference to 'glocalisation', a process supposedly describing the new global-local intermingling or interpenetration. In cultural studies in particular this term has come to denote a new hybrid blend or fusion (for example, in the 'localising' of McDonalds in Korea). Perhaps there is a somewhat too benign flavour to this metaphor when applied to the de-industrialised city in the era of globalisation. Ash Amin has, however, referred interestingly to 'the urban social fragments and hybridity generated by "in here-out there" mingling' (Amin, 1997: 134). If the response hitherto has been to make the city work in the interests of those 'out there', there is no reason why we cannot start from the interests of those 'in here' (*i.e.* the city). As Amin puts it, 'the challenge is to mobilise diversity as a source of both social cohesion and urban economic competitiveness' (Amin, 1997: 134). The big issue today in debates on the future(s) of capitalism is 'trust' (see Fukuyama, 1995). A shared sense of reciprocity, trust and citizenship can be and is being generated in cities. That is a resource in terms of 'social capital' and political confidence that cannot be neglected.

To be provocative we could now plausibly reverse the feminist and environmental movement slogan of the 1970s which bade us 'Think globally, act locally'. Local politics is not just given or predetermined by global aggregation of interests. The much-vaunted 'death of distance' due to the time-space compression (Harvey, 1989) inherent in globalisation can certainly be exaggerated. A recent study of city politics concludes that 'local politics in a global era are best understood in terms of the ideas, institutions and interests shaping local policy processes' (Clarke and Gaile, 1997: 28). Certainly the new economics of globalisation sets the parameters in which any city operates but so also does the regional and sub-regional level. There is no reason why a Liverpool cannot develop a northwest of England perspective, or a Glasgow a European perspective, and not just sink into the globalisation blues. Globalisation has created a far greater degree of social polarisation at the local level but it has also generated a new localism that can knit together a social and political alliance to meet human needs at a local level. Globalisation is the context but not the sole horizon of possibilities if we consider the benefits of increased international transactions at all levels of human existence.

What we call globalisation has affected cities everywhere, even those we call 'provincial,' in making them more permeable to 'outside' factors, be it migration, global consumerism or the global mass media. Michael Prike refers to cities as 'places of multiple connections' which can no longer be thought of in isolation or as having some mythical 'fixed coherence' (Pryke, 1999: 326). A city is not just a place on the map: it is a site of power, difference and contestation. The city is cut across by multiple economic, social, political and cultural flows and interconnections. This relational perspective is also, necessarily, fluid, since these interconnections are constantly changing as well as intensifying in scope and depth. Amin and Graham usefully conceptualise cities as 'places of intersection between many webs of social, cultural and technological flow, and the superimposition of these relational webs in the physical space of cities' (Amin and Graham, 1999: 9). Another (more chronological) way of seeing the city is as a palimpsest, a manuscript or text in which layers of writing (or meaning?) are superimposed on the original. Except that, rather than effacing the original, the new layers of the city often co-exist with the earlier ones.

The global city analysis strengthens these points in a number of ways, even if Liverpool's entry into this category must be open to debate. The new globalised professional classes need to find in a city the residential amenities, the services and the low-paid (often informal) workers to provide these. Much of Liverpool's 'regeneration' seems to be directed to this purpose as much as 'empowering' the poor. Today's urbanisation (as against suburbanisation) is driven largely by the needs of this professional class, which generates a growing demand for central city space and luxury enclaves. Thus the global city can be seen not only as a site in strategic cross-border circuits but also as a set of contested social spaces where the politics of place becomes the main axis of city dynamics.

If cities must necessarily be conceived of as 'open' in the era of globalisation, they must also be understood as diverse and conflictual in essence. In relating to a city such as Liverpool we have two main prejudices to contend with. First, there is a long-standing myth of the classless northern city characterised by tight-knit 'communities'. A casual acquaintance with the TV serial *Coronation Street* will give you the picture. Secondly, as Logan and Molotch write, there is a certain tradition of Marxism which gives little attention to neighbourhood life, but when it does it has assumed a homogeneity among almost all neighbourhoods, regardless of race, ethnicity or location (Logan and Molotch, 1987: 101). This would derive either from a productivist and economistic perspective that believed the 'class struggle' only occurred between labour and capital in factories, or from the 'Castells school' in its structuralist phase. From that perspective there was a belief that sharing use of the same services would generate a struggle dynamic based on 'collective consumption' issues. We are now more sensitised to differences based on age, gender, ethnicity, sexual orientation and locality amongst others. Our Rowntree Project on two Liverpool neighbourhoods, indeed, placed these differences at the centre of our research and analysis.

The city is inevitably always a gendered and a racialised space. As one Liverpool woman told us 'The men put on the suits and try to be helpful but basically the women run the homes [...] they also run all those types of [community] groups' (Andersen et al., 1999). When it came to the spatial definition of a neighbourhood, many residents of a predominantly 'white' area stressed that they were not part of the contiguous well-known 'black' area. Every aspect of social life, street life and political life in the city is cut across by racial and gender differences. Age, too, is a constant feature in social differentiation. Youth has come to symbolise 'social exclusion' and elders have come to signify 'dependency'. Our study cut across widely cherished stereotypes. Many young people were reflective on their 'troublesome' image and had a general vision for their area. Elders seemed well aware of the frustrations of youth in their area and were not keen to scapegoat them.

In a recent reader on the city, Gerry Mooney argues that Britain's deprived council estates are:

> all too frequently portrayed as intense, uniform locales of conflict and unrest, housing homogeneous groups of 'socially excluded' people. Little thought is given to their internal social and spatial differentiation and heterogeneity, to the strategies which residents adopt to 'cope', and to residents' day-to-day struggles with public agencies. (Mooney, 1999: 73)

It is important to note finally, that the Liverpool Rowntree study, while stressing social differentiation and the diverse perspectives, did find that 'in the last instance' (apologies to Marx) there was a shared working-class identity and a local identity of considerable coherence, especially when faced with what were perceived as external threats.

Regenerating the City

Liverpool has been the recipient of almost every urban regeneration initiative in Britain since the 1960s. Liverpool, along with the north of England generally, has been seen as a prime candidate for regeneration given the consistently higher than average rates of unemployment, homelessness and poverty in the city region. The problem has been seen to lie with the estates, those sites where popular and academic attention (Power, 1998) have focused on crime, poor housing and a supposed general social and moral decline. The culmination of many failed initiatives has been New Labour's New Deal for Communities, which in the course of 1999 began to promulgate the concept of 'joined-up' thinking and action to deal with problems that are, indeed, clearly interrelated. The New Deal for Communities was pledged to 'target money on the most deprived neighbourhoods to: improve job prospects; bring together investment in buildings and investment in people; and, improve neighbourhood management and the delivery of local services' (DETR, 1998: 7). The mechanisms for its delivery would be through local partnerships and there was a commitment to sustain community involvement. While the major focus was, as always, on jobs, housing and health, there was a new emphasis on 'neighbourhood management' and on 'anti-social behaviour'.

What has emerged, in the long trial and error process of urban regeneration initiatives, is an integrated approach to sustainable improvements in urban life. It would seem that national-level initiatives could only achieve their objectives through local-level actions. Indeed, a Joseph Rowntree Foundation review of area-regeneration programmes found that each area was different, with its own distinctive problems and opportunities (Joseph Rowntree Foundation, 1998). Nevertheless, this research did highlight certain general patterns and the need for regeneration initiatives to address certain key issues, including:

1. Understanding disadvantaged neighbourhoods—including the views of local people and the local assets available;
2. Bringing residents to the centre of regeneration-building skills and enhancing confidence to undertake projects with professionals;
3. Transforming mainstream services at the local level—developing a clear neighbourhood focus for services through partnerships;
4. Targeting economic development services—to create the training, jobs and finance to link growth with local regeneration;

5. Strengthening communities—to build community capacity so that long-term income is ensured;
6. Ensuring a long-term commitment to sustainable neighbourhood regeneration—policy integration and visionary city leadership. (Joseph Rowntree Foundation, 1998)

While this would appear to be a coherent recipe for progressive transformation of deprived communities, we need to examine the broader context of who is actually involved in urban regeneration. Clearly, the communities themselves are interested, but business and government (both local and national) are the key players. In the era of globalisation, cities are becoming major competitive players. These cities are now 'managed' as are businesses and not 'planned' as in the heyday of modernist urban planning. Michael Porter has codified what the new managed competitive city needs to do to succeed: 'We must stop trying to cure the inner city's problems by perpetually increasing social investment and hoping for economic activity to follow. Instead an economic model must begin with the premise that inner city businesses should be profitable' (Porter, 1999: 313). The cornerstone of this regeneration model is to seek the competitive advantage a modern city may enjoy and help it find a niche that is hard to replicate. This has led to the scramble to package and repackage cities across the world to make them more attractive to business. This model, which first sprang to prominence in Reagan's America, is now the accepted common sense lying behind most inner-city regeneration initiatives. That it is essentially a 'beggar thy neighbour' philosophy does not seem to concern its advocates.

What have emerged in many cities since the early 1980s are 'urban growth coalitions' committed to 'boosterism'. The classic definition is that of Molotch and Logan who refer to the new urban coalitions as 'a set of actors who push for local growth maximisation to increase returns from real estate manipulation and other business activities specifically dependent on local grown—collectively making up the "growth machine"' (Molotch and Logan, 1985: 144). That these policies are often socially regressive and environmentally destructive does not detract from the overall goal. Competition between places seems to take over from competition between businesses and the city becomes a growth machine committed to boosting its local fortunes against other cities. Logan and Molotch call this 'the battle of the growth machines' (Logan and Molotch, 1987: 35). However, it is not at all clear whether this battle actually benefits the citizens of the places that are supposedly 'winning' nor, for that matter, the public good in any generally recognisable way. What is clear is that community organisations can gain resources for redevelopment of their areas through entering these coalitions, in the same way that businesses and local government can gain through obtaining 'community support' for their growth machines when seeking, for example, to access European funding where the discourse of community 'participation' prevails.

The ideologies of the 'growth machines' tell us that a city is a place where 'people learn better and develop faster' (Rossabeth Moss Kanter, cited in Thrift, 1999: 283) if they develop the 'three Cs': concepts (new ideas or technologies), competence (high-quality products) and connections (international trade). If 'world class' status in one of the three Cs is not achieved the city inevitably becomes residualised or marginalised. To some extent this is the fate of Liverpool and other cities in the north of England; it is not exaggerating to see in Engels' descriptions of mid-nineteenth century Manchester a prescient picture of today's run-down housing estates in these northern cities. Taylor, Evans and Fraser refer eloquently to 'the silence or indifference—at least in public, political discussion—as to the lived character of these residualised places and territories' (1996: 291). The people living in these places feel forgotten and find regeneration to be somewhat hollow as far as their direct experience is concerned. Their expectations are hardly radical or unrealistic:

> We want to be recognised, to have the same things as other people, to be equal with the others. That's not asking a lot. We want our own shops, we want things to entertain the children rather than make a mess out of everything. We want councillors who will work for us rather than against us. (Andersen et al., 1999: 25)

What is remarkable is that research had to be commissioned in the late 1990s to find out what people wished for in these places.

While cities are now 'managed' to make them competitive in the world market they must also be governed. The issue of governance in the era of globalisation is a troubled one, and nowhere more so than in relation to the city. Governance today has a political but also a social and economic dimension; it involves governmental but also non-governmental institutions. Parts of the global economy are escaping control by direct political governance. National governments can come to office—as with New Labour—claiming that globalisation constrains their governmental choices. Yet cities have to be governed and not just managed because citizens live in them. It is not surprising that cities are sites of 'boosterism' and competitive advantage but also for social movements and radical democratic discourses. The city is a site for the powerful in their global quest for hegemony but it is also where the powerless live, dream and struggle. Nigel Thrift refers in this context to how the 'global cities can be seen as strategic sites within which hierarchies of power are most striking *and* most open to challenge' and refers to grass-roots economic innovations such as LETS as 'possible economic contributions to the redefinition of citizenship as a more global-local concern' (Thrift, 1999: 305).

We find in regime theory an interesting new perspective on power and governance in the contemporary city (see Stoker, 1999) that helps us understand the complexity and the interdependence of the modern urban system. While it focuses on the role of business and government it does not neglect the role of disadvantaged groups and argues that 'politics matter'. For regime theory the internal politics of coalition building is crucial in determining the mode of governance in the city. While stressing the relationships between business interests and local government it also embraces the knowledge professionals (for example, urban planners and consultants of various kinds) and communities or their 'representatives'. In his model of urban governance, Jon Pierre distinguishes four ideal types:

> *Managerial*
> Its objective is efficiency, its style pragmatic, its key instrument the contract and its evaluation criterion efficiency;
> *Corporatist*
> Its objective is distribution, its style ideological, its key instrument deliberations and its evaluation criterion participation;
> *Pro-growth*
> Its objective is growth, its style pragmatic, its key instrument partnerships, and its evaluation criterion growth;
> *Welfare*
> Its objective is redistribution, its style ideological, its key instrument networks, and its evaluation criterion equity. (adapted from Pierre, 1999: 388)

For many cities we can recognise some of these models for particular periods, even if, in practice, they may be 'impure' or combined in their application. It is certainly possible to deploy this model, for example, in Liverpool to see how an alliance of pro-growth city councillors and officers, business interests, urban regeneration professionals and community 'representatives' has been created in recent years. We must also understand that this is a contingent political alliance and not necessarily a natural given. Equally, a common situation of de-industrialisation, for example, will not generate the same type of regime as Di Gaetano and Lawless's corporate study of Birmingham, Sheffield and Detroit shows. They found, rather, that 'despite remarkably common economic experiences, the structures and processes of governance developed in the three de-industrialised cities from 1980 to 1997 varied considerably both across cities and over time' (Di Gaetano and Lawless, 1999: 569). While corporatism has been a common international mode, managerialism is a mainly British phenomenon and clientelism more a US mode. It is inevitably local politics, even with a similar broad regime model being applied, that determines the precise contours, modalities and effectiveness of a given mode.

Finally it may be useful to stand back reflexively from the complex issues of regeneration and governance in the contemporary city and begin to think of the actual language of these discourses. For example, if we examine Liverpool First's Action Plan ('New Commitment to Regeneration'), we read at the start that: 'In the last decade, the political landscape of Liverpool has changed beyond recognition. Since the 1990s a spirit of pragmatism and co-operation has been evident' (LPG, 1999: 5). Later we are told that the three key 'drivers' for regeneration will be competitiveness, social justice and environmental sustainability. Not only is competitiveness placed first but its compatibility with the other two 'drivers' might at least be questionable. But we can assume that 'pragmatism' will prevail and cooperation will be secured from the community for the overriding need to build 'competitiveness' (itself a deeply ambiguous term). When later in the document we find a discussion of 'Local Community Empowerment Strategies' we must dig beneath the surface but it would seem that 'empowerment' is essentially about a partnership agreement: 'This will promote ways to engage communities and businesses and help them to become confident and informed partners' (LPG, 1999: 15). Language always reflects the power arrangements in a given society; it is never 'innocent' or transparent, and it gains authority from the discursive terrain it is embedded within.

As Rob Atkinson has pointed out, the competitiveness drive and the partnership model are 'firmly rooted in a discourse which prioritises the provision of a stable environment for business and the control of social protection costs' (Atkinson, 1997: 7). Thus we find that when official discourse refers to a 'partnership' the concept is usually seriously under-defined. It is bathed in a positive glow but its precise contours and nature are not really specified, beyond general aspirations to a form of 'synergy'. A dominant discourse is also well able to absorb and defuse contestatory elements that might challenge it. For example, the notion of 'empowerment' can be seen as quite radical as applied in Third World contexts, but when applied to urban regeneration the terms become even vaguer than those of 'partnership'. As Atkinson argues,

> If we are to move beyond such a position then it is essential [...] that genuine community empowerment requires not merely that the community be allowed to participate but that we rethink the language of participation in order to tackle imbalances in social, economic and political power. (Atkinson, 1997: 9)

In our Rowntree project *Neighbourhood Images in Liverpool* we found, indeed, that at all levels of the community and in local government there was a disputed discursive terrain around such concepts as 'participation' and the whole nature of 'regeneration'.

(Re)Presenting the City

To put it polemically, there is no such *thing* as a city. Rather, *the city* designates the space produced by the interaction of historically and geographically specific institutions, social relations of production and reproduction, practices of government, forms and media of communication, and so forth [...] *The city*, then, is above all a representation (Donald, 1992: 417).

Reacting against the excesses of the structuralist vision of the 1970s there is now considerable attention paid to 'the city as text. Rather than seek a false coherence and unity in today's city we need to 'read' it, and that implies that we can read it in different ways. In part, we are dealing with a paradigm shift here in terms of how we interpret the discourse of the city. Anthony King explains how the city was once the privileged territory where white Western male sociologists and urban planners inscribed their pet theories and models, but that it has now become 'the happy-hunting ground of film theorists, poets, art historians, writers, television producers, literary critics, and postmodern connoisseurs of all kinds' (King, 1996: 2). A degree of theoretical diversity and even disagreement may be necessary to move beyond outdated visions of the city and its discontents.

If someone were to arrive in Liverpool from Mars they would definitely have heard of the Beatles and the Albert Dock (the Slavery Museum?). If they were lucky they would have seen Alan Bleasdale's *Boys from the Blackstuff* and if they were unlucky they would have watched *Brookside*. The point is that we have a cultural image of places. That culture and history are also embodied in the buildings of Liverpool through which we can also 'read' the histories of colonialism, Irish emigration and urban decline. It is through these readings that we produce representations of the city. They exist at a discursive level even if they also have material representation. The cultural dimension of the city is vital in a number of ways. The 'cultural turn' in the social sciences and humanities, referred to above, leads to a situation where '[the] city as an object of analysis has been unbound' (Jacobs, 1993: 827). Furthermore, if we examine the recent history of cities such as Glasgow and Dublin, we see to what extent their cultural revival has led to real economic regeneration given the strong cultural element in globalisation.

It is also important to understand what the 'cultural turn' is not. When anthropologists ran out of exotic 'others' to study in the non-Western world (including the west of Ireland), they turned to the cities. In the new urban settings they did ethnography and they engaged in what Fox called an 'undignified scramble to find substitute savages in slums' (cited in Hannerz, 1980: 2). In the new exotic setting we could rediscover 'community' or rail against 'alienation' in the modern city. It is hardly surprising that radical urban sociologists such as Castells (1997) and Harvey (1973) rejected 'culturalism' in the 1970s. Today, it is more an issue of foregrounding language in that loose family of methods known as discourse analysis (see Howarth, 2000). The emphasis is on the interrelationship between language and power over representation. Michèle Barrett summarises Michel Foucault's *The Archaeology of Knowledge* admittedly 'a little polemically' as 'the production of "things" by "words"' (Barrett, 1992: 131). A discourse can thus be seen as a practice that forms the object of which it speaks. Thus 'Liverpool' as we know it, live it and (re)present it, is constructed historically, socially and politically, but also discursively in the films, plays and TV and newspaper reports about the city region.

As with other 'northern cities' Liverpool is often represented in the national media as symbolic locale for some horrific crime, an example of a worthy urban regeneration initiative, or the site of an inspiring drama about urban unemployment.

Yet there is very little basis for constituting 'the north' as a social/spatial site of special significance and we may, just as validly, refer to an east/west split in Britain. Yet the north exists discursively and George Orwell could refer in *The Road to Wigan Pier* to a 'strange country' above a line a little north of Birmingham where the 'real ugliness of industrialisation' began (Orwell, 1959). Certainly, the uneven development of British capitalism did result in a core and a periphery, in both economic and cultural terms. This spatial discourse marked and accentuated social divisions of power reflected in language and customs—in short, in culture. North of Watford lies the land of 'the British working class' as portrayed in films and plays. In these cultural products, the north becomes a real place: 'place becomes a signifier of character, a metaphor for the state of mind of the protagonists, in the well-worn naturalist tradition' (Andrew Higson, cited Shields, 1991: 216).

The north, as the land of 'the working class', is yet another ethnographic construction of an Other. As Rob Shields puts it, it is 'an invention cast as the foreign "Other" of the socially constructed orderliness of the British nation centred around London' (Shields, 1991: 218). These images are notionally class images rendered spatially, but also gendered images. The 'salt of the earth' northern worker is also male, preferably a docker, a miner or steelworker. As, say, with the north of Ireland, where gender and religion are symbiotic in cultural images (Catholic/female; Protestant/male) so here manliness and northernness go hand in hand. Boss politics and labour politics in Liverpool have always been gendered, as epitomised in the macho-Marxism of the dismal Militant period. Now, it would be wrong to think that these discourses are simply distortions. Rob Shields is perfectly correct to stress 'the fact that the myths were not simple fictions but related in a complex manner with tangible conditions. In many cases, the images accentuated these conditions; in others, the images became self-fulfilling prophecies' (Shields, 1991: 245). This last point is essential to understanding the difficulties a city like Liverpool has in (re)presenting itself anew as an image-place given the long history of myth-making and 'deviance amplification'.

It is always also in the imagination, though, that a city can be reimagined. Discourse on the city has always been permeated with utopias, images of the 'good city'. Sociological language is somewhat 'cold' in this regard, and in its vain concern for 'scientificity' it often refuses to engage with change. In academic circles, as Taylor and co-authors argue, there has been 'an absence of the kind of engagement shown by the urban regeneration coalitions or from the pessimistic concerns of the urban retreatists' (Taylor, Evans and Fraser, 1996: 312). While it is easy to critique and deconstruct some of the millenarian fantasies of the urban planners, alternative urban imaginaries are less easy to find. Yet we need to understand that a city is not just its buildings, its highways, its parks and its housing estates. As Nestor García Canclini writes in relation to Mexico City: 'Cities are also configured through images. These may be the plans that invent and order the city. But also, the sense of urban life is imagined through novels, songs and films, press stories, radio and television. The city becomes dense as it is loaded with heterogeneous fantasies' (García Canclini, 1997: 109). The programmed or managed city is overloaded as it overflows with multiple, individual and collective stories.

We can now go back to the theme of reading the city as a text. When Engels represented the Manchester of the 1840s in *The Condition of the Working Class in England* (Engels, 1969), 'This reading of the city, this perception and construction of it as a signifying structure, may be regarded [...] as prototypical for the nineteenth century, and the first part of the twentieth' (Marcus, 1973: 232). Yet the late twentieth-century/early twenty-first-century city seems literally 'illegible'. It may be simply because the modernist paradigm has been exhausted, along with totalising illusions that we can 'grasp' the city in its wholeness. Many writers on the city now complain that their language seems inadequate to the tasks of analysis (and change) at hand. The decentred city of today can only be grasped through the critical and pluralist tools of an affirmative or emancipatory postmodernism (see Sousa Santos, 1999). The city of today is but a metaphor for the strange new postmodern globalised world we are entering. Following Sharpe and Wallock I would, finally, note that, as the examples of Engels and Orwell (in his own way) show, 'learning how to read the city is a necessary part of learning how to change it' (Sharpe and Wallock, 1987: 39).

Transforming the City

There is now a widespread acceptance among policy makers and researchers that urban regeneration requires the cooperation of urban residents. A Joseph Rowntree Foundation report by Marilyn Taylor (1995) is entitled *Unleashing the Potential: Bringing Residents to the Centre of Regeneration.* Consultation with the community or its representatives is now mandatory for most national and European regeneration initiatives. Yet there is a widespread feeling in many of these 'disadvantaged' communities that residents are not in fact properly consulted and that, certainly, they have little actual power in relation to regeneration of their areas. In our Liverpool Rowntree study it was common for us to hear comments like the following:

> Consultation is a poor thing [...]. Involvement from the beginning is by far preferable.
>
> People do get involved but, whatever you say, it doesn't make any difference. You spend all that time in a committee discussing and trying to help the area to get better but then it's decided by someone who doesn't even live here [...]. (Andersen et al., 1999)

So, while we may all agree in a general sense that 'It's all down to the people' (the subtitle of the Liverpool Rowntree study), we are still not clear on how citizens may be part of the overall project to transform the city in a democratic development direction.

One important response to the perceived ravages of globalisation is communitarianism, which argues that local community solidarity can provide coherence to a given area and create the resources denied or even destroyed by the state. The theory of 'social capital' explicitly charges the state with 'crowding out' the informal networks that could help regenerate communities. This does not stop enlightened state policies (such as those of New Labour) from seeking to co-opt the notion of social capital to state-led regeneration initiatives. This is 'helping people to help themselves'. But whatever the positive features of the new localism in terms of the empowerment of communities, communitarianism must remain a flawed model for social transformation. 'Community' is a political and highly contested concept (see Hoggett, ed., 1997) so it simply cannot be taken innocently or at face value. Furthermore, as David Harvey puts it, '"community" insofar as it exists is an unstable configuration [...] insofar as it does acquire permanence it is frequently an exclusionary and oppressive social form that can be as much at the root of urban conflict and urban degeneration as it can be a panacea for political-economic difficulties' (Harvey, 1989: 439). Indeed, our Liverpool Rowntree study found a constant allusion to 'close' communities also being 'closed' communities intolerant of 'difference'.

If 'community' or, more precisely, communitarianism is no panacea for urban problems this does not mean that the state is either. For one thing, in the era of globalisation, the nation-state is too 'small' to cope with international pressures and too 'big' to deal with local issues. The urban growth coalition, referred to earlier, has the potential to create a social and political alliance for redevelopment. It is possible to conceive of a 'synergy', as Peter Evans writes in relation to international development strategies, in which 'civic engagement strengthens state institutions and effective state institutions create an environment in which civic engagement is more likely to thrive' (Evans, 1996: 1034). Networks of civic engagement with local state support can create new norms of trust and reciprocity. Bureaucratic local states can be reformed as the current British engagement with a democratising local government agenda demonstrates. Nor do 'communities' and community activists need to be permanently suspicious of the 'suits' as planners are dubbed in the vernacular of Liverpool (and doubtless elsewhere). John Friedmann is probably speaking for many when he declares: 'I see urban planners being passionately engaged in a transformative politics for inclusion, opportunity for self-development and social justice. It is a politics driven by the energies of a civil society that is beginning to reassert itself in all of its diversity' (Friedmann, 1998: 35).

The discourse of civil society is a broader one than that of 'social capital', and has a definite technocratic edge to it. A flourishing civil society means more than community 'representatives' sitting on regeneration boards. Indeed, it may well be the case that the whole 'participation' drive in regeneration politics has actually demobilised civil society. Structures that become formalised, relationships of patronage and clientelism, and a 'soft' funding-driven development strategy are not good for the health of civil society. The development of state-civil society synergy would seem to be essential to a democratic transformation strategy that could avoid both the futility of an abstract revolutionism and the co-option of a lukewarm reformism. The sustainable city depends on the emergence and consolidation of such structures and processes. It is certainly the only way that a genuine democratic development plan can replace the current fashion for the 'management' and 'selling' of great cities. In its progressive aspect, planning has always included a social vision as well as the spatial dimension. As Blowers and Pain note, 'Space itself does not determine the sustainability of cities, but the configuration of social relations does' (1999: 291). The quest for sustainability, though, faces a major challenge from the forces unleashed by globalisation.

It is one of the great myths of the era that globalisation is an all-powerful tidal wave sweeping away locality and nation-state and putting a lock on any form of contestation. Even the relative autonomy of the state is removed by internationalisation and the city can only compete with other cities to court favour with the agents of globalisation. Yet, as Harvey notes, the spatialisation of globalisation is, in reality, part of 'the space-place dialectic [which] is ever a complicated affair, that globalisation and historical (spatio-temporal) development that creates a variegated terrain of anti-capitalist struggle' (Harvey, 1996: 439). For every door that is closed by globalisation another one is opened. From the protests against the World Trade Organisation in Seattle 1999 to international campaigns against child labour, from social movement unionism challenges to the transnational corporations, to inter-city networks in Western Europe, globalisation is being challenged by many social forces. The 'information city' with its networked citizens, the 'post-colonial city' with its socially diverse populations, and even the 'rustbelt' or de-industrialised city striving to reinvent itself, all have a positive role to play in reasserting social control over capital.

A city in transformation will have a mobilised civil society, will be committed to sustainability (social as much as spatial), and will avoid the twin pitfalls of communitarianism and globalism. It will also, by necessity, and arguably by choice, be an 'open' city. We have already seen the necessary openness of cities in the era of globalisation but 'open' can also denote a new radical democratic space. Michael Pryke writes in this regard on how the open nature of cities makes them 'spaces of instability and contingency' but also 'offer[s] them the potential to become space of opportunity and empowerment' (Pryke, 1999: 334-35). While Pryke seems to give priority to the first element there is no reason why we should not explore the second aspect in more detail. It is not just the powerful who live in the great cities but a great mass of people with hopes, aspirations and energies. There is a new cultural politics of the city emerging with contestation at all levels, from the city council to the schools, from court rooms to public spaces, from community organisations to the places of work. There is in the city a new frontier—more complex, nuanced and contradictory than the old capital-labour opposition—where democracy contests the unfettered rule of capital.

This final section began with the theme that 'it's all down to the people'. In current British regeneration discourse this conception would seem populist at best, co-optive in intent at worst. Certainly we have tried to deconstruct this language and develop a more adequate theoretical and political perspective. A city such as Liverpool is more than 'a suitable case for treatment', a laboratory for 'social inclusion' experiments, its people cannon fodder for participation exercises or social capital calculations. This is an argument made powerfully by Saskia Sassen in her Foreword to this volume. There is still a common assumption abroad that 'disorderly places' such as the urban ghetto, the Third World shanty-town, or the inner-city estate in Britain, breed 'disorderly people' (Mooney, 1999: 81). There is a whole underclass industry examining these people through what Edward Said has referred to as the new 'urban orientalism', an exoticising of the Other. In fact, the attitudes of the young people in the

Liverpool Rowntree Study were remarkably 'ordinary' for people living in an area where one-third of the working population were unemployed:

> They think we are all dead common and rough. They say don't come here because they rob your car [...]. If they go to places where they hire stuff they won't let you [...]. People think we are all druggies [...].
>
> I want to get a good job really and just be happy. I don't want to be on the dole.
>
> If they did up all the houses, yeah, make it look pretty [...] people aren't afraid of pretty things [...].

REFERENCES

Amin, A. (1997), 'Placing Globalisation', *Theory, Culture and Society,* 14(2).

—— and Graham, S. (1999), 'Cities of Connection and Disconnection', in J. Allen, D. Massey and M. Pryke (eds.), *Unsettling Cities,* London: Routledge.

Andersen, H., Munck, R., et al. (1999), *Neighbourhood Images in Liverpool: 'It's All Down to the People',* York: Joseph Rowntree Foundation.

Appadurai, A. (1999), 'Globalisation and the Research Imagination', *International Social Science Journal,* 160 (June).

Atkinson, P. (1997), 'Discourses of Empowerment and Partnership in Contemporary Urban Regeneration', paper presented at the conference 'Discourse and Urban Change: Foregrounding language in housing and urban research', University of Glasgow.

Barrett, M. (1992), *The Politics of Truth: From Marx to Foucault,* Cambridge: Polity Press.

Blowers, A., and Pain, K. (1999), 'The Unsustainable City?', in S. Pile, C. Brook and G. Mooney (eds.), *Unruly Cities?,* London: Routledge.

Cameron, G. and Crooke, S. (1992), *Liverpool—Capital of the Slave Trade,* Liverpool: Picton Press.

Castells, M. (1996), *The Information Age Volume 1: The Rise of the Network Society,* Oxford: Blackwell.

—— (1997), *The Urban Question,* London: Edward Arnold.

Clarke, S. and Gaile, G. (1997), 'Local Politics in a Global Era: Thinking Locally, Acting Globally', *Annals AAPSS,* 551 (May).

Cox, K. (1997), *Spaces of Globalisation: Reasserting the Power of the Local,* New York: The Guildford Press.

Davis, M. (1990), *City of Quartz: Excavating the Future in Los Angeles,* New York: Verso.

—— (1992), 'Fortress Los Angeles: The Militarisation of Urban Space', in M. Sorokin (ed.), *Variations on a Theme Park,* New York: Noonday Press.

DETR (Department of the Environment, Transport and the Regions) (1998), *New Deal for Communities*, London: DETR.

Di Gaetano, A. and Lawless, P. (1999), 'Urban Governance and Urban Decline, Governing Structures and Policy Agenda in Birmingham and Sheffield, England and Detroit, Michigan, 1980-1997', *Urban Affairs Review*, 34(4).

Engels, F. (1969) [1844], *The Condition of the Working Class in England*, London: Panther.

Evans, P. (1996), 'Development Strategies across the Public-Private Divide', *World Development*, 24(6).

Friedmann, J. (1998), 'The New Political Economy of Planning: The Rise of Civil Society', in M. Douglass and J. Friedmann (eds.), *Cities for Citizens. Planning and the Rise of Civil Society in a Global Age*, Chichester: John Wiley & Sons.

Fukuyama, F. (1995), *Trust? The Social Virtues and the Creation of Prosperity*, New York: Free Press.

García Canclini, N. (1997), *Imaginarios Urbanos*, Buenos Aires: Eudeba.

Garreau, J. (1991), *Edge City: Life on the New Frontiers*, New York: Doubleday.

Hall, P. (1966), *The World Cities*, New York: McGraw Hill.

Hannerz, U. (1980), *Exploring the City: Inquiries Toward an Urban Anthropology*, New York: Columbia University Press.

Harvey, D. (1973), *Social Justice in the City*, London: Edward Arnold.

—— (1989), *The Condition of Postmodernity*, London: Blackwell.

—— (1996), *Justice, Nature and the Geography of Difference*, London: Blackwell.

Hoggett, P. (ed.) (1997), *Contested Communities*, London: Policy Press.

Howarth, D. (2000), *Discourse*, Buckingham: Open University Press.

Jacobs, J. (1993), 'The City Unbound: Qualitative Approaches to the City', *Urban Studies*, 50(4/5).

Joseph Rowntree Foundation (1998), *Regenerating Neighbourhoods: Creating Integrated and Sustainable Improvements*, York: Joseph Rowntree Foundation.

King, A. (1996), 'Introduction: Cities, Texts and Paradigms', in A. King (ed.), *Re-Presenting the City. Ethnicity, Capital and Culture in the Twenty-First Century Metropolis*, London: Macmillan.

Lane, T. (1997), *Liverpool, City of the Sea*, Liverpool: Liverpool University Press.

LPG (Liverpool Partnership Group) (1999), *Liverpool First. New Commitment to Regeneration. Action Plan Phase 1*, Liverpool: Liverpool Partnership Group.

Logan, J., and Molotch, H. (1987), *Urban Fortunes: The Political Economy of Place*, Berkeley: University of California Press.

Marcus, S. (1973), 'Reading the Illegible', in H.J. Dyos and M. Wolff (eds.), *The Victorian City: Images and Realities*, London: Routledge.

Meegan, R. (1995), 'Local Worlds', in J. Allen and D. Massey (eds.), *Geographical Worlds, Vol. 1*, Oxford: Oxford University Press.

Molotch, H. and Logan, J. (1985), 'Urban Dependencies: New Forms of Use and Exchange in US Cities', *Urban Affairs Quarterly*, 21(2).

Mooney, G. (1999), 'Urban "Disorders"', in S. Pile, C. Brook and G. Mooney (eds.), *Unruly Cities?*, London: Routledge.

Orwell, G. (1959), *The Road to Wigan Pier*, London: Secker and Warburg.

Pierre, J. (1999), 'Models of Urban Governance: The Institutional Dimension of Urban Politics', *Urban Affairs Review*, 34(3).

Porter, M. (1999), 'The Competitive Advantage of the Inner City', in J. Allen, D. Massey and M. Pryke (eds.), *Unsettling Cities*, London: Routledge.

Power, A. (1998), *Estates on the Edge: The Social Consequences of Mass Housing in Northern Europe*, Houndmills: Macmillan.

Pryke, M. (1999), 'On the Openness of Cities', in J. Allen, D. Massey and M. Pryke (eds.), *Unsettling Cities*, London: Routledge.

Raban, J. (1974), *Soft City*, New York: Dutton.

Sassen, S. (1991), *The Global City: New York, London, Tokyo*, Princeton, NJ: Princeton University Press.

—— (1994), *Cities in a World Economy*, Thousand Oaks: Pine Forge Press.

—— (1999), 'Whose City Is It? Globalisation and the Formation of New Claims', in J. Holston (ed.), *Cities and Citizenship*, Durham, NC and London: Duke University Press.

Sharpe, W. and Wallock, L. (1987), 'From "Great Town" to "Nonplace Urban Realm": Reading the Modern City', in W. Sharpe and L. Wallock (eds.), *Visions of the Modern City. Essays in History, Art and Culture*, London: Johns Hopkins University Press.

Shields, R. (1991), *Places on the Margin: Alternative Geographies of Modernity*, London: Routledge.

Soja, E. (1989), *Postmodern Geographies: The Reassertion of Space in Critical Social Theory*, London: Verso.

Stoker, G. (1999), 'Regime Theory and Urban Politics', in S. Pile, C. Brook and G. Mooney (eds.), *Unruly Cities?*, London: Routledge.

Sousa Santos, B. (1999), 'On Oppositional Postmodernism', in R. Munck and D. O'Hearn (eds.), *Critical Development Theory: Contributions to a New Paradigm*, London: Zed Books.

Taylor, I., Evans, K. and Fraser, P. (1996), *A Tale of Two Cities, Global Change, Local Feeling and Everyday Life in the North of England. A Study in Manchester and Sheffield*, London: Routledge.

Taylor, M. (1995), *Unleashing the Potential. Bringing Residents to the Centre of Regeneration*, York: Joseph Rowntree Foundation.

Thrift, N. (1999), 'Cities and Economic Change: Global Governance?', in J. Allen, D. Massey and M. Pryke (eds.), *Unsettling Cities*, London: Routledge.

7

Towards Apartheid? Policies of Segregation and Deprivation in Delhi

HANS SCHENK
schenk1937@planet.nl
AGIDS, University of Amsterdam, The Netherlands.

Starter

From the early 1960s onwards, squatter settlements in Delhi have been demolished, and squatters have been re-settled elsewhere. The modes of re-settlement, and the impacts these re-settlements have had on the squatters, have changed, however, over the decades. A relatively clean and wealthy core city is now surrounded at a safe distance by rejected urban poor in the urban periphery, living in dismal conditions and with little hope for a better future. Do current policies imply apartheid-like conditions for the poor in India's capital city?

Introduction: an overview of events

Urban Delhi counts approximately 13 m. inhabitants[1] (2001 Census). Its growth has been phenomenal since India's independence in 1947, when the city counted 1.4 m. citizens. In every decade from 1951 onwards, the growth has been in the order of magnitude of 50%. This growth rate implies a continuing stream of in-migrants into the city, as natural growth has been responsible for some 20% per decade only.

Delhi's first major experience with in-migration was in 1947. After the partition of British India into two new states, India and Pakistan, millions of Indian Muslims fled to Pakistan, while even more Pakistani Sikhs and Hindus sought refuge in India. Not less than 500,000 of them went to Delhi, and its population almost doubled between 1941 and 1951: from 900,000 to 1,750,000.

Though some newcomers in Delhi could be housed in the abandoned homes of refugees to Pakistan, most of them were given shelter in temporary camps in open spaces in the central and at that time peripheral parts of the city. Gradually the more remote camps developed into housing colonies. This incidental wave of in-migrants has been followed by a much more structural one: rural migrants. Landless labourers and marginal landholders in the densely populated and extremely poor states in Northern India—mainly Uttar Pradesh and Bihar—started their move to the cities: many of them to Delhi. As in other cities in Asia, Africa and Latin America, they tried to find unskilled jobs in what has later been called the informal sector: in services and workshops and in the construction industry. And as in these cities, they tried to find shelter nearby. Some of them found accommodation in dilapidated houses in the old core of the city, while other ones started settlements on squatted land in or near the urban centre. In the late 1950s about 300,000 people squatted in the city which counted then about 2.3 million inhabitants: some 13% of the total population. Many more lived in substandard slum houses.

The Delhi administration[2] became alarmed by the massive flow of in-migrants and in the late 1950s policy discussions on this topic started. These discussions resulted in a 20-year Master Plan for Delhi in which future land use, and further development were outlined for the period 1962-1982. In this plan a stated objective was the elimination of slums and squatter settlements and the provision of adequate housing and related community facilities through large scale resettlement of squatters of the central parts of the city: the 'Jhuggi-Jhompri Removal Scheme'.[3]

> It goes beyond the scope of this paper to enter into most of the details of the J.J. scheme ideas and activities of the 1960s and early 1970s. A few characteristics will be mentioned as they seem relevant here. A distinction was made between 'eligible' squatters and others. Eligible squatters were those who squatted on public land before 1960. This category

> was to be provided with developed plots of some 80 sq. yards (appr. 67 sq.m.) on a 99 year leasehold and with sufficient basic amenities at relatively close distances to the central parts of the city. More recent squatters were provided with a plot of 25 sq. yards only (21 sq.m.) with less amenities and in the periphery of the then city.
>
> Another major characteristic of the objectives of the Master Plan was that re-settlement colonies were to be planned in the middle of high and middle income residential areas, in order to make these colonies an integral part of a neighbourhood (Kundu, Schenk & Dash, 2002, 67-68). As Verma (2003) expresses it: "*The Plan envisages integration of the poor, not their segregation in large areas just for them. This is explicated in the stipulation that their 25% housing be ensured not at city level but at the level of 1 lakh* (100,000; HS) *population* [...]."

What matters here also is that the re-settlement schemes have not been very successful in the 1960s and early 1970s. Till the late 1960s some 50,000 families have been given a serviced plot against a low rent in 18 re-settlement colonies after which the plan was abandoned for lack of funds.[4] It has been estimated, moreover, that 40% of the allottees had illegally transferred their plots to middle classes and have come back to the city centre (Sundaram, 1978, 138). Not surprisingly, the number of squatter settlements rise from 300 in 1961 to over 1100 in 1973 (Kundu, Schenk & Dash, 2002, 67).

During the ill-famous Emergency period (1975-1977) when democratic and legal rights were upheld in India, some politicians and bureaucrats close to the then Prime Minister Indira Gandhi, her son Sanjay Gandhi and their immediate surroundings, 'could do what they liked to do', a major activity in Delhi became massive bulldozing of squatter settlements and eviction of their inhabitants, not seldom at gun point. Not less than 700,000 persons were removed from the old core of the city and its immediate surroundings. Some were re-settled in developed plots, but many others were just dumped outside the municipal limits.[5] Vice Chairman of the DDA, Jagmohan played an important role in the resettlement activities. In the next section, more attention is given to Jagmohan.

The end of the Emergency brought a 'regime change' in India and in Delhi, and a policy change as well. Demolitions and re-settlements were largely banned, so to say, and attempts to *in situ* upgrading of existing squatter settlements were undertaken through a variety of fresh programmes by the Delhi Municipal Corporation. The coverage was not large, though: in all 5,000 households were covered under these programmes in the 1980s and some evictions and re-settlements continued.

Not surprisingly, the number of squatters in Delhi increased after the end of the Emergency. In 1977, 70 colonies were counted, while in the early 1990s, the number of settlements had risen till over 1000, in which 20 to 25% of the urban population lived.[6] The increase was mainly a result of vague and inconsistent policy signals about the future of the settlements which encouraged squatters to come to the city and to stay. To some extent they were even encouraged to stay as squatter settlements—encroaching on public or private land-developed more and more into convenient vote banks.

> Vote banks function optimally with politicians who can exercise power. The Indian district (constituency) system of 'the winner takes all' shows interesting characteristics when a party in power loses the elections and its representatives in a legislative assembly find themselves suddenly at a loss. This happened *e.g.* in 1999 (demolitions had started again, see below) when Congress party politicians and members of the Delhi's Legislative Assembly had to transfer power to the BJP. Kota Neelima wrote in *The Indian Express* under the heading: *"MLAs panic as their vote banks are demolished"*: *"[...] With the encroachers demanding to know what has the Congress done for them, the MLAs are desperate to protect their loyal vote-banks"*, and one asks: *"Why is none of the encroachments in BJP constituencies being touched?"*

The year 1996 can be seen as a crucial one regarding 'squatter policies', and in some ways it resembles the start of the Emergency in 1975. In 1996, a court ruled that certain polluting industries could be replaced from the urban centre to its periphery.[7] In the wake of this ruling, an effective attack on unauthorized squatter settlements started again, now under the banner of cleaning the city from pollution and other environmentally nuisances. This renewed attack on Delhi's squatters was—again—organized by Jagmohan, at that time Minister of Urban Development of the National Union Territory of Delhi. It lasted till 2002, for the time being.

This brief account of event leads to a number of questions. The first one is obvious: which are the major reasons to bulldoze squatter settlements and re-settle squatters or even dump them somewhere? This question is discussed in the next section. A next question is on the impact of the periodic and massive cleaning operations in Delhi whereby squatters —largely the urban poor—are dislocated. What happens to re-settled or dumped squatters; where are they re-settled or dumped; how does this dislocation affects their livelihood; how does it affect the urban social structure at large? These questions are discussed—rather touched upon in the framework of this brief paper—in the final section.

Analysis

It is difficult to find one single major denominator to 'explain' the re-settlement activities and their absence in the history of Delhi of—say—the last 50 years. A number of factors will be introduced first.

Modernization and globalization

From India's independence in 1947 till the late 1960s, India followed a path of modernization of its economy and its society. India's first Prime Minister Jawaharlal Nehru—who was the major architect of independent India's course of development during the 1950s and early 1960s—was deeply convinced that India's future should be that of a secular, democratic state, guided by the West European examples of the welfare state, together with the Soviet experiences with a planned economy. Moreover, he was confident that India—and other newly independent Third World countries—could develop rapidly in this direction hence the colonial yoke was thrown off. India's first three five-year plans (from 1951 to 1966) were drawn along these ideological lines. In these plans, urban development would allow the urban poor to become incorporated into the modern urban society and its means of earning a livelihood. Subsequently, living conditions would improve, and decent housing would become an affordable issue for the rank and file of the urban population. This approach implied that existing squatter settlements would be of a temporary nature only and would be replaced by 'modern' housing. The massive influx of migrants (see above), however, made the local authorities decide for re-settlement, though with little vigour till the Emergency.

Modernization can also be named as a denominator of specific evictions of squatter settlements in the post-Emergency era, though with one major difference. The belief that India's poor could hook on to the modernization ideals of the 1950s and 1960s had gone; the poor have become a burden and a danger since the 1970s. However, not a general idea was the guiding principle of action, from the mid 1970s till the mid 1990s, but rather concrete 'problems'. The Asian Games (1982), and increasing traffic, led to infrastructural works into and in the city, often at the cost of squatters. The construction of the underground railway of the city led to the following ironical statement: *"Wherever there are rich residential colonies, it goes underground. Where there are slums, it goes over ground"* (quoted by Joshi, n.d.).

> India was more or less bankrupt around 1990; the state had a huge budget deficit. Seeking for money, the IMF and the World Bank made it clear that India had to restructure its economy before it could be eligible for loans. One of the item of the demanded restructure was the lift on foreign investors in its economy. From 1991 the so-called New Economic Policies, prevailed, and multi-nationals and other entrepreneurs were welcomed to start an enterprise, alone or under a joint venture arrangement. Another measure was that the ban on starting an industry in the major cities—in order to promote a more balanced urban structure—was lifted. Foreign investors did come (though fewer than hoped for), and they settled in the major urban centres of the country. Initially most

> capital was invested in Greater Bombay (now Mumbai), but from the mid 1990s onwards, Delhi and surroundings attracted most of the foreign capital (Oldenziel, 1998, 27).[8]

"Delhi in the 1990s may be described as a postcolonial city with a first world desire" (Nigam 2001, 40). This opening statement in Nigam's essay reflects the dream of Delhi's policy makers and elites. Delhi was to become a global city, a city that mattered, a city that welcomed *"multinationals like Sony, Samsung, Daewoo, Motorola and Nokia, which were moving into Delhi in a big way—apart from international banks, financial companies and fast food chains"* (Nigam, 2001, 41).

The concept of globalization of the 1990s brought bulldozings and evictions back on the ideological level. The concept had in common with the modernization ideology that it looked to the 'West'. It differed, however, in some fundamental ways. Neither the welfare state, nor the planned economy are icons in nowadays India, but the expected benefits of the market, and preferably a free market. During the modernization era, there was the recognition that the state was somehow responsible for the victims of the aspirations of the elites—though this responsibility did not materialize substantially. The bulldozers that did their work in a squatter settlement that had to be sacrificed in the name of modernity, did the same job as those who came in the name of globalization. However, the modernization-victims were provided with some sort of alternative place to stay, while the victims of globalization were left to the market. Needless to say, the massive supply of poorly paid, poorly looked after urban citizens does not generate market steered provisions in terms of housing and basic facilities for this category. The question now arises how a global Indian city should look like.

Beautification and cleanliness

Beautification is a possible catchword to describe another and closely related emerging trend from the 1990s onwards. This trend has led to the expulsion of polluting industries and filthy squatter settlements. Delhi should look modern and attractive in the eyes of foreign investors.[9] As such beautification and cleaning up the incredibly filthy Indian cities seems laudable.[10] Especially cleaning up, however, has its secret agenda.

> From the mid 1800s, the British in urban British India were obsessed with setting up new and safe environments for the British men and women who increasingly settled in the colony. This obsession was partly based on physical safety, since the 1857 revolt of Indian soldiers in the colonial army made it clear that the representatives of the British Empire were not loved by all Indians. A second element was the conviction that the 'natives' would bring contagious diseases such as malaria and cholera, unless they be kept at a safe distance. These fears brought about urban planning concepts based on spatial segregation: 'native' towns versus British 'civil lines' and 'cantonments', separated by a field of fire.[11] Nigam (2001, 42) refers to this historical fear when discussing the history of re-settlement policies in independent Delhi: *"There is no doubt that the early efforts at town planning in Delhi were all characterized by this fear of disease. The document prepared by the Town and Country Planning Organization (TCPO) in the 1970s, implemented with an unprecedented brutality during the Emergency, and witnessed in the large scale demolitions of urban slums—was framed by this fear. It was the designation of these areas of 'plague spots' and 'dense of vice' that underlay the entire discourse of town planning."* An underlying motive to bulldoze squatter settlements in the more central parts of the city is then not only the fear for plague or other contagious diseases, but also social and political fear, as Nigam indicates. From the 19th century onwards, the elites have explicitly feared 'the other' urban citizens: colonizers versus colonized, elites versus the poor, etc. An immediate translation of fear is spatial segregation, the re-location of the urban poor to sites as far as possible into the urban periphery.

Cleaning and beautification in the context of Delhi means primarily the removal of poor inhabitants and possibly obnoxious economic activities from certain parts of the city. This policy was immensely helped and sanctioned by a 1996 court order implying that the *"health of some is more important than the livelihood of others"* (Nigam, 2001, 43). This order intensified the removal of obnoxious ('non-conforming') industries and squatter settlements from the more central parts of Delhi to the urban periphery. Thus, during the 1990s, massive activities have taken place to create in essence two Delhi's. The first one is relatively clean and well serviced, and is occupied by the better off of the city, while the second one is inhabited by the poor and is dirty and substantially less serviced, to say the least. In the next section this aspect stands central. In this section, some attention is finally given to a remarkable person in the debate and policy action regarding, filth, squatters, demolishing and re-settlement: Jagmohan.

> If one person can be singled out who inspired and managed the eviction drives of both the 1970s and those of the 1990s, the name of Jagmohan has to mentioned. Jagmohan was Vice-Chairman of the DDA during the Emergency, and in charge of the re-settlement activities at that time. In his book Rebuilding Shahjahanabad (1975), he argued for a large scale upgrading and beautification of the old walled city of Delhi. He was explicitly inspired by Haussmann who reshaped Paris in the mid 19th Century by demolishing dilapidated housing and cutting broad boulevards across the medieval street pattern of that city. Jagmohan can be seen as an exponent of the Western-oriented modernisation approach that dominated India's policy from its independence till the late 1960s.[12] After the Emergency he was sacked from his DDA post. An official inquiry into the misuses of power during the Emergency, led to the conclusion that: *"Shri Jagmohan grossly misused his position and abused his authority. He, during the Emergency became a law unto himself and went about doing the biddings of Shri Sanjay Gandhi without care or concern of the miseries of the people affected thereby"* (Government of India, 1978, 252: see also a prominent example of

> research journalism: Dayal & Bose, 1977).[13] Jagmohan defended himself in a second book (1978). From the 1980s onwards, Jagmohan was active again in public positions, and in 1996 he was elected as a member of the Lok Sabha—the Indian Lower House and most important legislative assembly. In 1999 he became Minister of Urban Development at national level until 2001, when he was side-tracked to the national ministry of Tourism and Culture.[14] His reign as Minister of Urban Development coincided with the intensified bulldozing and re-settlement campaigns of the late 1990s. As a Minister of Tourism, he just continues his life-long ideals. The daily *The Hindu* (7-9-2001) quotes him: *"Why should a foreign tourist visit Humayun's Tomb if it is surrounded by slum clusters?"*.

Which truth prevails? Jagmohan has a point when he stresses that filth is an eyesore and a threat to health for every urban citizen: visitor or inhabitant, rich or poor. He has a point that clean cities are attractive cities, again to everyone involved. However, he seems to miss the point when advocating removal, bulldozing, etc. to reach his goals. His approach seems an ultimate Nimby solution, and not relevant, or even counter productive for the needs of the poor citizens of Delhi. The impacts of his contributions to Delhi's future will be discussed in the next section.

Impacts

Delhi is a city of middle classes, perhaps more than any other Indian city. It has no industrial tradition unlike Mumbai (Bombay) or Kolkata (Calcutta), no industrial proletariat and no powerful trade unions. It is characterized by its many (petty) civil servants and by employees working in semi-public and private sector undertakings. This complex of middle class citizens has been surrounded by a kaleidoscopic category of small scale industries and service oriented enterprises and workers.

> In the traditional Indian urban setting, the economic, political and social elites of the urban population were spatially separated from the lower classes, though the small scale of separation admitted easy functional

contacts: household servants lived around the corner of the better-off, so to say, or even in the back side of their compounds.[15] One could speak of a fine grained urban socio-spatial pattern.

A number of events has gradually changed this pattern. Rapid population growth is a first 'event'. As long as spatial 'involution' was an option, the growth of the urban population could be absorbed in the traditional spatial units. When the limits of involution were reached, bombs burst. First, the better-off started to move out of their central city positions. From the late 1950s onwards, the urban elites went to the South of the city. In the 1960s and especially in the 1970s (Emergency) many poor were driven out of the central parts, to resettlement colonies to the North and the East. The elitist desire to segregate is a second factor. As has been discussed above, the permanent fear among the better-off for the urban poor, has promoted segregation, especially when the numbers of nearby poor became frightening. This feeling has raised a dilemma: some poor are needed (household servants, etc.) but not too many. Modern technology and modern institutions, however, tend to solve this problem: some erstwhile needed servants became superfluous when modern inputs became available to the middle classes: washing machines replaced washermen and hence their presence nearby[16]; self-service food stores have similarly replaced many food vendors, etc.

The middle and higher classes have, moreover, clearly prioritised their perceptions of safety above convenience. They have not protested when nearby squatter settlements that housed their servants were removed and parachuted far away. They seem prepared to pay for the bus fares of their remote servants and have sealed off their neighbourhoods against unwanted persons rendering services.[17]

From the point of view of the better-off in Delhi, the replacements of the urban poor from their immediate surroundings to far away locations is considered as an improvement. What about the other point of view: that of the squatters who have become residents in re-settlement colonies? Squatters have been re-settled since the 1960s. As has been seen above, the conditions of re-settlement were not bad for in the early years: up to a 67 sq. m. plot, security of tenure, and a location at a reasonable distance to places of work. Gradually these conditions have changed for the worse. The re-settlement campaign from the mid 1990s onwards means re-location on small plots (12 to 18 sq. metres) to far remote places, and under unclear or temporary security of tenure (say five or ten years).

> An example is formed by a large re-settlement colony in the far Northwest of Delhi. The DDA has demarcated plots by laying a brick or cement outline of the house to be built. Many of these plots have been occupied (early 2002) and houses of durable materials (*pacca*) have been built. Some plots are still empty, while some houses are not occupied. The houses have been built with a loan from the Housing and Urban Development Corporation (HUDCO), India's largest developer and credit supplier of house construction loans. HUDCO finances to some extent also low budget housing. In this re-settlement colony it appears that its loan conditions are tough, tougher perhaps than in the past and tougher perhaps than elsewhere. A few houses were locked by HUDCO and the inhabitants thrown on the street as a result of arrears in instalments. The major complaint of the inhabitants is the lack of work, and thus of income, in this remote area. A bus ride to the more central locations of the city where the inhabitants used to have their jobs would take two to three hours; a return trip half a day's wages. Especially women have lost their jobs, while many of their husband stay overnight in the workshops etc. in the centre or elsewhere, and come home once a week. Anyway the loss of household income is severe. Relations with a nearby village are tense. A small pond next to the village is traditionally used for irrigation purposes. The DDA used it as the end-station of a sewerage system in the re-settlement colony; the pond is now severely polluted. The few men and women in the village who are engaged in the scarce non-agricultural jobs in the area meet the competition of newcomers from the colony.

A major aspect of the nowadays re-settlement practices is that it cuts off the lifelines between the poor and the city. The urban poor of Delhi have come from the countryside of the Northern India states, notably Uttar Pradesh and Bihar. They have become superfluous in the rural agricultural economy and could only survive by going to an urban place and offering their unskilled hands to any poorly paid job. They have settled in cities such as Delhi and most of them just survived.[18] The squatters have experienced the varying moods of policy makers: sometimes their illegal settlements were nourished against a vote for a politician; sometimes the DDA came with bulldozers. However, during the 1960s, the 1970s, and the 1980s, evictions were a nuisance but they could be overcome. It seems that those of the 1990s have passed a limit. This limit cannot be overcome anymore for very basic and perhaps trivial reasons: distance, time and money.[19]

Re-settlement colonies are not only located further and further away from the central city. Geography plays another role. South of the traditional core of Delhi (Shahjahanabad) the British built the new capital of their Indian Empire in the first half of the 20th Century: New Delhi. In New Delhi the offices of the colonial government were established and the British administrators, etc. were housed there as well as some of the Indian political elites.[20] After Independence, the Indian political elite took the places of the British. As New Delhi knew very rigid land use controls, population growth among the middle classes and elites found an natural and nearby outlet South of New Delhi. From the late 1950s onwards, the tracts South and Southwest of New Delhi have become the hunting grounds for housing by the better off.[21] South Delhi has subsequently become the location of many upper and middle class wards,[22] while settlement colonies of squatters can be found to the North, the East and the Southeast.[23] This geographical segregation is very rigid: squatters in the South (and in the central areas) are easily chased away, and relatively easy tolerated elsewhere.

Residential segregation matters in particular with regard to the relation between suppliers of domestic labour and consumers of daily necessities on the one hand, and the domestic labourers, washermen, gardeners, roadside traders, etc. It was mentioned above that this relation is weakening as a result of societal changes. However, most squatters and inhabitants in re-settlement colonies have casual or regular work in industry and trade—predominantly informally. It matters hence, where these places of work are located. Many small scale industries and workshops have been relocated from Delhi's central areas to industrial estates in its fringes. On the map of Greater Delhi there is some similarity between the new locations of the workshops, etc. and several re-settlement colonies. However, map wisdom can be far remote from field realities. It has been proven once more that labour relations are not mechanical ones. A small scale employer does not recruit workers as such: he recruits known workers, from his native area, speaking the same language, being perhaps related, being a patron in a dependency relation, etc. Hence, very often the new industry and workshop owners lost their known workers, did not want to recruit nearby 'strangers' and hence recruited fresh boys and men from their networks in the countryside. In many other cases, the workers stay on the work premises during the week and go home to their re-settlement colony during weekends.

The new industries that came to Delhi settled also in the periphery, with only headquarters in more fashionable parts of (South) Delhi. Again, on the map, their locations are in industrial estates in Delhi State, but in particular in those of the bordering states of Haryana (Gurgaon, Faridabad) and Uttar Pradesh (NOIDA, Ghaziabad). These estates are often not too remote from the re-settlement colonies. Especially the estates in Uttar Pradesh, East of Delhi seem to match with the many re-settlement colonies in the East of Delhi. However, large scale, and 'formally' operating industries require skilled labourers. Most of the re-settled squatters do not qualify for a skilled job. The leftover jobs are available—but not many after all: sweepers to clean the factory, etc. And even then, unskilled workers are given a temporary job only—for less than six months, thus avoiding claims on a permanent tenure, according to labour laws.

In this context, it is important to note that not only re-settlers have come to the periphery. Contrary to a few decades ago, fresh in-migrants into Greater Delhi hardly try their luck in the central parts of the city any more, as their chances of being left in peace are meagre. They try their luck directly in the urban fringes: near the industrial estates in Delhi, Uttar Pradesh and Haryana, but also in and nearby existing villages (see Bentinck, 2000).[24] The resulting emerging pattern is that two streams of poor Indians 'meet' in Delhi's fringe: the first originates from the inner parts of the city, the second from the countryside. The pattern is one of despair.

One might expect that the infrastructural amenities such as access to (drinking) water, the provisions of sewer, etc. are better in the planned re-settlement colonies that in the previous inner city squatter colonies. The opposite was found (Kundu, Schenk & Dash, 2002). It appears clearly that inner-city squatters could 'rely' on political protection and on more facilities than peripheral re-settlement colonies. The un-authorized squatter colonies in the fringes are in an even worse condition.

> In a squatter settlement in NOIDA, in the neighbouring state of Uttar Pradesh, no facilities at all were provided by the state or the local government. The settlement was just tolerated as long as the pressure on land was not very high, and as long as neighbouring industrialists found it convenient to have some unskilled temporary workers nearby. In a re-settlement colony in Delhi state, security of tenure beyond five years was not given by the DDA, and hence, no investments in the physical and social infrastructure of the area took place.

Kundu (in: Nelissen & Schenk, 2002) speaks outright of a 'degenerated periphery' when characterizing the Delhi fringe. Not only has the periphery been cut off from the city, it witnesses either a new unregulated squatter habitat without any services and any security of tenure, or a hardly regulated re-settlement colony, with some services and some security only. The new squatters are often young men. When they are married, they tend to leave their wives at home in their villages. Kundu considers these clusters of single men, living and working in abject conditions, as social and political time-bombs.[25]

Summing up: inhabitants of re-settlement colonies in the periphery of Delhi, and squatters in these tracts, face a regime of segregation and deprivation that comes close to Apartheid[26], a wilful set of measure that clears the inner city of its poor, cleans it from their 'ugliness', and keeps the poor at a safe distance. The poor in the periphery—either se-settled or just squatting—have few options: they have been rejected from their agricultural existence and have fled to the city. They are rejected again in globalizing Delhi, and the question is where they have to go and where and how they can survive.

REFERENCES

Basu, Somnath (1994). *Land Use and Land Prices in Semi-Controlled Land Market: a Case Study of Delhi.* Unpublished Ph.D., School of Social Studies, Jawaharlal Nehru University, New Delhi.

Baviskar, Amita (2002). *The Politics of the City.* http://www.india-seminar.com

Bentinck Johan (2000). *Unruly Urbanisation on Delhi's fringe; changing patterns of land use and livelihood.* Netherlands Geographical Studies, no. 270. RU Groningen.

Bose, Ashish (1973). *Studies in India's Urbanization 1901-1971.* Tata McGraw-Hill, New Delhi.

Bruijne, G.A. & H. Schenk (1992). Where do the poor live?; an analysis of residential patterns of poor inhabitants in Indian cities, in, *The Indian Geograpical Journal,* Vol. 67, No. 2, 1-16.

Dayal, John & Ajoy Bose (1977). *For Reasons of State: Delhi Under Emergency.* Orient Vision, New Delhi.

Dupont, Veronique (2000). Spatial and Demographic Growth of Delhi since 1947 and the main migration flows, in, Veronique Dupont, Emma Tarlo and Denis Vidal (eds.) *Delhi, Urban Space and Human Destinies.* Manohar, New Delhi.

Government of India (1978). *Shah Commission of Inquiry. Third and Final Report.* Government of India Press, New Delhi.

Jagmohan (1975). *Rebuilding Shahjahanabad, the walled city of Delhi.* Vikas, New Delhi.

—— (1978). *Island of Truth.* Vikas, New Delhi.

Joshi, Sharmila (n.d.). *To go global, evict the poor.* http://www.humanscapeindia.net

King, Anthony D. (1976). *Colonial Urban Development: culture, social power and environment.* Routledge & Kegan Paul, London.

Kundu, Amitabh, Hans Schenk & Bal Paritosh Dash (2002). *Changing Role of State in Urban Governance; Provision of basic amenities in the context of unplanned growth in metropolitan peripheries of Delhi and Hanoi.* Report to IDAD. Institute of Human Development, New Delhi.

Neelima, Kota (1999). MLAs panic as their vote banks are demolished, in *The Indian Express*, February 3.

Nelissen, Bert & Hans Schenk (2002). *Delhi: towards a new urban order.* Video. Debert Media. Amsterdam.

Nigam, Aditya (2001). *Dislocating Delhi: a city in the 1990s.* Sarai Reader 2001. http://www.sarai.net/journal.

Oldenziel, Joris (1998). *Investing in India, Experiences of multinationals in the National Capital Region.* M.A. thesis, Department of International Relations, University of Amsterdam.

Schenk, Hans (1994). Het Recht op Riolering; de longpest in India komt rechtsstreeks uit de goot, in, *NRC/Handelsblad, Zaterdags Bijvoegsel.* October 8.

—— (2002). Urban Fringes in Asia: Markets versus Plans, in, I.S.A. Baud & J. Post (eds.), *Realigning Actors in an Urbanizing World, Governance and Institutions from a Development Perspective.* Ashgate, Aldershot. 119-36.

—— & Michael Dewit (2001). The Fringe Habitat of Bangalore, in, Hans Schenk (ed.), *Living in India's Slums, a case study of Bangalore.* IDPAD/ Manohar, New Delhi, 113-33.

Sundaram, K.V. (1978). Delhi: the National Capital, in, R.P.Misra (ed.), *Million Cities of India*, Vikas, New Delhi, 105-54.

Tarlo, Emma, (2000). Welcome to History: A resettlement colony in the making, in, Veronique Dupont Emma Tarlo & Denis Vidal (eds.), *Delhi, Urban Space and Human Destinies.* Manohar/Centre de Sciences Humaines. New Delhi, 51-75.

Verma, Gita Dewan (2003). *Slumming Delhi: evictions, endowments and entitlements.* Lecture at the Indian International Centre, New Delhi, January 18, 2003. http://www.architexturez.net.

NOTES

1. Urban Delhi refers to the agglomeration formed by the area under the Delhi Municipal Corporation, that under the military: the Delhi Cantonment, and finally under a few more remote townships within Delhi State (formerly the National Union Territory, now the National Capital Territory). Besides, one speaks of the Delhi Metropolitan Area, an area that includes some urban tracts of the neighbouring states of Uttar Pradesh and Haryana, with a 2001 population of approximately 15 m. Finally, the much larger National Capital Region—a planning region—counts 30 m. inhabitants.
2. The term Delhi Administration may be confusing. The Union Territory of Delhi was at that time governed by the central Indian government, unlike the Indian states which have been granted quite some autonomy in 'local' matters. Hence, local policies and national policies can hardly be distinguished. Even now, when Delhi has the status of a Indian state, the influence of politicians at national level on the state and local affairs of Delhi is substantial.

3. The re-settlement policy was not implemented by the municipal corporations within the National Union Territory of Delhi, but by a semi-autonomous union-level authority: the Delhi Development Authority (DDA) (see Sundaram, 1978, 105-54 for details). The DDA functions as a land acquisition authority and subsequently as a land developer and seller (see Basu 1994).
4. Of these families, 46,000 were provided by small (21 sq. m.) plots on a non-regular basis, *i.e.* without much security of tenure, and 3,700 families only got a plot of 67 sq. m. with services, and on a 99-year leasehold basis. The latter category consisted of registered squatters who had stayed in a settlement for a long time.
5. A detailed and impressive account of the birth of one re-settlement colony has been given by Tarlo (2000).
6. Perhaps this percentage is far too low. It was said—though not confirmed —that the number of inhabitants in squatter settlements increased between 1995 and 1999 from 4 million to 6 million, *i.e.* 40 to 50% per cent of the urban population.
7. It has been estimated that this measure involved some 100,000 industrial units and two million people (Baviskar 2002).
8. Being close to the bureaucracy matters in order to avoid lengthy procedures and delays to get needed licences for almost everything to start an enterprise.
9. Or, in at least in those parts of the city where expatriates stayed and foreign offices were located.
10. One may remember that some ten years ago an almost medieval outburst of plague took place in Surat, a million city in Western India. Not taken care of liquid and solid waste was largely held responsible for the spreading of the disease by rats (see Schenk 1994 for details).
11. Indeed, in some cities, canons were positioned towards the native parts of the city and covering a 'field of fire'. Many fields of fire a still exist, a good example can be seen in Bangalore.
12. Jagmohan remained a stubborn modernisation advocate. He went on to pursue modernisation ideals when it had become clear to India's intelligentsia and its political leaders, that this path of development was unrealistic for a long time, and that immediate policy priorities had to be given to the eradication of poverty. He was at that time supporting the policies of the secular Congress party. Later on he switched to the Hindu fundamentalist and nationalist Bharatiya Janata Party.
13. Sanjay Gandhi was the youngest son of the then Prime Minister Indira Gandhi. He was deeply involved in the campaigns to bulldoze the squatter settlements in central Delhi, and became even more infamous as the driving force of the sterilisation campaigns that terrorized Delhi and Northern India.
14. For details: see Jagmohan's biographical sketch: http://alfa.nic.in/lok13/biodata/13DL01.htm

15. See: G.A. de Bruijne & H. Schenk (1992) with specific attention to Madras (Chennai) and Calcutta (Kolkata).
16. Some washermen have changed their trade and have become ironers, and hence needed and thus tolerated in middle class neighbourhoods.
17. See: Nelissen & Schenk (2002). An increasing number of middle class and elite neighbourhoods has sealed off their areas with fences and gates and watchmen, who check visitors.
18. The idea of upward social and economic mobility as advocate by John Turner for Latin America in the 1970s is just a myth in the Indian context. Almost all (rural) in-migrants in the cities remain poor and so do their children.
19. Many squatters worked in the small scale non-conforming industries that were replaced since 1996 as well. There has been no coordination, however, between relocation of workshops, etc. and relocations of (their) workers.
20. The colonial town planners and administrators were very precise about the location of the several layers of the British administration in New Delhi. Details are given in King (1976).
21. See Ashish Bose (1973) for an account of the semi-illegal penetration of urban land use into agricultural villages.
22. The irony will that the soil upon which large parts of South Delhi are built (*e.g.* the huge Vasant Kunj area) has a very low holding capacity of groundwater. This matters, even though a piped water distribution net does exist. Its capacity is very limited and hence, many inhabitants of blocks have collectively drilled deep bore wells and have organised private water distribution networks. The underground water level is, however, rapidly falling, as a result of over-exploitation of this resource, and water has become a scarce commodity for even many of the better off in South Delhi.
23. See Dupont (2000) for a clear visualization of this pattern.
24. This rather recent trend can also be observed in other major Indian cities, such as Bangalore. See: Schenk & Dewit (2001) and Schenk (2002).
25. It goes beyond the scope of this contribution to enter into details of the history of social and political unrest in India. Here it suffices to note that politicians regularly mobilize inhabitants of squatter settlements and other housing areas of the urban poor, for their political ambitions. The riots following the murder of Prime Minister Indira Gandhi, and the killing of many poor Sikhs in Delhi, is one example; the mass killing of Muslims in Ahmedabad in 2002, following a fabricated assault on a train carrying pious Hindus back home, is an other.
26. Apartheid in its former South African setting was clearly 'racial' determined. In Delhi (and in urban India in general) the large majority of urban squatters and inhabitants of re-settlement colonies are 'untouchables' (Dalits) by caste. Both in former South Africa and in India, population categories are stigmatised and treated accordingly by referring to ascribed characteristics, not achieved ones.

8

The Fiscal Sociology of Decentralisation: The Impact of Decentralisation on Tax Capacity and Pro-Poor Policy[1]

AARON SCHNEIDER
a.schneider@ids.ac.uk
Research Fellow, Institute of Development Studies, University of Sussex, Brighton, England, United Kingdom.

EXECUTIVE SUMMARY

This project studies patterns of decentralisation and public finance in 68 countries in 1996. Six indicators of decentralisation clustered around fiscal, administrative, and political dimensions, and these dimensions had independent and surprising relationships with how much governments taxed and what they did with their money. First, politically decentralised regimes taxed less overall and spent less on social policies. Second, administrative decentralisation showed a positive impact on social policies, but neither administrative nor fiscal decentralisation had a systematic relationship to tax capacity. These results suggest that multi-level governance might best be pursued in a partial fashion. Political centralisation favours the actors and interests who seek large amounts of progressive public action; administrative decentralisation allows competition, information, and innovation to lead to efficient and effective public policies. Together, political *centralisation* and administrative *decentralisation* may offer the optimal combination to achieve large quantities of effective, efficient, and redistributive public action. Fiscal decentralisation had no statistical impact in any of the models.

1. Introduction

Decentralisation biases political conflict. By redrawing the political-administrative division of the state, decentralisation changes the geographical boundaries of political contestation, alters the relative power of different actors, and changes the location of government interaction with society.[2] The current project seeks systematic cross-national patterns in the ways that shifting resources and power from the centre to the local level affects policy outputs. The project proceeds by examining public finance by looking at two public finance decisions: tax capacity and pro-poor expenditure. The chief hypothesis is that political centralisation provides those with preferences for greater public action and more progressive public policy with certain organisational and material advantages that they either lack at the local level or possess only in scattered jurisdictions. In contrast, their opponents do not depend on political centralisation to advance their preferences, and they can wield influence at both the local and the national level.[3] Of course, cleavages focused on these issues do not define all types of political conflict, but when they do, this paper argues that, other things being equal, the amount of political decentralisation is a deciding factor in the outcome of struggle.

Many studies have attempted to explain how public finance varies across countries. It is beyond the scope of the current study to examine all the literature, but it is worth noting that valuable advances have been made through studies of welfare states, economic growth and distribution, and interest group politics. Still, we have far too little understanding of the independent impact of differences in the level and kind of decentralisation.[4]

The need to consider multilevel government institutions has increased in recent decades, as many central governments have decentralised functions and resources to lower levels. To test the impact of these changes, the project builds on measures of decentralisation that make conceptual and empirical distinctions between three dimensions of decentralisation: fiscal, administrative, and political.[5] Fiscal decentralisation refers to how much central governments cede fiscal impact to non-central government entities. Administrative decentralisation refers to how much autonomy non-central government entities have relative to central control. Finally, political decentralisation refers to the degree to which non-central government entities satisfy the political functions of governance, such as representation. The dimensions are related to each other, but the current analysis suggests the independent impact of each dimension on public finance that can be estimated and evaluated.

In terms of public finance, the study looks at (a) the resources that government raises and (b) what it does with them. To paraphrase a well-known definition of politics, this is the study of 'Who gets what from whom?' The resources raised by government are addressed in the concept of tax capacity, which is the degree to which government can tap into the wealth of society. The uses to which public resources are put are addressed by the concept of pro-poor policy, which is the degree to which government spends its money on social policy. The analysis offers lessons to those seeking to fine-tune systems of multi-level governance in order to boost tax capacity and pursue pro-poor policy. The study suggests that the greatest degree of progressive public action is associated with *centralised* politics and *decentralised* administration.

To develop this argument, the paper examines data from 1996 for 68 countries (see Appendix A). A factor analytic exercise confirmed the conceptual validity and improved the accuracy of measures of three dimensions of decentralisation (Schneider 2002b). Here, the project applies regression techniques to these indicators to test the impact of decentralisation on tax capacity and pro-poor policy. By distinguishing between fiscal, administrative, and political decentralisation, the paper draws out the independent, and, at times opposite, impact of each dimension of decentralisation.

2. Conceptual frameworks for public finance

This project tests the impact of decentralisation on public finance, specifically tax capacity and pro-poor expenditures. Others have used public finance to reflect broad social science concepts, such as state-building (Tilly 1992) or reflections of economic structures (Goldscheid 1958). Here, public finance is used as a measure of the sum of various kinds and levels of state-society interaction. In particular, tax capacity and pro-poor expenditures are chosen to focus attention on those aspects of public finance that are likely to reflect the impact of decentralisation. More specifically, tax capacity reflects the relative size of the public sector, its administrative capacity, and the ability of government to call on private wealth for public purposes. Pro-poor expenditures are equally as rich for the information they convey: they reflect the social contract that ties citizens to the state; government attempts to target and transform society; and interest group demands for benefits.

Some might suggest that to truly test the way public finance links to these concepts, greater attention should be paid to social outcomes, such as social conditions or individual behaviours, rather than a focus on policy outputs, such as taxation or pro-poor expenditures. On this, the project is less ambitious; it limits itself to a partial understanding of the impact of decentralisation. Attempting to trace the impact of decentralisation through to its social conclusion would require accounting for the many other variables that determine social outcomes.[6] Nevertheless, the project views tax capacity and pro-poor expenditure as interesting in and of themselves. In addition, they provide useful information about broader concepts associated with public finance.

Tax capacity indicates a fiscal choice about the size of government relative to the economy. How much economic wealth belongs in public hands? Indeed, some have posed this question within a general argument that a large public sector "crowds out" the private sector (Barro 1974). This perspective guided leaders in Europe and the United States during the 1980's, and has been at the root of opposition to taxation since. For neo-Marxists, by contrast, growth in government parallels the growth of the private sector. As capitalism progresses, it faces ever greater monopoly and instability, and a larger and larger government is needed to manage crises of accumulation (O'Connor 1973).

Tax capacity also reflects the ability of government to administer and enforce tax rules. Milka Casanegra of the IMF made the oft-quoted statement that 'tax administration is tax policy'. Executing tax policy requires tax administration to accomplish the complicated task of monitoring economic activities in such a way that government can categorise and quantify the surplus possessed by economic actors and generated in economic activities. By itself, this requires a vast effort of administrative resources and effort.[7] Even if tax administration can calculate the value of privately held wealth, extraction also requires tax handles that effectively tap into bases. These bases, inevitably, attempt to avoid, and perhaps evade, taxes. Curbing such behaviour requires enforcement, and many countries have turned to revenue authorities in an attempt to patch the holes in a porous administration.

Finally, taxation is also an indicator of the level of quasi-voluntary compliance—the degree to which citizens are willing to pool their private resources to attain collective goods (Levi 1988). Governments cannot expect to monitor and enforce every single transaction and apply all tax rules; at a certain point governments depend on citizens accepting the legitimacy of tax payments and handing over their wealth. The principles that underlie taxation (*e.g.* ability to pay) and the justification offered (*e.g.* democratic rights and social benefits) must be enough to convince citizens to accept levies. The breakdown of this quasi-voluntary compliance leads more and more citizens to skirt the tax net and undercuts the ability of government to finance itself.

Like taxation, pro-poor expenditure offers a rich story about the way we think about governance.[8] Some approach pro-poor expenditure in terms of universal rights and the establishment of a basic social contract. Others view pro-poor expenditures as targeted attempts by government to transform society, while others suggest that pro-poor expenditures are particularistic responses to interest group demands.

Each of these perspectives has a long intellectual history. Briefly, the social contract and universal view of pro-poor expenditure sees in social spending a contract that defines the relationship between citizen, state, and market. Each society must decide on the kind of protections that public actors provide for citizens, and the resulting view of universal rights can be read in pro-poor expenditures. These range from minimal safety nets to widespread protection from uncertainty and want. Some of the most vivid discussions of this conceptualisation can be found in the work of people who looked at societal responses to the early dislocations created by marketisation and industrialisation (Polanyi 1944). Later analysts focused on the compromises made to create welfare states during more advanced stages of development (Esping-Anderson 1990).

A second conceptualisation of social policy reads pro-poor expenditures as government attempts to shape and transform society. This reflects the statist perspective of early writers, who saw social policy as part of a wider phenomenon in which government bureaucratised social relations (Weber 1968: 956-89). Later, more neo-Marxist perspectives saw social policies as the means by which government removed obstacles to capitalist development (Cameron 1978). Both perspectives, albeit from different ideological origins, tended to see the state acting above and on society.

From a slightly different angle, more pluralist writers viewed pro-poor expenditures in terms of particular responses to the demands of interest groups. Unlike the universalistic social contract view, pluralists saw government action as the complex aggregation of social forces (Dahl 1961). Social policy was simply the sum of the particularistic benefits that interest groups had demanded and government had targeted.

Tax capacity and pro-poor expenditures are central to a fiscal sociology of governance. Measuring tax capacity tells us that governments have made a fiscal choice about the relative role of government and are able to implement that vision with administrative capacity and legitimacy. Measuring pro-poor expenditures tells us that governments and citizens have negotiated a social contract that defines the relationship between citizens and the state. In so doing, both are given shape. Governments pursue policies to transform society and allow production and power to continue; citizens form interest groups to obtain particularistic benefits. The sum of government and societal interactions is contained in the lines of public finance. Past theorists of public finance set lofty goals in analysing fiscal sociology:

> The spirit of a people, its cultural level, its social structure, the deeds its policy may prepare—all this

> and more is written in its fiscal history, stripped of all phrases. He who knows how to listen to its messages here discerns the thunder of world history more clearly than anywhere else. (Schumpeter, as cited in Swedberg 1991: 100-01)

If Schumpeter is right, then there are powerful insights to be drawn from a fiscal sociology of the state. The current analysis begin with a narrow question, 'who pays what for whom?'. It approaches that question in the context of comparing centralised and decentralised regimes, and it reads in fiscal policy much larger social science concepts. Before turning to this task, it is necessary to look a little closer at the concept of decentralisation.

3. Decentralisation in vogue

The current fondness for decentralisation began during the 1980s and represented a striking reversal from advice that dominated earlier ideas of development.[9] In the 1950s and 1960s, military coups and regime breakdowns occurred across Latin America and instability followed decolonisation in much of Africa. Observers understood these circumstances as evidence that escalating demands and mass mobilisation had outstripped the capacity of state institutions (Huntington 1968). Centralised decision-making was seen as a way to rationalise scarce resources and depoliticise the masses; by contrast, decentralisation was viewed as likely to heighten political, racial, ethnic, and religious cleavages.

During the 1980s, the tide began to turn and pressure to decentralise began to rise. Stagnant economies and inefficient central bureaucracies led researchers to reconsider centralisation as a solution to the problems of developing countries, and multilateral institutions began to include decentralisation components in many of their programmes.[10] Additionally, freer trade, international treaties, and loan conditions led central governments to choose, or be forced, to abdicate their traditional roles, and left critical functions to non-central government entities if they were to be performed at all.[11] There were domestic pressures for decentralisation also, as local politicians and civil society actors sought to capture power from central governments, and national leaders granted access to central power and resources as a means of purchasing support from local allies or meeting demands for democratisation.[12] As we enter the next decade, zeal for decentralisation has become more tempered, though a positive hue continues to tint most evaluations:

> An overall conclusion of the paper is that decentralised fiscal structures are more suitable in the institutional environment of developing countries, especially so if careful attention is paid to the design of institutions vital for the success of decentralisation policies such as the rule of law, conflict resolution and coordination, charter of rights, effective limitations on the authority of governments beyond their designated spheres of influence, accountability and institutional capacity for evaluation at all levels. (Shah and Huther 1998: 1)

The fervour that surrounded decentralisation both encouraged and reflected processes that were already under way on the ground. Developed countries had already become increasingly decentralised by the 1970s; and over the 1980s, developing countries began to narrow the gap. In the developed world, sub-national revenues as a percentage of total revenues stood at 23.3 per cent of total revenues in the 1970s and 23.9 per cent in the 1990s. In the developing world, the sub-national percentage of total revenues rose from 11.6 per cent to 13.2 per cent. Including all countries, including those in transition, the average sub-national percentage of total revenues rose from 16.1 per cent in the 1970s to 18.3 per cent in the 1990s.[13]

As governments shifted resources downward, they also created new administrative apparatuses to implement programmes and make decisions at the local level. In developing countries, 63 of 73 countries surveyed had governmental institutions that administered sub-national jurisdictions (World Bank 2000: 109).

Many of these jurisdictions also provided the ground for political representation, holding elections and organising civil society associations at the sub-national level. For example, in 1999, 94 of 127 countries (74 per cent) elected at least one sub-national tier of government (World Bank 2000: 216-17).

In short, sub-national governments are now doing a larger share of the work of government in both developed and developing countries. As more and more countries move away from centralised government institutions, the concept of decentralisation is studied in new contexts. Still, though many of these countries share characteristics of decentralisation, there are stark differences in the kind and degree of decentralisation that has occurred.

4. Conceptual confusion in decentralisation research

To their credit, researchers have been careful about the way they define decentralisation and the contexts in which they would like to study it. Yet, the differences in kind and degree of decentralisation have produced a conceptual muddle. The muddle has multiplied the conceptualisations of decentralisation; associated the concept with varied meanings; imbued it with positive normative value; conflated it with other concepts; and ignored its multi-dimensionality.[14]

A survey of the voluminous literature on decentralisation suggests that decentralisation has been approached by a variety of intellectual traditions with little agreement.[15] Cohen and Peterson (1997: especially Annex I) offer a useful categorisation of disciplinary approaches based on what decentralisation achieves. Geographers and planners discussing spatial decentralisation focus on reducing concentration in urban areas by promoting regional growth poles. Political scientists discussing political decentralisation focus on bringing decision-making to low levels of aggregation. Economists discussing market decentralisation focus on the smallest unit that can efficiently produce goods and services that meet the revealed preferences of individuals. Lawyers and public administration professionals discussing administrative decentralisation focus on decreasing the hierarchical and bureaucratic control of central government units.[16] In short, there are multiple approaches to decentralisation, and each carries implications about the most useful ways to define the concept. By way of contrast, decentralisation's antonym, centralisation, has a much more precise and accepted usage, which is the concentration of power, resources, and authority in a single head or centre.[17]

Two problems tend to arise with concepts given varied meanings. The concept can be associated with too many meanings (over-specified) or too few (under-specified).[18] Either extreme produces conceptual muddle and causal uncertainty, as observers can approach the concept by delimiting the meanings and indicators that match their belief systems.[19] This is especially problematic when the beliefs associate the concept with normative values, as in the case of the generally positive value associated with decentralisation.

In many cases, the original concept, decentralisation, becomes simply conflated with other evaluative concepts. For example, much research has included democracy or market reforms in the definition of decentralisation.[20] The problem, of course, is that the relationship between decentralisation and these other concepts is a causal hypothesis, subject to empirical test. Indeed, one can certainly imagine democratic regimes that are centralised or decentralised regimes in which market reforms do not occur. When researchers try to be careful about mixing their concepts, they often end up substituting words for decentralisation that do not carry the normative implications; for example, multi-level government, de-centred governance, multiple centres, etc.

The types of problems that arise are typical of poorly defined concepts more generally.[21] The first problem is that one observer can claim that decentralisation exists in a given case, while another observer claims the opposite.[22] This leads to disagreement simply about where to study the phenomenon. Second, the role of decentralisation in causal analysis becomes muddled. One observer claims decentralisation comes from one cause while another observer points to a different or opposite cause. Likewise, one observer can claim that decentralisation causes an outcome while another observer claims it causes a different or opposite outcome. In sum, the result is complete uncertainty about the appropriate universe of cases for comparison and the causes and effects of decentralisation.

This has contributed to a stand-off between cheerleaders and detractors of decentralisation. To take one example, cheerleaders argue that decentralisation leads to greater efforts at progressive public policies while detractors argue that decentralisation leads to a "race to the bottom" and more regressive public policies.[23] Among other arguments, the arguments of the cheerleaders include some combination of the ideas that decentralisation (a) allows experimentation, (b) makes government more accountable, and (c) targets small communities in which citizens empathise with each other. As a result, citizens will pay for public services, including progressive public policies.[24] The detractors argue quite the opposite. Among other arguments, they suggest that decentralisation (a) fragments the political voice of progressive actors, (b) increases the possibility of elite capture, and (c) leads to competition among jurisdictions for a tax base. As a result, narrow interests will avoid paying for progressive policies and governments will not attempt to implement them.[25]

The current project suggests that some of the inconsistency between cheerleaders and detractors is caused by the two camps talking past one another. The most careful researchers from each camp specify a definition and stick to it within an individual context or study. Still, the abundance of research, not all of it careful, has led to an abundance of definitions and an abundance of research strategies. The evaluative nature of the concept intensifies the debate. People attempting to draw implications from the research, such as policymakers, cannot help but be confused.

Take the example of careful researchers studying West Bengal state in India. One researcher applauds decentralised administration that allowed local administrations to target post-flood reconstruction and relief through local administered Food for Work programmes (Charvak 2000: 12-14). A second researcher highlights the role of a centralised, Leftist political structure that directed decisions towards progressive outcomes even as it penetrated society through decentralised administration (Webster 1992). Both researchers were careful in their use of the decentralisation concept, but their studies talk past each other in terms of the ways in which they interpret the case.

The example in the previous paragraph reminds us to be careful in the emphasis placed on different dimensions of decentralisation. Both the cheerleaders and the detractors could find evidence for their arguments in the West Bengal case. Cheerleaders could argue that the autonomy enjoyed by local units makes West Bengal a case of decentralisation. Detractors could argue that West Bengal is actually a case of centralisation in which a centralised political party shapes what gets done, even in local jurisdictions. Is it possible for both to be right?

This project suggests that some of the conceptual and causal tangle can be undone by distinguishing among the multiple dimensions of decentralisation. If there are multiple dimensions, then decentralisation along one dimension could be related to one set of causes and effects, and decentralisation along another dimension could relate to a different or opposite set of causes and effects. Alternatively, decentralisation along one dimension could interact or combine with decentralisation along another dimension to relate to a set of causes and effects. Researchers who do not explicitly look at each dimension or who haphazardly aggregate dimensions will mis-measure the type and degree of decentralisation in a case and will draw incorrect inferences about the relationship between decentralisation and other phenomena. To disentangle these relationships it is necessary to conceptualise and measure the dimensions separately and calculate their interactions. Only then can we identify examples of more or less decentralisation and begin to undertake causal analysis.

5. Conceptual frameworks for the decentralisation concept

One way to understand the core meanings of decentralisation is in terms of the uses to which the concept has been put.[26] Some of the most successful conceptualisations and categorisations in the literature have concentrated on decentralisation in terms of decentralisation *to*. They define and distinguish dimensions of decentralisation in terms of who receives the power and resources that are being decentralised. Thus, democratic devolution identifies the category of cases in which decentralisation occurs to elected local authorities (Crook and Manor 1998). Privatisation defines the category of cases in which decentralisation occurs to organisations outside the government sector (Rondinelli *et al.* 1989). The non-governmental sector has been further disaggregated into private sector organisations that are for-profit versus non-governmental, voluntary associations (Leonard 1982). Each of these distinctions, and others, has been useful for understanding causes and effects of decentralising *to* one kind of unit or another. What is the impact of decentralising to an elected local government or to a private sector, for-profit organisation? Conceptualisations that apply these categories offer a useful beginning, but do not answer a more fundamental question. Where does decentralisation come from, and is it an improvement on centralisation?

In the following paragraphs, care will be taken to conceptualise and define the dimensions in ways that produce categories useful for these more basic questions. Therefore, we are concerned with decentralisation *from*. Each dimension is conceptualised in terms of the degree to which power and resources are taken away from central governments. Such a conceptualisation is clearly directed to studying the causal impact of shifting power and resources away from the central government. This will allow us to measure and evaluate decentralisation as compared to centralisation. Unlike prior conceptualisations, here the recipients of decentralisation are left ambiguous. Rather than be concerned with the many varieties of decentralisation to, the current conceptualisation focuses on the one thing they all share: all forms of decentralisation, regardless of the recipient, involve shifting power and resources away from the central government.

This approach builds on applications of the decentralisation concept in theories of fiscal federalism, public administration, and political science. Briefly, fiscal federalism theories view decentralisation in terms of the welfare effects of giving resources to one level of government or another. Fiscal decentralisation indicates a greater proportion of fiscal impact at levels other than the central government (Oates 1972: 17).[27] Administrative arguments focus on the administrative effects of granting local jurisdictions autonomy from central control. This autonomy refers to general policymaking authority and personnel control, as well as control over what is done with public finances (Rondinelli, Nellis and Cheema 1984).[28] Finally, political arguments focus on the effects of conducting political activities such as participation, organisation, elections, and representation at the local level as opposed to the national level. Decentralised political systems are those in which political actors and issues are significant at the local level and at least partially independent from those at the national level (Fox and Aranda 1996). These conceptualisations can be understood within the broader theoretical frameworks to which they are to be directed.

5.1 Fiscal federalism

Fiscal federalism theories dealing with decentralisation focus on maximising social welfare, which is portrayed as a combination of economic stability, allocative efficiency, and distributive equity. The precise combination and importance attached to each goal will depend on the context, but the challenge of decentralisation is essentially to locate resources at the level of government that optimises social welfare (Musgrave 1958: 132-33, 175-78).

Definition 1: Systems that are fiscally decentralised locate a greater proportion of fiscal resources at a level other than the centre.

In stabilisation policy, governments pump money into the economy (or withdraw it) to influence the overall level of economic activity. Generally, governments can be expected to seek a stable, but relatively high, level of activity. Fiscal decentralisation of stabilisation suggests that non-central entities spend or absorb a greater proportion of the resources that influence the amount of economic activity. This activity is reflected in macroeconomic aggregates, such as employment, inflation, and growth.[29]

In allocation policy, governments choose to direct resources towards one activity or another, for example, shifting resources from agriculture to industry or from one region to another. Generally, governments strive for the use of resources that generates the greatest amount of wealth and services for a given amount of spending and taxing, *i.e.* provides allocation efficiency. Fiscal decentralisation of allocation suggests that non-central units spend or extract a greater proportion of the resources that influence allocative efficiency.[30]

In distribution policy, governments choose to channel wealth, which is the return to economic activity, to a particular group, region, or set of individuals. It is difficult to determine the optimal distribution of wealth, but most fiscal federal theories focus on moving towards a more equal distribution of wealth. Fiscal decentralisation of distribution suggests that non-central entities spend or raise a larger proportion of resources that influence who gets what.[31]

Essentially, what distinguishes among these dimensions is the concept of fiscal impact. Which level of government exerts the greatest influence over fiscal outcomes such as stabilisation, allocation, and distribution? If resources have been ceded to sub-national units, then sub-national units are, to one degree or another, influencing these outcomes. One of the chief ways in which fiscal impact is perceived is in terms of collateral for credit. Governments that handle large amounts of resources, whether those revenues are tied to expenditures or not, are able to draw on credit resources. Intentionally, this conceptualisation has focused on fiscal impact and ignored the autonomous control that local units possess in exercising that capacity. Autonomy is the focus of the next dimension, administrative decentralisation, which draws on theories of public administration.

5.2 Public administration

Public administration theories dealing with decentralisation broadly focus on achieving modern bureaucracies, which are perceived as efficient, effective, and rational (Weber 1968 esp. 926-39 and 956-89). There is significant debate about whether these goals operate in tandem or if there are trade-offs, and the combination will probably depend on individual cases. The specific challenge of decentralisation, however, is to locate administrative authority at the level of government that will optimise efficiency, effectiveness, and rationality.

Definition 2: Systems that are administratively decentralised locate a greater proportion of administrative autonomy at a level other than the centre.

In terms of administrative efficiency, governments seek to match policy packages of taxes and services to the preferences of citizens within a budget constraint. For example, some citizens prefer a package of high taxes and high services, while others prefer low taxes and low services. More administratively decentralised systems grant non-central entities greater autonomy in deciding what policy package to offer.

In terms of effectiveness, governments seek to attain the goals of their programmes. For example, governments seeking to improve literacy can use multiple strategies, from pre-school preparation to adult literacy campaigns. More administratively decentralised systems grant non-central entities greater autonomy in deciding how they are to attain goals.

In terms of administrative rationality, governments seek to obey the norms of ration-legal authority, in which personnel are professional, oriented by rules and make decisions according to rational norms. This differs from systems operating according to patrimonial or charismatic forms of authority. More administratively decentralised systems grant non-central entities greater autonomy in setting the orientations of their administrations.

The amount of administrative decentralisation varies continuously across systems, from systems in which the centre grants little autonomy to those in which the centre grants large amounts. Previous literature has categorised administrative decentralisation in categorical terms, most commonly labelled deconcentration, delegation, and devolution (see Rondinelli 1990).[32] The current approach to decentralisation sees these categories as nothing more than break-points along a continuum of administrative autonomy. Deconcentration involves the least amount of autonomy, delegation slightly more, and devolution the most. The following paragraphs discuss the categories found in the literature and make the case for treating them as a continuum of administrative autonomy.

Deconcentration refers to a central government that disperses responsibility for a policy to its field offices. This transfer changes the spatial and geographical distribution of authority, but does not significantly change the autonomy of the entity that receives the authority. Under deconcentration arrangements, the central government retains authority over the field office, and exercises that authority through the hierarchical channels of the central government bureaucracy. Deconcentration allows only moderately more autonomy than centralised systems.

By contrast, delegation transfers policy responsibility to local governments or semi-autonomous organisations who are not controlled by the central government but remain accountable to it.[33] The main difference between deconcentration and delegation is that the central government must exercise its control through the contractual relation that enforces accountability on the part of local government. This represents a slightly higher level of administrative autonomy for local entities than under deconcentration.

Finally, under devolution, the central government allows quasi-autonomous local units of government to exercise power and control over the policy responsibility being transferred.[34] Compared to the other two types of administrative decentralisation, devolution provides the greatest degree of autonomy to the local unit. The local unit is only accountable to the central government in so far as the central government can impose its will by threatening to withhold resources or responsibility that the local unit needs.

The concept that discriminates among these categories of administrative decentralisation is the relationship between the central government and the entity that receives power and resources. Deconcentration involves a bureaucratic, hierarchical relationship; delegation involves a contractual relationship; and devolution involves an arm's length relationship.[35] The differences in kind among these relationships, between hierarchy, contract, or arm's length, are a syndrome of factors. The best way to summarise that syndrome is in paying attention to the degree of autonomy granted by the central government. Such a simplification perhaps misses some of the conceptual richness of the different relationships, but is sufficient for measuring the continuum of administrative autonomy.[36]

The devolution category deserves further attention because it is often defined as decentralisation to democratically elected local bodies. Such a definition includes patterns of representation in the administrative dimension. This shifts focus, however, and introduces aspects not associated with administrative autonomy. Representation deserves attention in its own right, however, and belongs appropriately to the next dimension, political decentralisation.

5.3 Political decentralisation

Political science theories dealing with decentralisation focus on mobilisation, organisation, articulation, participation, contestation, and aggregation of interests. All political systems must perform these functions, and the way in which this occurs will depend on individual contexts. The specific challenge of decentralisation, however, is to resolve these political processes at the level of government that allows the greatest degree of institutionalisation.

Definition 3: Systems that are politically decentralised institutionalise a greater proportion of political functions at a level other than the centre.[37]

The best way to summarise political functions might be in terms of representation, which refers to the way political institutions 'map the multiplicity of citizen interests onto policy decisions' (Litvack *et al.* 2000: 6). To have an impact on policy, interests in society must be mobilised, organised, and articulated through institutions that carry interests to the state (Berger 1983). Some systems of representation operate through civil society institutions, such as non-governmental organisations, social movements, or interest organisations. Other systems of representation, such as political parties, aim to bring interests directly into positions of official political power through elections. Finally, some systems of representation bring interests into direct negotiation with the state bureaucracy, as in corporatist bargaining.[38] All systems of representation are bounded by institutions of the state itself, which set the rules for representation and thus shape what issues get politicised and how. Under politically decentralised systems citizens define interests and form identities on the basis of local concerns, and organisations such as parties and social movements operate locally and compete over local issues and in local elections.

5.4 Interrelations among the dimensions

The preceding discussion of theoretical approaches to decentralisation provides clear dimensions for analysis: fiscal decentralisation, administrative decentralisation, and political decentralisation. What is not clear, but still pertinent, is the degree to which these dimensions are interrelated. This interrelationship contributes to conceptual confusion, as decentralisation along one dimension may influence or cross-over into decentralisation along another dimension. There are also measurement effects of ignoring the interrelationship, as measures will overestimate or underestimate the amount of decentralisation in a case if they do not account for their interrelationship.

First, we can consider the range of possible ways that dimensions could interact. One possible pattern is that increasing decentralisation on one dimension leads to an increase in decentralisation in another dimension. A second pattern is that increasing decentralisation on one dimension leads to a decrease in decentralisation on another dimension. With three dimensions, there are six different combinations.[39]

Without getting too caught up in speculation, it makes sense to describe how a few of these interactions might operate. For example, fiscal decentralisation might generate greater administrative decentralisation. This would occur if local units used increased resources for a power grab and asserted administrative autonomy from the centre.[40] Alternatively, fiscal decentralisation might lead to less administrative decentralisation. This would occur if central governments systematically tried to counteract any release of resources with an increase in bureaucratic or regulatory controls.[41] Similar scenarios could be described for the relationships between each dimension.

6. Hypotheses linking decentralisation to public finance

The current analysis highlights a diverse economic and political literature about the determinants of fiscal policy.[42] In particular, there are competing views about the impact of decentralisation. For some, decentralised regimes imply smaller governments, while for others decentralisation implies larger ones. In part, these different hypotheses arise from conceptual differences about what fiscal policy represents. Is it a reflection of the relative power of different groups in protecting their interests; is it an indicator of state administrative capacity; and/or is it a reflection of the legitimacy of the state and citizen willingness to pay for public purposes? These conceptual differences are borne out in the different hypotheses that surround fiscal, administrative, and political decentralisation. In testing these hypotheses empirically, the analysis here will separate the different types of decentralisation, and as a result, allow empirical examination of these different approaches to public finance. In particular, the analysis focuses on the way decentralisation affects the ability of government and those without wealth to tap into the resources of those who hold wealth and the willingness and capacity to redistribute.[43]

6.1 Fiscal federalism approaches to public finance

There are a number of ways in which fiscal decentralisation could affect public finance, and many of the most important hypotheses have emerged from theories of fiscal federalism. The main insights from fiscal federalism follow from notions of competition among jurisdictions. In fiscally decentralised settings, any attempt to redistribute wealth in one jurisdiction will result in the migration of its wealthy citizens to another jurisdiction (Tiebout 1956). Brennan and Buchanan (1980) follow this approach and argue that fiscal decentralisation heightens the competition among jurisdictions to retain their tax base. Such competition forces restraint on political elites, even if they would like to maximise revenues or engage in pro-poor expenditures.[44]

If decentralisation heightens competition among jurisdictions, then jurisdictions will be tempted to attach their revenue streams to those tax handles that will produce the least negative response, which may not be the most lucrative.[45] One implication is that jurisdictions will be forced to target those sources of wealth that are least easy to move, such as immovable property and perhaps labour. Mobile capital, by contrast, will be least likely to be targeted. Services will also be targeted towards holders of mobile capital, who will receive subsidies to invest, even if it means lower pro-poor expenditures. Critics have labelled this tendency to avoid redistribution a 'race-to-the-bottom' (Musgrave 1958, 1997; Inman and Rubinfeld 1997).

In addition to the race-to-the-bottom problem, fiscal federalists argue that decentralisation lowers capacity to tax or target pro-poor expenditures across regions because jurisdictions are "stingy". In short, rich regions are unlikely to shift resources to poor regions or address needs in poor regions (Buchanan and Wagner 1977; Oates 1972; Prud'homme 1995).

Centralisation implies the opposite effects. Centralisation lowers competition among jurisdictions and reduces the possibility of migration by the wealthy to escape policies in a sub-national unit. This allows greater overall levels of taxation and also taxation of goods with higher elasticities of demand and more mobile wealth. It also lowers pressure to subsidise mobile capital and allows greater pro-poor expenditures. Further, central governments can use fiscal transfers to equalise resources across regions or to address specific regional needs.

Of course, if the decentralisation-competition argument does not hold, then these propositions are invalid. In the context of increased liberalisation and globalisation, some argue that national governments are just as likely to race-to-the-bottom as a result of competition with other nations. The causal connection may not be between decentralisation and competition, but between capital mobility and competition (Swank 1992; Wallerstein 1997).

Also, even when they are not constrained by international capital, central governments may be equally as stingy as regional governments. Central governments are only likely to shift wealth across regions if poor regions can exert pressure at the central level.

Finally, sub-national governments themselves might not be as stingy as previously assumed. Rich regions may view it as beneficial to pass resources to poor regions. For example, sub-national governments from rich regions may wish to end the spill-over effects of poverty in neighbouring regions, such as migration or environmental degradation. In addition, some might argue that wealthy citizens will favour redistributing resources at the local level because they feel more empathy for poor neighbours than they do for the poor in distant regions (Pauly 1973).

6.2 Administrative approaches to public finance

Administrative approaches direct their attention to the ways in which decentralisation influences administrative performance. Administrative decentralisation gives local units autonomy, which entails flexibility to experiment and innovate. Further, decentralisation allows them to imitate successful examples from other regions. In effect, this replicates the benefits of competition highlighted by fiscal federal theories, this time with an emphasis on competition for efficiency. The implications for tax capacity and pro-poor expenditure, however, are ambiguous.

For some, competition forces jurisdictions to provide more services for lower cost (Rondinelli *et al.* 1984; Tendler 1997; Wildavsky 1984; Buchanan and Tullock 1962; Dye 1966; Toqueville 1969).[46] These governments will waste fewer resources on administrative bureaucracy. If they desire, these governments can simply collect lower taxes (Shah 1999). Alternatively, more pro-poor services could be provided at the same cost. As a result, efficiency helps the poor if it frees resources for services they would not otherwise receive (Litvack *et al.* 2000: 8).

A slightly different perspective looks at the impact of competition for administrative effectiveness. By keeping bureaucracy small and limited to local jurisdictions, decentralisation counters the tendency of large organisations to become rigid and unresponsive.[47] Limited geographical scope improves information flows and allows the state to monitor citizens more effectively, both in terms of their demands and their wealth. In addition, local units may be more agile when changes have to be made, making it easier for them to tap into elusive tax bases (Dye 1966; Toqueville 1969; Shah and Huther 1998; Fisman and Gatti 2000). At the very least, this enhances the capacity to collect taxes, and will lead to less *evasion* and avoidance. It is likely to be of particular benefit to the poor in circumstances in which centralisation had contributed to non-transparent and inflexible policies that systematically excluded the demands of the poor.

The beneficial effects of administrative decentralisation only hold if local administrations are capable. This kind of capacity requires resources and professionalism which are unlikely to exist in uniform quantities across a territory, and are often concentrated in higher status and higher paying central bureaucracies. Further, administration may operate with economies of scale and be more efficient in single national units (Prud'homme 1995: 201-03). In addition, decentralisation disconnects local welfare from national welfare in ways that encourage lower levels to shirk difficult tasks and push these tasks to their neighbours or to the national level. The difficulty of taxation, in administrative and political terms may be high, and local jurisdictions may prefer to depend on transfers from above (Petrei 1998; Shah 1991; Hommes 1995).

If these problems exist, they may undercut any advantages from the impact of decentralisation on administrative efficiency and accountability (Bird and Vaillancourt 1998). In fact, decentralisation may simply increase the number of governments attempting to extract wealth. Rather than competing by cutting taxes, they may compete to collect them, leading to an overall increase in taxation, with no connected improvement in services (Oates 1985).

6.3 Political approaches to public finance

The current project highlights the fact that both decentralisation and public finance are eminently political phenomena, with a central role being played by systems of representation.[48] Systems of representation are the institutions that link citizens to the state and map their interests into state policies. Under decentralised systems of representation, citizens direct their demands through local organisations and institutions, and representatives orient their appeals to local constituencies. The current project suggests that a local orientation to politics will manifest itself in public finance. Two issues arise here: first, who gets represented, and second, how does that representation translate into public finance decisions?

Decentralisation allows different interests to attain representation across a territory and thus provides representation to a more diverse array of interests than would otherwise occur. Centralised systems of representation are likely to exclude the interests of minorities unless affirmative mechanisms are in place for ensuring minority representation.[49]

This possibility only matters in the current analysis if decentralisation influences representation and policymaking with respect to groups interested in doing different things with taxation and expenditures. Advocates of decentralised representation suggest that decentralisation will allow a taxation structure that raises more revenues and allows them to be directed to more pro-poor activities.

First, in traditionally centralised, exclusionary regimes, decentralisation frees national governments from capture by narrow interests (Morris and Lowder 1992: 4-7).

Second, by creating smaller and more numerous institutions of representation, decentralisation increases opportunities for participation, multiplying the sites at which poor people participate and multiplying the interests that gain access to the public purse (Narayan, Chambers, Shah and Petesch 2000; Crook and Manor 1998).[50]

Third, some argue that people with similar preferences and levels of income tend to be concentrated geographically, thus decentralisation creates some jurisdictions in which the median voter prefers more tax capacity and more pro-poor expenditures (Gandmont 1978).

Fourth, there are those who argue that decentralisation provides multiple training grounds for democracy, altering the culture of a polity, incorporating previously excluded groups, and raising citizen consciousness of the need for public action (Toqueville 1969).

By contrast, there are those who argue that decentralised systems privilege the interests of those with a preference for lower public action, including lower taxes and less pro-poor expenditures. In decentralised cases, national representative institutions are often simply the sum of locally oriented ones, and no mechanism links national institutions directly to citizens (Grodzins 1960). If only regional or local issues get politicised, those interests that favour higher taxes and more pro-poor expenditure may find it difficult to focus attention on problems that are supra regional (such as redistribution) and that require higher taxation.[51]

Decentralisation may more directly privilege holders of wealth. They use their wealth to purchase influence in government or to threaten government revenues by slowing economic production.[52] Political decentralisation does not change the tools available to the rich, nor does it change their effectiveness; decentralisation simply forces them to apply their political leverage to lower levels of government. The key is that decentralisation implies deconcentrating government, while capital remains concentrated.[53] These weapons of the wealthy are likely to be equally, if not more, effective at local as well as central levels of government.[54]

In contrast, political decentralisation weakens the influence of groups that do not hold wealth. The poor are not without economic leverage of their own, but the impact of their wealth depends on levels of centralisation. By definition, the poor do not hold enough wealth to purchase much influence, though they at least purchase some influence when they aggregate their wealth in a single organisation at the national level (McConnell 1970). Likewise, their threats to slow economic production are only credible if they are united across companies and across jurisdictions where withholding their labour cannot be easily side-stepped by shifting production.[55] In some contexts, peak level unions pool material resources and coordinate national strikes to pressure for pro-poor policy (Wallerstein 1997; Swenson 1991).[56]

The most important effect of decentralisation may be its detrimental impact on the ability of the poor to concentrate politically. Organisation is the main weapon of the poor, as it allows them to utilise the one resource they have in abundant quantities, their numbers. Organisation is no easy task, however, it requires leadership, discipline and mobilisation, and these resources are often in short supply. Decentralisation spreads these scarce organisational resources, and forces the poor to organise in multiple jurisdictions for multiple contests. Further, organisational resources that exist in one jurisdiction are not easily transferred or leveraged to another.[57] The key for the poor is an institutional structure that can overcome resource and collective action constraints to press demands (Hicks and Swank 1992). Political decentralisation forces the poor to organise in multiple jurisdictions for multiple contests, electoral and otherwise, and spreads thin their organisational resources (Garrett 1995: 657-87). Though the poor may find the leaders to discipline and mobilise them in some cities or regions, they are unlikely to be able to replicate this success in all jurisdictions.

The preceding discussion has focused mostly on the way in which political decentralisation shifts the balance of power between different interest groups. There is an additional political dynamic that deserves attention, however, and that is the degree to which decentralisation influences the links between state and society. For some, public finance decisions are an indicator of government accountability and governance more generally (Moore 2001). Citizens are willing to hand over their wealth if and only if they believe they can hold government accountable. Simply increasing the sites of contact by decentralising may enhance the ability of citizens to monitor and hold government accountable.[58] The result, it is argued, is greater willingness to contribute and more collective action to combat problems like poverty.

Of course, monitoring and accountability may be less forthcoming at the local level than at the national level.[59] Legislatures, judiciaries, civil society organisations, and the press act as monitoring mechanisms to deliver information to citizens, but these institutions may actually be inhibited at the local level by their smaller scale (not to mention the fact that they are usually much more recent at the local level than their national counterparts). In addition, small scale and distance from central authority allows clientelism and private power to survive in local contexts (Bardhan and Mookherjee 2000: 2-7).[60]

The preceding paragraphs presented a series of relationships between decentralisation and public finance. How then do we proceed in testing these arguments? The sections below describe the use of cross-national statistical data to obtain measures of the three dimensions of decentralisation, tax capacity, and pro-poor expenditure.

7. Measuring fiscal decentralisation

Fiscal federalism theories dealing with decentralisation focus on the location of resources. These theories highlight social welfare, which is portrayed as a combination of economic stability, allocative efficiency, and distributive equity. The precise combination and importance attached to each goal will depend on the context, but the challenge is to locate resources at the level of government that optimises these fiscal categories of social welfare (Musgrave 1958: 132-33, 175-78).

Expenditures and revenues form the two main components of fiscal activity.[61] These two elements are central to any system of public finance, and they summarise the total amount of money that governments put into or take out of an economy as well as where governments put the money and where they take it from. The current study hypothesises that the best indicator for the level of fiscal centralisation or decentralisation is the share of sub-national expenditures and revenues.

The choice of focusing on fiscal instruments rather than regulatory or financial policies is partly methodological and partly substantive. Governments influence the amount of wealth in society and its distribution through various instruments. Regulatory instruments are built into the formal and informal institutions that govern civil society and private sector behaviour; thus, they are extremely complex and context specific. Financial instruments are similarly difficult to measure with statistics, and their impact on distribution is not so direct as fiscal policy. Fiscal policy offers the most accessible window into levels of fiscal decentralisation, and regulatory or financial mechanisms will have to be taken up in closer country studies.

Despite being easier to measure, fiscal instruments still present some methodological difficulties. Though the IMF attempts to standardise its definition of local versus national resources, it is extremely difficult to attain accurate measurement using self-reported national statistics.[62] What is measured as a local expenditure or revenue in one context may be scored as a national government resource in another.

Nevertheless, there are several advantages to a focus on revenues and expenditures. First, revenues and expenditures offer the best measures available without detailed study of each and every country. Second, errors are not likely to be correlated with other variables of interest thus they introduce no bias into estimation. Finally, by using both expenditures and revenues, we tap into the main attributes implied by the concept of fiscal decentralisation. The key attribute that defines fiscal decentralisation is the fiscal impact of sub-national governments relative to the overall impact of government.

Expenditures focus on the amount of government activity that sub-national governments undertake, and revenues focus on the quantity of resources that pass through them.

Expenditures are all cash outlays made by a given level of government. They can be examined as a whole, over time, in terms of revenues, as a percentage of GDP, in distinct sub-sections, in sub-sections as a percentage of some other variable, in constant values, in current values, or as done here, as a percentage of all government outlays. Each treatment cuts a slightly different perspective on spending policy, but sub-national expenditures as a percentage of total expenditures is the most appropriate to gauge fiscal decentralisation.[63] A larger proportion of the expenditures spent by lower level governments indicates decentralised fiscal impact.

The revenue side of fiscal decentralisation is composed of all cash inflows to sub-national governments, including taxes, loans, and grants. As in the case of expenditures, these can be examined in a number of ways and with respect to other variables, and each treatment offers a different view of revenue policy. Similar to the choice for expenditures, the indicator chosen is sub-national revenue as a percentage of total government revenue, which focuses on the fiscal revenues passing through sub-national governments as opposed to those revenues that remain at the centre.[64] A larger proportion of revenues passing through sub-national governments indicates decentralised fiscal impact.

8. Measuring administrative decentralisation

As discussed above, the concept that discriminates among degrees of administrative decentralisation is the autonomy granted by the central government to other levels of government. Despite interesting differences in kind (deconcentration, delegation, and devolution), the current measurement seeks a continuous measurement of the one dimension that underlies administrative decentralisation: autonomy.

One way to measure levels of local administrative autonomy is in the control exercised over local revenue. The percentage of local revenues from taxes provides an indicator of sub-national autonomous control over resources. Taxes are different from the total amount of resources, which is more a measure of wealth than a measure of control. As mentioned before, sub-national revenues are a combination of taxes, transfers, grants and loans. Taxes offer the greatest degree of autonomy, grants and loans offer somewhat less, and discretionary transfers probably offer the least. Transfers, even supposedly automatic ones, can be withheld, and grants and loans generally arrive with conditions or with expenditures earmarked.[65]

A second measure of sub-national autonomy is the percentage of total grants and revenues not accounted for by transfers. This could conceivably include taxes, loans, fees, sales of assets, or informal contributions. There are some drawbacks to excluding all transfers, which does not distinguish between transfers over which lower levels of government have total control, such as block grants, and transfers that are tied to central government priorities, such as ear-marked transfers, or transfers that require certain behaviours by sub-national governments, such as matching or some other condition. Still, the treatment of all revenues aside from transfers gives an indication of the degree to which sub-national governments autonomously raise their own funds, through taxes, loans, fees, or sales of assets.

9. Measuring political decentralisation

Political science theories dealing with decentralisation focus on the location of mobilisation, organisation, articulation, participation, contestation, and aggregation of interests. All political systems must resolve the challenges of institutionalising these processes, and the way in which this occurs will depend on individual contexts. The challenge of decentralisation is to resolve these political functions at the level of government that allows the greatest degree of institutionalisation. The key political function measured here involves representation.

In elections, the electorate votes; the votes are aggregated; and candidates take power. Elections at the local level indicate that some portion of representative activity is being undertaken at the local level and parties must organise for local contests. Candidates must compete and make appeals in local jurisdictions, and citizens participate at the local level. Citizens may organise and participate through non-electoral channels, but these are harder to characterise, and probably do not have as direct an impact on representation. Of course, simply holding elections does not automatically mean that national forces do not overwhelm local ones, but local elections at least increase the likelihood that some political functions will be decentralised.[66] The existence of elections at the municipal level or the state/provincial level is hypothesised here as an indicator of political decentralisation.

Though there are other political functions, the electoral components offer the most valid indicators of political decentralisation as they tap into fundamental aspects of political authority. Elections address the issue of representation, which is the way interests gain possession of legislative and executive power. Table 1 displays the concepts, measures and sources used for the different dimensions of decentralisation.

TABLE 1: Decentralisation Indicators and Dimensions

Dimension	Indicator	Source
Fiscal decentralisation	1. Sub-national expenditures as per cent of total expenditures.	Decentralisation statistics. World Bank website.
Fiscal decentralisation	2. Sub-national revenues as per cent of total revenues.	Decentralisation statistics. World Bank website.
Administrative decentralisation	3. Taxation as a percentage of sub-national revenues.	IMF government finance statistics.
Administrative decentralisation	4. Non-transfer income as a percentage of sub-national revenues.	IMF government finance statistics.
Political decentralisation	5. Municipal elections	Database on political institutions. Library of Congress country facts. CIA world factbook.
Political decentralisation	6. State elections	Database on political institutions. Library of Congress country facts. CIA world factbook.

10. Using the indicators to obtain accurate aggregate measures

For the concept of decentralisation, factor analysis generates more accurate scores of the three dimensions than other techniques. Measuring decentralisation dimensions is complicated by the fact that core attributes are difficult to measure, and any metric for one dimension is likely to simultaneously pick up elements of the others. In part, this is because there are causal relationships among the dimensions (political decentralisation may contribute to fiscal decentralisation etc.) but also because any quantitative measure is likely to be somewhat imprecise. No single indicator can capture the decentralisation concept fully, and no simple combination of indicators, such as an average or sum, could capture the multidimensionality of the concept. To avoid the mistakes that might arise from other methods, factor analytic techniques both confirmed that there were three dimensions to the decentralisation concept (fiscal, administrative, and political) and quantified the amount that each case had decentralised along each dimension.[67] The scores for the cases and the factor analysis are included in Appendix B. To make the scores more intelligible, they were normalised to a zero-one scale, and can be read in terms of decentralisation units. Thus, the United States scored .80 fiscal decentralisation units, .56 administrative decentralisation units, and .84 political decentralisation units.

11. Tax capacity: taxation as a percentage of GDP

Many of the fiscal, administrative, and political hypotheses relate decentralisation to the fiscal size and administrative capacity of government. To measure these outputs, overall tax levels as a percentage of GDP reflect the size of government with respect to overall economic activity. Governments that possess the capacity to extract resources and whose leaders make the decision to extract will score high on taxation as a percentage of GDP. Other denominators, such as total expenditures or tax as a percentage of total revenues, would also measure aspects of the size and capacity of government, but would bring in other conceptual interpretations, such as the efficiency of government administration. Here, the analysis is most concerned with the concepts of fiscal size and administrative capacity.

In measuring tax capacity, the study was careful to measure all of the taxes collected. Many datasets include only central government tax revenues, missing those taxes collected by local and regional governments. Data from the *Government Finance Statistics* was used to add central, regional, and local taxes when considering total tax capacity.[68]

The relationship between total taxes and total economic activity, measured as taxation as a percentage of GDP, focuses on the willingness and ability of governments to tap into private wealth for public action. This directs attention to those decentralisation hypotheses that degrees of decentralisation affect the administrative capacity of government, change the incentives facing fiscal actors, alter the accountability of government, and shift the relative power of interests. The average amount of tax capacity is 30.10 per cent of GDP, with a standard deviation of 10.54, a minimum of 8.04, and a maximum of 50.88.

12. Pro-poor expenditures

One way that the impact of decentralisation can be measured is in terms of the policy steps taken by government. Policy steps can be expenditure policies, revenue policies, and regulatory policies, and each kind of policy can be pro-poor or anti-poor. In general, policies that offer services used by the poor, redistribute wealth, or improve the treatment of poor within society are pro-poor.

Here, the project uses the proportion of expenditures directed towards social policy as an indicator of pro-poor policies. Social policy expenditures are a particularly good measure of pro-poor policy effort as they incite vehement distributive conflict and require an active effort on the part of government to transfer resources. In addition, social policies come together as a meaningful configuration of government actions that other studies have examined to understand the nature of state-society relations in terms of a social contract between citizens and government.[69]

To measure pro-poor policy, data is taken from the IMF Government Finance Statistics. The data from multiple levels of government categorise expenditures according to expenditures on health, education, social security and welfare, and housing and community amenities. The total social policy effort is the sum of social spending at all levels of government divided by the total amount of resources spent.[70]

Among the 68 countries for which decentralisation data was available, 64 had data from all levels of government on the amount spent on social policy. The mean percentage spent on social policy was 51 with a standard deviation of 16.

13. Research design

The current project asks whether government has greater capacity to act progressively under centralised or decentralised systems. More specifically, the study attempts to trace the causal mechanism between decentralisation and tax capacity and decentralisation and pro-poor expenditure levels by looking at different kinds of decentralisation. In particular, are differences in the progressive capacity of government due to patterns of fiscal, administrative or political decentralisation?

The broader literature on the determinants of public finance offers a large number of hypotheses in addition to decentralisation. An effort was made to include a number of these rival explanations while maintaining the principal focus, which was to test the marginal impact of decentralisation on taxation and expenditure policy.

The first rival hypothesis focused on the level of development. Though it is an imprecise concept, the level of development reflects in one way or another (a) the amount of resources available to extract, (b) the organisation of social interests, and (c) the resources available for government administration. Each of these variables could potentially influence tax capacity and pro-poor expenditure effort. To control for the impact of development, the model includes the log of GDP per capita in 1995 US$.[71]

A second rival hypothesis involved globalisation. Globalisation certainly puts pressure on public finance. For some, this pressure militates for a decrease in taxation as countries must shrink the size of government and lower labour costs. For others, globalisation forces the state to increase pro-poor expenditure to compensate or insure those dislocated by international competition.[72] To control for levels of globalisation, the model included an indicator of trade openness. Trade openness was measured as the total value of imports and exports as a percentage of GDP.[73]

A third rival hypothesis involves the major claimants on government. The proportion of resources that are required for government are likely to depend on the demographic and political weight of key dependants. One group that clearly depends on and benefits from government policy is the elderly. To control for the weight of state dependants, the analysis includes a measure of the proportion of the population aged 65 and over.

Finally, the model also acknowledges the possibility that the dimensions of decentralisation interact. Fiscal decentralisation may combine with administrative decentralisation and/or political decentralisation to create changes in tax capacity and pro-poor policy beyond the impact of any single dimension alone.[74]

The analysis incorporates the theoretical possibility that many of the hypotheses depend on a regime variable that intervenes between decentralisation and public finance outputs. Especially those hypotheses revolving around political decentralisation would be likely to operate most powerfully in democratic political systems, in which citizens have more freedom to organise and governments are perhaps more likely to answer to citizens. To control for this potential confounding variable, the final application removes countries that are not democratic from the sample. Democracies were defined as those countries that the Polity IV dataset scored more democratic than authoritarian.[75]

The analysis was conducted in a series of models that test the different permutations of variables. All models include the control for level of development, as it is likely to have the biggest single impact on tax capacity and pro-poor expenditure. The first model examines the impact of factor scores on dimensions of decentralisation. The second model examines the impact of the decentralisation dimensions after including all the control variables and the interaction term.

The third model applies the full analysis to democratic countries alone. A fourth model chooses an indicator for each dimension of decentralisation rather than use the factor scores. Though worse measures, the indicators alone offer more explicit implications for those uncomfortable with the factor analysis terminology. The dependent variable in Table 2 is tax capacity, measured as 100 times the total amount of taxation divided by GDP.[76] The dependent variable in Table 3 is pro-poor expenditure effort, measured as 100 times the total amount of health, education, housing, and social security divided by total expenditures. Both tax capacity and pro-poor effort were calculated from the combined finances of national and sub-national units.

13.1 Results

The results of regression analysis demonstrate that dimensions of decentralisation have independent effects on tax capacity and pro-poor expenditure. Notably, the impact of political decentralisation was consistently negative, leading to both lower tax capacity and lower pro-poor expenditure effort. Administrative decentralisation had a positive impact on pro-poor expenditure, and fiscal decentralisation did not appear statistically significant in any analysis. The results for the two dependent variables will be considered in turn.[77]

Table 2 displays the results from the different models for tax capacity. If we compare across models, the statistical significance, the approximate size, and the direction of impact of the coefficients stay relatively constant. The coefficient for administrative decentralisation does change signs across the models, but it is not significantly different from zero in any model. As might be expected, the explanatory power of the models increases when we add variables to the models, but all of the models provide a reasonably good fit with an adjusted R^2 above .53.

In each model, political decentralisation was negatively related to tax capacity and was statistically significant. For example, model three suggests that democratic countries that were .1 unit lower on the scale of political decentralisation were .98 lower in taxation as a per cent of GDP.

Models that included the control variables did not change the significance, the approximate size, or the direction of impact of the primary hypotheses. The interaction term was not significant in any model, nor was the impact of globalisation. Analysing democratic countries alone did not change most of the results about the impact of different kinds of decentralisation. The weight of state dependants and the level of development were significant in all models, and had the predicted impact of increasing tax capacity. For example, democratic countries with an average per capita income collected 30.10 per cent of GDP in taxes while countries with $100 higher in per capita income collected 32.65 per cent.[78] Also, countries with 1 per cent more of the population over 65 collected 1.41 percentage points more of GDP in taxes.

The final model repeats the analysis using a single indicator for each dimension of decentralisation. The coefficients are consistent with those using the factor analysis. For example, there were no significant impacts of fiscal and administrative decentralisation but political decentralisation had a negative impact. Countries in which local legislatures were elected collected a proportion of GDP that was 4.31 lower than those in which there were no local legislative elections.[79]

The results of the second regression analysis reaffirm that dimensions of decentralisation have independent, and at times, opposite effects, this time when tested for their impact on pro-poor expenditures. Again, the impact of political decentralisation was negative—consistently in the direction of less pro-poor expenditure effort. Unlike the model for tax capacity, administrative decentralisation had positive effects. Once again, however, fiscal decentralisation did not appear statistically significant in any model.

Table 3 displays the results from the different models for pro-poor policy outputs. If we compare across the models, one can see that the size of the coefficients changes slightly, but the statistical significance and direction of impact was robust to the different model specifications. The R^2 statistic was reasonably good (.32 in the simplest model); and, as one might expect, it rose when more of the control variables were included.

TABLE 2: Decentralisation and Tax Capacity

	Model 1: decentralisation dimensions	Model 2: decentralisation dimensions and controls	Model 3: decentralisation dimensions and controls, democratic regimes		Model 4: single indicators
Constant	-15.63* (8.34)	-.953 (8.72)	-5.81 (12.02)	Constant	-8.72 (5.70)
Fiscal decentralisation units	-6.75 (5.46)	11.88 (14.49)	.749 (19.59)	Sub-national revenues as a percentage of total	-9.97E-02 (.064)
Administrative decentralisation units	4.20 (7.10)	8.11 (13.91)	-2.73 (18.69)	Sub-national tax as percentage of revenues	1.45E-02 (.042)
Political decentralisation units	-15.53*** (6.37)	-12.38*** (4.31)	-9.76* (4.99)	Municipal elections	-4.31*** (1.24)
Interaction among decentralisation terms		-30.71 (29.69)	-4.75 (42.43)		
Development (log GDP per capita)	6.15*** (.87)	2.38*** (.75)	2.55*** (.84)	Development (log GDP per capita)	3.07*** (.72)
State claimants (senior citizens)		1.63*** (.24)	1.49*** (.26)	State claimants (senior citizens)	1.40*** (.22)
Globalisation (trade openness)		3.68E-02 (.023)	3.23E-02 (.025)	Globalisation (trade openness)	3.75E-02* (.021)
Adjusted R-squared	.53	.82	.77	Adjusted R-squared	.83
Cases	42	42	37	Cases	42

*Indicates statistically significant at .10 level, **at .05 level, and ***at .01.

Note: Standard errors in parentheses.

In each specification, political decentralisation was negatively related to pro-poor expenditure and was statistically significant. For example, in democratic countries, an increase from .1 to .2 in political decentralisation led to a drop of .21 in the proportion of total expenditures spent on pro-poor expenditures. Administrative decentralisation, by contrast, had a positive relationship to social policy for democratic countries; an increase from .1 to .2 in administrative decentralisation was correlated with an increase of .27 in the proportion of total expenditures spent on social policy. Fiscal decentralisation was not statistically significant.

The control variables behaved as expected though they were not always significant. The interaction term was not significant in any model, nor was the impact of globalisation. The weight of state dependants and the level of development were significant in all models, and had the predicted impact of increasing pro-poor expenditures. For example, democratic countries with per capita $100 above the average spent per cent more on pro-poor expenditures.[80] Also, countries with 1 per cent more of the population over 65 spent 1.47 percentage points more of GDP on pro-poor expenditures.

TABLE 3: Pro-Poor Expenditure Effort

	Model 1: decentralisation dimensions	Model 2: decentralisation dimensions and controls	Model 3: decentralisation dimensions and controls, in democratic regimes		Model 4: single indicators
Constant	-.11 (.10)	9.88E-02 (.13)	4.00 (.14)	Constant	2.30E-02 (.11)
Fiscal decentralisation	-1.69E-02 (.067)	6.77E-02 (.19)	8.37 (.20)	Sub-national revenues as percentage of total	6.86E-04 (.004)
Administrative decentralisation	.27 (.070)***	.26 (.13)**	.25 (.14)*	Sub-national tax as percentage of revenues	3.23E-03*** (.001)
Political decentralisation	-.16 (.061)**	-.14 (.060)**	-.17 (.067)**	Municipal elections	-5.47E-02** (.023)
Log of GDP per capita	6.79E-02 (.011)***	3.39E-02 (.015)**	3.12E-02 (.015)*	Log GDP per capita	3.79E-02** (.014)
Age-proportion over 65		1.41E-02 (.005)***	1.47E-02 (.005)***	Age-proportion over 65	1.30E-02*** (.005)
Trade openness		3.90E-04 (.00)	4.44E-04 (.00)	Trade openness	3.77E-04 (.000)
Decentralisation interaction		-.22 (.38)	-.21 (.41)		-.32 (.46)
R^2	.41	.46	.45	Adjusted R-squared	.48
N	61	59	49	Cases	59

*indicates statistically significant at .10 level, **at .05 level, and *** at .01.

Note: Standard errors in parentheses.

The final model repeats the analysis using a single indicator for each dimension of decentralisation. The coefficients are consistent with those using the factor analysis. For example, there was no significant impact of decentralised fiscal resources, but higher levels of administrative decentralisation and lower levels of political decentralisation were associated with more pro-poor expenditure. Countries with sub-national units that collected 10 per cent more of their revenue in taxes spent .32 per cent more on pro-poor expenditures. Countries in which local legislatures were elected spent .055 less on pro-poor expenditure than those in which there were no local legislative elections.

A graphical representation in Figure 1 brings together the measurement model from the factor analysis with the linear regression results from this section. The figure uses conventions common in linear-structural relations analysis (Hayduk 1987). Squares indicate that variables were observable, and ovals, like the decentralisation dimensions, show that concepts had to be derived from other indicators. The left side of the figure shows a measurement model in which the three abstract dimensions of decentralisation in ovals at the centre are connected by arrows to the six measurable variables in squares to the left. Above the decentralisation ovals are squares representing the control variables in the regression analysis. Arrows connect the control variables and the decentralisation ovals to the dependent variable on the right, tax capacity and pro-poor expenditure outputs. The arrows indicate the causal relationship between each explanatory variable and the outcome.

13.2 Implications

The main concern of this exercise was to understand the impact of decentralisation on public finance. Unlike other potential influences, decentralisation offers a unique opportunity to policymakers and policy advisors who could conceivably take steps to precise a system of intergovernmental relations to improve tax capacity and pro-poor expenditure. Other determinants, such as level of development and aged percentage of the population, had a positive impact on tax capacity and pro-poor expenditure, but these are hardly instruments of policy.

FIG. 1: Linear Structural Model of Pro-Poor Outputs

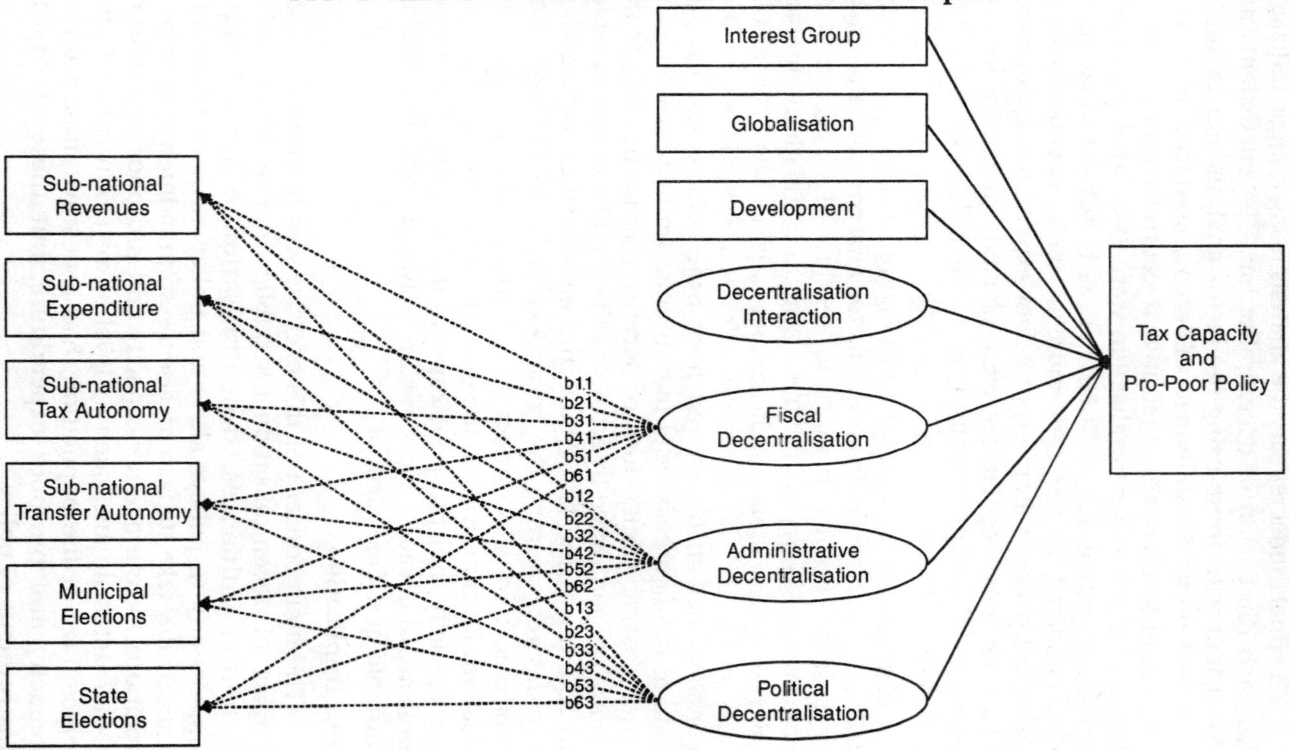

The dimensions of decentralisation, however, are attributes that governments can potentially alter with less difficulty. Though the dimensions may be fundamentally related, they did not combine in a systematic way to influence tax capacity. This suggests that centralisation along one dimension might be combined with decentralisation along another dimension to fine-tune the conditions for expanding tax capacity.

The regressions confirmed a negative impact of political decentralisation and, at least for pro-poor expenditures, a positive impact of administrative dimension. The negative relationship between political decentralisation and tax capacity suggests that decentralisation lowers the political resources available to those who favour greater public sector action and strengthens the political influence of those who do not. The negative relationship between political decentralisation and pro-poor expenditures suggests that the organisational and material resources that allow the poor to advance their demands are less powerful at the sub-national level than at the national level.

The positive relationship between administrative decentralisation and pro-poor expenditures suggests that competition, information, and innovation resulting from decentralisation may have efficiency benefits that increase pro-poor spending. One interpretation is that by being able to do more with less, efficient administrations free up resources that are used for pro-poor expenditures. Another interpretation is that sub-national jurisdictions compete to retain their citizens by providing services, including those services directed to the poor. The two results together suggest that that administrative decentralisation and political centralisation led to the outcomes policy advisors might like. This is especially the case as there were interaction effects among the dimensions.

One policy step that might be taken would be to encourage governments to strengthen the institutions that centralise political functions, especially those institutions that might represent the poor. To centralise politics, advisors could encourage organisation in national political parties, unions, and interest groups. Of course, national organisations cannot be created overnight, but institutional changes may encourage national collective action. For example, governments can create arenas in which associations gather and take binding decisions, as was the practice in peak level bargaining in corporatist systems. To encourage similar centralisation in political parties, governments could adjust electoral institutions to favour issues and contests with national scope. Timing national and local elections at the same time and linking national and local nomination and financing procedures might have such an effect. The point is not that local political competition is bad. Rather, the point is that national issues of redistribution and poverty have to be fought and advanced at all levels of government. These issues are not likely to be brought to the table, however, unless there are national level organisations that allow poor people to organise, articulate their interests, and gain representation.

A second policy step that might be taken would be to grant administrative autonomy to local units. Immediate efforts that might advance this autonomy would be giving sub-national units greater control over their resources, for example through the use of block grants rather than ear-marked or conditional grants, and granting local units access to professional staff from central bureaucracies. To promote competition among sub-national units, central governments could loosen national mandates and allow greater experimentation, innovation, and specialisation. Those behaviours that produce efficiencies can be rewarded and best practices can be exported, for example through administrative exchanges across sub-national units. Of course, all of these mechanisms of administrative efficiency will work only if information, monitoring, and oversight are in place at the local level. This means that local ombudsmen, press, and political actors should be encouraged to challenge administration and hold it accountable. Accounts tribunals or other oversight bodies at the sub-national level can play an important role.

The distinction to be understood here is (a) the values that decide how much public action should be undertaken versus (b) the efficiency with which government takes action. Other things equal, political centralisation allows poor people and those who favour public action to overcome obstacles to collective action and influence the values that direct government. It is not that these actors cannot do the same at the local level, indeed, they often do; it is simply that centralised political systems allow those who favour public action to shape the values of government more than decentralised systems.

Other things equal, administrative decentralisation allows efficient implementation of political values. It is not that central governments are not efficient; they are often the repositories of the best and the brightest from government bureaucracy. On the other hand, centralised bureaucracies may not be able to encourage the innovation and competition that promote efficiency in sub-national units.

In sum, administratively decentralised systems achieve more efficient public policies than administratively centralised systems. At the same time, in comparison with politically decentralised systems, politically centralised systems direct policies with values that favour more public action and more pro-poor action. Taken together, then, administratively decentralised and politically centralised systems offer the greatest amount of progressive public action.

APPENDIX A

Factor Analysis for Decentralisation[81]

The model proposed here conceptualises decentralisation as three distinct but interrelated dimensions that can be measured using the six indicators described above. Factor analytic techniques applied to the indicators can calculate the unique and interrelated characteristics of the different dimensions of decentralisation and test whether the model is accurate. This technique of proposing and testing a measurement model using factor analysis is known as confirmatory factor analysis, and it rests on the intuition that underlying concepts, such as the dimensions of decentralisation, are difficult to measure, but they are manifest in empirically observed indicators.[82]

The specific hypotheses to be tested are (a) decentralisation consists of three abstract dimensions; and (b) each of the six indicators is closely related to one of the three dimensions. To test the first hypothesis, confirmatory factor analysis separates the unique characteristics of each indicator from the characteristics shared with other indicators. If the most statistically accurate grouping of shared characteristics divides the indicators into three clusters, the analysis confirms that there are three underlying dimensions, as opposed to two or four (or some other number).[83]

Next, factor analysis uses the correlations among the variables to measure their relationship to underlying dimensions. The shared characteristics can be divided into the portion explained by each dimension, given as a factor coefficient for each dimension. If the model is correct, the largest factor coefficients should relate indicators to the dimension they are hypothesised to measure. For example, the largest factor coefficient on sub-national percentage of expenditures should be the coefficient related to the fiscal decentralisation dimension. These steps confirm the measurement model. They also produce improved and more precise measures of the concepts.

This is possible because the analysis generates factor coefficients relating each indicator to all the dimensions. Partly, this is because the measures are imprecise, and they will pick up some of the relationships to other dimensions. In addition, the coefficients reflect the fact that the dimensions are related. For example, politically decentralised systems might find local political weight used to allocate more resources to lower levels of government. As a result, part of the sub-national revenues indicator should not be attributed to fiscal decentralisation but reflects characteristics derived from the political decentralisation dimension.

Factor analysis uses this information to improve measurement in ways that simple aggregation or indexes cannot. Factor analysis separates the relationship to each dimension and calculates its size in the factor coefficients. This allows us to use only the information from each indicator that is relevant to a single dimension and ultimately obtain better measures of the dimensions.

A second output of the analysis is an accurate measurement of each dimension in each case. The factor coefficient measures the intensity of the relationship between each variable and each dimension and can be multiplied by each case score on each variable. The sum of the coefficients multiplied by the case scores gives a factor score for each case on each dimension. In other words, we can produce a measure of fiscal decentralisation, administrative decentralisation, and political decentralisation in each case. In fact, this measure is superior to other methods of measurement that do not take as many indicators into account and/or that do not attempt to separate the unique and shared characteristics of each indicator.[84]

A1: Cases and data

The current project applied confirmatory factor analysis to decentralisation data collected from 68 countries in 1996. The data included fiscal indicators from IMF Government Finance Statistics, obtained from the World Bank website on decentralisation, and filled in missing values with data from the 2001 IMF hardcopy publication where available. Other data were collected in the Database of Political Indicators collected by researchers at the World Bank and the Government of Switzerland. Missing political data was obtained from country constitutions, Library of Congress Country Facts, and the CIA Factbook.[85]

In cases in which there was no fiscal data available from 1996 but data from other years in the 1990s were available, linear trends obtained through regression analysis of available data filled the 1996 data. As most fiscal indicators are variables that change incrementally over time, if at all (expenditures, revenues, etc.) this practice was not likely to change the results. The findings were robust to using data from a single year data alone (1995, 1996, 1997), but pooling the data into a single year increased the number of cases available.

Special care was also taken with relation to indicators that were related to variables that might confound the analysis, such as the type of regime. This was particularly the case for the political decentralisation indicators that focused on elections and electoral rules. Some non-democracies held elections and data was therefore available on the political decentralisation indicators. Nevertheless, some might argue that the representation that occurs in non-democracies, however decentralised, is substantively different than that occurring in democracies. A local election in which the national government is authoritarian or in which only one party competes can hardly be called competitive, and probably does a poor job of decentralising political functions.[86] To address this issue, the analysis was conducted after removing non-democracies. No significant changes in results occurred.[87]

A2: Factor analysis

Confirmatory factor analysis was used to test the hypothesis that three dimensions of decentralisation (fiscal, administrative, and political) that underlay measurable indicators. The six indicators were: (1) sub-national expenditures as a percentage of expenditures; (2) sub-national revenues as a percentage of total revenue items; (3) the relative importance of tax as a percentage of sub-national revenues; (4) the relative importance of transfers as a percentage of sub-national revenues; (5) the existence of municipal elections; and (6) the existence of state or provincial elections. The hypothesis was that the first two indicators mostly measured fiscal decentralisation; the third and fourth indicators measured administrative decentralisation; and the last three indicators measured political decentralisation.[88]

The number of cases with data available on all indicators was 68. Among these cases, the mean percentage of expenditures as a percentage of total expenditures was 22.27 and the mean percentage of revenues was 17.24. The mean percentage of sub-national revenues from taxes was 44.65 and the mean percentage from transfers was 34.60. Twelve of the cases had no municipal elections, and 26 had no state elections.

Principle factor analysis of the data confirmed the assertion that three dimensions most appropriately organised the data. The eigenvalue for the third dimension was .92 with a cumulative per cent of variance explained of 88.29 (see Table A1).[89]

Next, the covariances among the variables were used to measure the relationship between variables and underlying dimensions.[90] As expected, sub-national expenditures as a percentage of total expenditures and sub-national revenues as a percentage of total revenues were highly correlated with each other and with what was labelled the "fiscal

TABLE A1: Eigenvalues

Component	Initial Eigenvalue	Cumulative % of variance explained
1	2.50	41.63
2	1.89	73.10
3	.92	88.29
4	.49	96.47
5	.18	99.42
6	3.45E-02	100.00

decentralisation" dimension. The factor coefficient of sub-national expenditures as a percentage of total revenues was .971 and the coefficient of sub-national revenues as a percentage of total revenues was .930.

Also as expected, the relative importance of tax and transfer revenues as a percentage of sub-national revenues were most highly correlated with each other and with what was labelled the "administrative decentralisation" dimension. The factor coefficient of tax revenues as a percentage of local revenues was .917 and the coefficient of non-transfer income as a percentage of local revenues was .931.

Finally, municipal elections and state elections were most closely related to each other and to the third dimension, which has been labelled "political decentralisation". The factor coefficient of municipal elections was .930, and the factor coefficient of state elections was .712 (see Table A2).

Factor analysis also allows us to determine the degree to which the dimensions are related to one another. Given the nature of the decentralisation concept, in which one kind of decentralisation is expected to influence other kinds, correlation among the dimensions was expected. Nevertheless, the factor analysis showed that the correlation between the dimensions was relatively small and statistically insignificant. Between fiscal decentralisation and administrative decentralisation, the correlation coefficient was -.13. Between administrative decentralisation and political decentralisation the correlation coefficient was .11, and between fiscal decentralisation and political decentralisation, the correlation coefficient was 0.

TABLE A2: Fiscal, Administrative and Political Decentralisation

Dimension	Observed variable	Coefficient	Factor coefficient
Fiscal decentralisation	Sub-national expenditure per cent	b_{11}	.971
Fiscal decentralisation	Sub-national revenue per cent	b_{21}	.930
Administrative decentralisation	Sub-national tax per cent	b_{31}	.251
Administrative decentralisation	Sub-national transfer per cent	b_{41}	2.629E-02
Political decentralisation	Municipal elections	b_{51}	-4.282E-02
Political decentralisation	State elections	b_{61}	.412
Fiscal decentralisation	Sub-national expenditure per cent	b_{12}	3.867E-02
Fiscal decentralisation	Sub-national revenue percent	b_{22}	.315
Administrative decentralisation	Sub-national tax per cent	b_{32}	.917
Administrative decentralisation	Sub-national transfer per cent	b_{42}	.931
Political decentralisation	Municipal elections	b_{52}	-2.818E-02
Political decentralisation	State elections	b_{62}	-.172
Fiscal decentralisation	Sub-national expenditure per cent	b_{13}	.144
Fiscal decentralisation	Sub-national revenue per cent	b_{23}	6.375E-02
Administrative decentralisation	Sub-national tax per cent	b_{33}	-2.766E-02
Administrative decentralisation	Sub-national transfer per cent	b_{43}	-.140
Political decentralisation	Municipal elections	b_{53}	.930
Political decentralisation	State elections	b_{63}	.712

None of the coefficients were statistically significant. Though this result was somewhat surprising, it supported the assumption that the dimensions could be analysed as though they were orthogonal.

Finally, the factor coefficients for each variable were used to obtain a score for each case along each dimension. For each case, the factor scores are the sum of the products of the factor coefficients and the indicator scores. To make them easier to interpret, the factor scores were normalised to a zero to one scale, and can be read in terms of decentralisation units. Thus, Albania has a score of .35 fiscal decentralisation units, 0 administrative decentralisation units, and .42 political decentralisation units. Appendix B displays the factor score on each dimension for the different countries in the study. The average amount of fiscal decentralisation, on a zero to one scale, was .42. The average amount of administrative decentralisation was .54, and the average amount of political decentralisation was .54.[91] These factor scores were used as the measures for fiscal, administrative, and political decentralisation in the causal analysis of pro-poor policy. The scores for each country are listed in Appendix B for those who would like to reproduce this analysis or examine other hypotheses.

We can test the face validity of these measures by comparing these scores with what we know from more qualitative research on decentralisation. For example, the data from 1996 gave Argentina high scores on all three dimensions of decentralisation (.70, .80, .90). Qualitative information offers details not picked up in the factor analysis, but the overall picture of 1996 Argentina is an extremely decentralised federation. For example, though not indicated in the factor analysis, Argentine sub-national fiscal capacity was greatly enhanced by the ability to borrow. Restrictions on borrowing were largely administrative and could be decided with the agreement of local legislatures. Many local jurisdictions also had the luxury of taking loans from their own banks. On the other hand, international loans required central government approval and all loans were restricted to investment or to restructuring.[92] Administratively, sub-national units enjoyed a great deal of autonomy in terms of what policies they pursued.

Central government had little ability to withhold finances from sub-national units as most transfers were an automatic percentage of domestic taxes, encoded by law, and distributed according to a predetermined formula or amount. For example, a portion of VAT and property tax were distributed to the provinces and municipalities according to the number of beneficiaries in the jurisdiction. Some of the transfers, though not all, were tied to specific expenditures, such as 50 per cent of asset tax being earmarked for education. Still, provinces and local jurisdictions enjoyed significant autonomy with respect to the amount, structure, execution, and supervision of various social services, including housing and education (except university). The public health system was controlled by the central government though hospitals were largely controlled by provinces. Politically, nomination and financing of candidates occurred at each level of government, and parties had internal factions that reflected bases of politicians in different provinces. On the other hand, a relatively dominant president and party leader added a degree of political centralisation not reflected in the factor analysis. Overall, the qualitative information on Argentina confirms what the factor analysis uncovered.

Were there any countries that seem to score oddly on the factor analysis? Netherlands Antilles appears odd, as it scored very high on fiscal decentralisation, very high on administrative decentralisation, and the lowest on political decentralisation (.93, .93, 0). It is possible for a country to decentralise fiscally and administratively while retaining political functions at the centre; still, it demands a closer examination. One explanation could be the small size of the Netherlands Antilles; decentralised political functions may simply not register in the indicators used. Indeed, the country is a strange one to characterise. It is a federation of five islands that are part of the Dutch Kingdom but autonomous in their internal affairs. The Dutch government manages defence and foreign affairs and the queen of the Netherlands remains the chief of state. She appoints a governor general who is the chief executive, and a parliament with 22 members selects a prime minister who carries out executive responsibilities. Each island has its own legislature, though the central government can overrule any council decision that it deems against the public interest. The odd scoring produced in the factor analysis may be attributable to the fact that the indicators used for political decentralisation did not detect the nuance presented by the individual island legislatures. The fiscal and administrative indicators, by contrast, did detect the autonomy of the islands. Fortunately, excluding Netherlands Antilles from the sample did not significantly change the ratio order of the other countries.[93]

APPENDIX B

Factor scores from confirmatory factor analysis—countries and decentralisation dimensions

Country	Fiscal decentralisation	Administrative decentralisation	Political decentralisation
Albania	0.38	0	0.44
Argentina	0.7	0.8	0.9
Australia	0.75	0.42	0.57
Austria	0.6	0.59	0.62
Azerbaijan	0.53	0.61	0.05
Belarus	0.57	0.63	0.04
Belgium	0.3	0.41	0.67
Bolivia	0.44	0.46	0.58
Botswana	0.19	0.17	0.5
Brazil	0.64	0.55	0.88
Bulgaria	0.25	0.66	0.98
Canada	0.96	0.67	0.82
Chile	0.15	0.92	0.44
Croatia	0.32	0.75	0.26
Czech Rep.	0.43	0.52	0.49
Denmark	0.71	0.53	0.87
Dom. Rep.	0	0.67	0.68
Estonia	0.35	0.75	0.37
Fiji	0.14	0.77	0.14
Finland	0.61	0.62	0.29
France	0.29	0.63	0.8
FRG/German	0.66	0.64	0.88
Georgia	0.49	0.66	0.06
Guatemala	0.35	0.02	0.01

Country	Fiscal decentralisation	Administrative decentralisation	Political decentralisation
Hungary	0.34	0.38	0.59
Iceland	0.38	0.81	0.8
India	0.77	0.49	0.42
Indonesia	0.27	0.27	0.33
Ireland	0.4	0.12	0.87
Israel	0.31	0.45	0.5
Italy	0.36	0.3	0.91
Kazakhstan	0.51	0.83	0.51
Kenya	0.15	0.68	0.12
Kyrgyzstan	0.51	0.54	0.19
Latvia	0.43	0.75	0.35
Lithuania	0.48	0.74	0.51
Luxembourg	0.3	0.51	0.35
Malaysia	0.42	0.39	0.19
Mauritius	0.1	0.41	0.65
Mexico	0.46	0.65	0.93
Moldova	0.58	0.76	0.32
Mongolia	0.6	0.5	0.45
Neth. Antil	0.93	0.93	0
Netherland	0.45	0.2	0.44
Nicaragua	0.09	0.94	0.71
Norway	0.48	0.56	0.75
Panama	0.01	1	0.91
Paraguay	0.06	0.81	0.43
Peru	0.38	0.13	0.45
Philippine	0.16	0.48	0.97
Poland	0.38	0.52	0.49
Portugal	0.23	0.55	0.36
PRC	1	0.5	0.36
Romania	0.19	0.69	0.67
Russia	0.67	0.83	0.91
S. Africa	0.55	0.1	0.85
Senegal	0.35	0.54	0.24
Slovakia	0.16	0.76	1

Country	Fiscal decentralisation	Administrative decentralisation	Political decentralisation
Slovenia	0.22	0.75	0.4
Spain	0.5	0.35	0.89
Sweden	0.58	0.83	0.5
Switzerland	0.8	0.61	0.85
Tajikistan	0.59	0.61	0.47
Thailand	0.12	0.72	0.68
Trinidad-T	0.18	0.04	0.59
UK	0.37	0.2	0.89
USA	0.8	0.56	0.84
Zimbabwe	0.32	0.49	0.06

REFERENCES

Afonso, J.R.R., 1996, 'Descentralizar e depois estabilizar: a complexa experiencia Brasileira', *Revista do BNDES*, Vol. 3, No. 5: 31-62.

Ahmad, E., 1997, *Financing Decentralized Expenditures—An International Comparison of Grants*, Cheltenham, UK: Edward Elgar Publishers.

Ames, B., 1995, 'Electoral rules, constituency pressures, and pork barrel: bases of voting in the Brazilian legislature', *Journal of Politics*, Vol. 57, No. 2: 324-43.

Ames, B. and Keck, M.E., 1998, 'The politics of sustainable development: environmental policy making in four Brazilian states', *Journal of Interamerican Studies and World Affairs*, Vol. 39, No. 4: 1-41.

Bardhan, P. and Mookherjee, D., 2000, 'Relative capture of local and central governments: an essay in the political economy of decentralization', unpublished.

Barro, R., 1974, 'Are government bonds net wealth?', *Journal of Political Economy*, Vol. 82, No. 6: 1095-1117

Bates, R.H. with Da Hsiang Donald Lien, 1985, 'A note on taxation, development, and representative government', *Politics and Society*, Vol. 14, No. 1.

Bendor, J. and Mookherjee, D., 1987, 'Institutional structure and the logic of ongoing collective action', *American Political Science Review*, March Vol. 81, No. 1: 129-54.

Berger, S., 1983, *Organizing Interests*, New York: Cambridge University Press.

Bird, R.M. and Vaillancourt, F., 1998, 'Fiscal Decentralization in Developing Countries: an overview', in R.M. Bird, F. Vaillancourt and eds., *Fiscal Decentralization in Developing Countries*, Cambridge: Cambridge University Press.

Block, F., 1977, 'The ruling class does not rule: notes on the Marxist theory of the state', *Socialist Revolution*, 33: 6-27.

Bollen, K., 1989, *Structural Equation Models with Latent Variables*, New York: John Wiley.

Brady, H., 1990, 'Traits versus issues: factor versus ideal point analysis of candidate thermometer readings', *Political Analysis*, 2: 97-129.

Brandt, L. and Ziaodong Zhu, 2000, 'Redistribution in a decentralized economy: growth and inflation in China under reform', *Journal of Political Economy*, Vol. 108, No. 2: 422-39.

Braun, J. von and Grote, U., 2000, *Does Decentralization Serve the Poor*, Washington, D.C.: International Monetary Fund.

Brennan, G. and Buchanan, J., 1980, *The Power to Tax: analytical foundations of a fiscal constitution*, Cambridge: Cambridge University Press.

Buchanan, J. and Tullock, G., 1962, *The Calculus of Consent*, Ann Arbor: University of Michigan Press.

—— and Wagner, R., 1977, *Democracy in Deficit*, New York: Academic Press.

Byskov, S., 2001, *Measuring Levels of Decentralization: the strengths and weaknesses of government finance statistics* <http://www1.worldbank.org/publicsector/decentralization/decent.doc>

Cameron, D., 1978, 'The expansion of the public economy: a comparative analysis', *American Political Science Review*, 72: 1243-61.

Campbell, J., 1993, 'The state and fiscal sociology', *Annual Review of Sociology*, 19: 163-85.

Campbell, T., 1997, *Innovations and Risk-Taking: the engine of reform in local government in Latin America and the Caribbean*, Washington, D.C.: World Bank.

Charvak, 2000, *From Decentralisation of Planning to People's Planning: experiences of the Indian states of West Bengal and Kerala*, Thiruvananthapuram: Kerala Research Programme on Local Level Development—Centre for Development Studies.

Cohen, J.M. and Peterson, S.B., 1997, *Administrative Decentralization: a new framework for improved governance, accountability, and performance*, Cambridge, MA: Harvard Institute for International Development.

——, 1996, *Methodological Issues in the Analysis of Decentralization*, Cambridge, MA: Harvard Institute for International Development.

Collier, D. and Adcock, R., 1999, 'Democracy and dichotomies: a pragmatic approach to choices about concepts', *Annual Review of Political Science* 2: 537-62.

——, and Mahon, J.E., 1993, 'Conceptual stretching revisited: adapting categories in comparative analysis', *American Political Science Review*, Vol. 87, No. 4: 845-55.

Crook, R.C. and Manor, J., 1998, *Democracy and Decentralization in South Asia and West Africa: participation, accountability, and performance*, Cambridge: Cambridge University Press.

——, and Sverisson, A.S., 2001, 'Decentralisation and poverty-alleviation in developing countries: a comparative analysis or, is West Bengal unique?', *IDS Working Paper* 130, Brighton: Institute of Development Studies.

Dahl, R.A., 1970, *After the Revolution: authority in a good society*, New Haven: Yale University Press.

——, 1961, *Who Governs?*, New Haven: Yale University Press.

DeMello, L.R., 2000, 'Fiscal decentralization and intergovernmental fiscal relations: a cross-country analysis', *World Development*, Vol. 28, No. 2: 365-80.

Dye, T.R., 1966, *Politics, Economics, and the Public: policy outcomes in the American states*, Chicago: Rand McNally.

Esping-Anderson, G., 1990, *Three Worlds of Welfare Capitalism*, London: Polity Press.

Evans, P., 1997, 'The eclipse of the state? Reflections on stateness in an era of globalization', *World Politics*, Vol. 50, No. 1: 62-87.

Fisman, R. and Gatti, R., 2000, 'Decentralization and corruption: evidence across countries', *World Bank Policy Research Working Paper* 2290, February, Washington, D.C.: World Bank.

Fox, J. and Aranda, J., 1996, *Decentralization and Rural Development in Mexico*, San Diego: Center for US-Mexican Studies, at the University of California, San Diego.

Fukasaku, K. and Hausmann, R., 1998, *Democracy, Decentralization, and Deficits in Latin America*, Washington, D.C.: Interamerican Development Bank.

Galasso, E. and Ravallion, M., 1999, 'Distributional outcomes of a decentralized welfare program', *World Bank Research Paper* 2316, Washington, D.C.: World Bank.

Gandmont, J.-M., 1978, 'Intermediate preferences and the majority rule', *Econometrica*, Vol. 46, No. II: 317-30.

Garrett, G., 1995, 'Capital mobility, trade, and the domestic politics of economic policy', *International Organization*, Vol. 49, No. 4: 657-87.

Gemmell, N. and Morrissey, O., 2002, 'The poverty impacts of revenue systems in developing countries', *Report to the Department for International Development*, Nottingham: Department for International Development.

Goldscheid, R., 1958, 'A Sociological Approach to Problems of Public Finance', in R.A. Musgrave and A.T. Peacock (eds.), *Classics in the Theory of Public Finance*, New York: The Macmillan Company.

Grodzins, M., 1960, 'American political parties and the American political system', *Western Political Quarterly*, Vol. XIII, No. 4: 974-98.

Hagopian, F., 1996, *Traditional Politics and Regime Change in Brazil*, Cambridge: Cambridge University Press.

Harberger, A., 1962, 'The incidence of the corporate income tax', *Journal of Political Economy* 70: 215-40.

Hausmann, R. and Stein, E., 1995, 'Searching for the right budgetary institutions for a volatile region', paper read at 'Securing Stability and Growth in Latin America: policy issues and prospects for shock-prone economies', Paris: Inter-American Development Bank Office of the Chief Economist.

Hayduk, L., 1987, *Structural Equation Modeling with LISREL*, Baltimore: Johns Hopkins University Press.

Hicks, A.M. and Swank, D.H., 1992, 'Politics, institutions, and welfare spending in industrialized democracies, 1960-82', *American Political Science Review*, Vol. 86, No. 3: 658-66.

Hommes, R., 1995, 'Conflicts and dilemmas of decentralization', Annual Bank Conference on Development Economics, Washington, D.C.

Huber, E. and Stephens, J.D., 1992, 'Internationalization and the social democratic welfare model: crises and future prospects', *Comparative Political Studies* 33: 353-97.

Huntington, S.P., 1968, *Political Order in Changing Societies*, New Haven: Yale University Press.

IMF, 2000, *Government Finance Statistics Handbook*, Washington, D.C.: International Monetary Fund.

Inman, R.P. and Rubinfeld, D.L., 1997, 'Rethinking federalism', *Journal of Economic Perspectives*, Vol. 11, No. 4: 43-64.

Kim, J.-O. and Mueller, C.W., 1978, 'Introduction to factor analysis: what it is and how to do it', *Quantitative Applications in the Social Sciences*, Vol. 13, Beverly Hills: Sage Publications.

Lakoff, G., 1987, *Women, Fire and Dangerous Things: what categories reveal about the mind*, Chicago: University of Chicago Press.

Leonard, D.K., 1982, 'Institutions of rural development for the poor: decentralization and organizational linkages', *Research Series* (University of California at Berkeley), Berkeley: Institute for International Studies.

Levi, M., 1988, *Of Rule and Revenue*, Berkeley: University of California Press.

Lindblom, C.E., 1977, *Politics and Markets*, New York: Basic Books.

Linz, J.J. and Stepan, A., 2000, *Inequality Inducing and Inequality Reducing Federalism: with special reference to the "Classic Outlier"—the USA*, Quebec City: International Political Science Association.

Litvack, J., Ahmad, J. and Bird, R., 2000, *Rethinking Decentralization at the World Bank*, Washington, D.C.: The World Bank.

Long, J.S., 1983, *Confirmatory Factor Analysis: A Preface to LISREL*, Los Angeles: Sage.

Mansbridge, J., 1980, *Beyond Adversary Democracy*, Chicago: University of Chicago Press.

McConnell, G., 1970, *Private Power and American Democracy*, New York: Vintage Books.

Michels, R., 1966, *Political Parties*, New York: Free Press.

Moore, M., 2001, 'Political underdevelopment: what causes bad governance?', *Public Management Review,* Vol. 3, No. 3.

Morris, A. and Lowder, S., 1992, *Decentralization in Latin America,* New York: Praeger.

Musgrave, R.A., 1997, 'Devolution, grants, and fiscal competition', *Journal of Economic Perspectives,* Vol. 11, No. 4: 65-72.

—— (ed.), 1958, *Multi-Level Finance,* New York: McGraw-Hill.

Narayan, D., Chambers, R., Shah, M.K. and Petesch, P., 2000, *Crying out for Change,* Washington, D.C.: World Bank.

Nice, D.C., 1987, *Federalism: the politics of intergovernmental relations,* New York: St Martin's Press.

Oates, W., 1985, 'Searching for Leviathan: an empirical study', *American Economic Review* 75: 748-57.

——, 1977, *The Political Economy of Fiscal Federalism,* Lexington: Lexington Books.

——, 1972, *Fiscal Federalism,* New York: Harcourt Brace Jovanovich.

——, and Schwab, R., 1991, 'The Allocative and Distributional Implications of Local Fiscal Competition', in D. Kenyon, J. Kincaid and eds., *Competition Among States and Local Governments: efficiency and equity in American federalism',* Washington, D.C.: Urban Institute Press.

O'Connor, J., 1973, *Fiscal Crisis of the State,* New York: St Martin's Press.

O'Donnell, G., 1993, 'Delegative democracy?', *Journal of Democracy,* Vol. 5, No. 1: 55-69.

Olson, M., 1965, *The Logic of Collective Action,* Cambridge, MA: Harvard University Press.

Pateman, C., 1970, *Participation and Democratic Theory,* Cambridge: Cambridge University Press.

Pauly, M.V., 1973, 'Income redistribution as a local public good', *Journal of Public Economics* 2: 35-58.

Petrei, H., 1998, *Budget and Control: reforming the public sector in Latin America,* translated by R.E. Petrei and Collaborator, Washington, D.C.: Inter-American Development Bank.

Polanyi, K., 1944, *The Great Transformation: the political and economic origins of our time,* Boston: Beacon Press.

Prud'homme, R., 1995, 'The dangers of decentralization', *World Bank Research Observer,* Vol. 10, No. 2: 201-20.

Quinn, D.P. and Shapiro, R.Y., 1991, 'Business political power: the case of taxation', *American Political Science Review,* Vol. 85, No. 3: 851-74.

Rodrik, D., 1996, 'Why do more open economies have bigger governments?', *NBER Working Paper* 5537, Cambridge, MA: National Bureau of Economic Research (NBER).

——, and Fernandez, R., 1991, 'Resistance to reform—status quo bias in the presence of individual uncertainty', *American Economic Review* 81 (December): 1146-55.

Rondinelli, D.A., 1990, 'Decentralization, territorial power, and the state: a critical response', *Development and Change,* Vol. 21, No. 3: 491-500.

——, McCulough, J.S. and Johnson, R.W., 1989, 'Analyzing decentralization policies in developing countries: a political-economy approach', *Development and Change,* Vol. 20, No. 1: 57–87.

——, Nellis, J.R. and Shabbir Cheema, G., 1984, *Decentralization in Developing Countries: a review of recent experience,* Washington, D.C.: World Bank.

Rosen, H.S., 1997, *Public Finance,* fifth ed., San Francisco: Irwin McGraw-Hill

Samoff, J., 1990, 'Decentralization: the politics of interventionism', *Development and Change,* Vol. 21, No. 3: 513–30.

Samuels, D.J., 2000, 'The gubernatorial coattails effect: federalism and congressional elections in Brazil', *Journal of Politics,* Vol. 62, No. 1: 240-53.

Sartori, G., 1970, 'Concept misformation in comparative politics', *American Political Science Review,* Vol. 64, No. 4: 1033–53.

Schattschneider, E.E., 1960, *The Semisovereign People: a realist's view of democracy in America,* 1st ed., New York: Rinehart and Wilson.

Schmitter, P.C., 1977, 'Modes of interest intermediation and models of societal change in Western Europe', *Comparative Political Studies* 10: 7-38.

——, 1974, 'Still the century of corporatism?', *Review of Politics* 36 (1 (January): 85-131.

——, 1971, *Interest Conflict and Political Change in Brazil,* Stanford: Stanford University Press.

Schneider, A., 2003, 'Different types and degrees of decentralisation: improving concepts and measures', *Studies in Comparative International Development.*

Scott, J.C., 1998, *Seeing Like a State: how certain schemes to help the human condition have failed,* London: Yale University Press.

Shah, A., 1999, 'Fiscal federalism and macroeconomic governance: for better or worse?', *World Bank Working Paper* 2005, Washington, D.C.: World Bank.

——, 1991, *The New Fiscal Federalism in Brazil,* Washington, D.C: World Bank.

—— and Huther, J., 1998, *Applying a Simple Measure of Good Governance to the Debate on Fiscal Decentralization,* Washington, D.C.: The World Bank.

Slater, D., 1990, 'Debating decentralization: a reply to Rondinelli', *Development and Change,* Vol. 21, No. 3: 501-12.

Snyder, R., 1999, 'After neoliberalism: the politics of reregulation in Mexico', *World Politics,* Vol. 52, No. 2: 173-204.

Sola, L., 1991, 'Heterodox shock in Brazil—tecnicos, politicians and democracy', *Journal of Latin American Studies,* Vol. V, No. 23: 163-95.

Steinmo, S., 1988, 'Social democracy vs socialism: goal adaptation in social democratic Sweden', *Politics and Society*, Vol. 16, No. 4: 403-46.

Stiglitz, J. and Heertje, A., 1989, *The Economic Role of the State*, Oxford: Blackwell.

Swank, D.H., 2002, *Global Capital, Political Institutions, and Policy Change in Developed Welfare States*, Cambridge: Cambridge University Press.

—— 1992, 'Politics and the structural dependence of the state in democratic capitalist nations', *American Political Science Review*, Vol. 86, No. 1: 38-54.

Swedberg, R., 1991, *Joseph A. Schumpeter: the economics and sociology of capitalism*, Princeton: Princeton University Press.

Swenson, P., 1991, 'Bringing capital back in, or social democracy reconsidered: employer power, cross-class alliances, and centralization of industrial relations in Denmark and Sweden', *World Politics*, July (43): 513-44.

Tanzi, V., 1995, 'Fiscal federalism and decentralization: a review of some efficiency and macroeconomic aspects', Annual Bank Conference on Development Economics, Washington, D.C.: World Bank.

Tendler, J., 2002, 'Small firms, the informal sector, and the devil's deal', *IDS Bulletin* 33 (July): 98-104.

——, 1997, *Good Government in the Tropics*, Baltimore: Johns Hopkins University Press.

Tiebout, C., 1956, 'The pure theory of local expenditure', *Journal of Political Economy* 64: 416-24.

Tilly, C., 1992, *Coercion, Capital and European States: AD 990–1992*, Oxford: Blackwell Books.

Toqueville, A. de., 1969, *Democracy in America*, translated by J.P. Mayer and (ed.), New York: Harper Perennial.

Wallerstein, M., 1997, 'Wage-setting institutions and pay inequality in advanced industrial societies', *American Journal of Political Science*, Vol. 43, No. 3: 649-80.

Wallis, M., 1991, 'Local government and development: a guide to the literature', *Environment and Urbanisation*, Vol. 3, No. 1: 121-29.

Weber, M., 1968, *Bureaucracy*, Berkeley: University of California Press.

Webster, N., 1992, 'Panchayati Raj in West Bengal: popular participation for the people or the party?', *Development and Change*, Vol. 23, No. 4: 129-63.

Weingast, B., 1995, 'The economic role of political institutions: market-preserving federalism and economic development', *Journal of Law, Economics, and Organization* 11: 1-31.

Wildavsky, A., 1984, *The Politics of the Budgetary Process*, fourth ed., Boston: Little, Brown and Co.

Williams, J.T. and Collins, B.K., 1997, 'The political economy of corporate taxation', *American Journal of Political Science*, Vol. 41, No. 1: 208-44.

World Bank, 2002, *World Development Indicators*, Washington, D.C.: World Bank Group.

—— 2000, *Human Development Report*, Washington, D.C.: World Bank Group.

Yilmaz, S. and Ebel, R.D., 2002, *On the Measurement and Impact of Fiscal Decentralization*, Washington, D.C.: World Bank.

NOTES

1. This article is based on IDS Working Paper#179 by Aaron Schneider, "Who Gets What from Whom? Decentralization, Tax Capacity and Pro-Poor Policy" [February 2003].
2. Schattschneider made a similar argument in the US case. See Schattschneider (1960). Schattschneider described political institutions as the mobilisation of bias, either organising interests into political institutions or organising them out.
3. A theoretical argument along these lines is made by Slater, in a critique of decentralisation during the 1980s (Slater 1990).
4. There have been studies of the impact of decentralisation on related areas, however. For example, Bendor and Mookherjee (1987) examine the impact on the ability to organise collective action, Braun and Grote (2000) examine the impact on poverty, and Brandt and Zhu (2000) examine the impact on redistribution in China.
5. This distinction is not new; the World Bank makes exactly this division of the decentralisation concept on its webpage: www1.worldbank.org/publicsector/decentralisation/. For a statistical verification and measurement of these three dimensions, see Schneider (2002b). The individual country measures can be found in Appendix B.
6. In the case of taxation, this would require studying incidence. For an early discussion, see Harberger (1962). More recently, see Gemmell and Morrissey (2002).
7. James Scott tells of the story of the origins of last names (Tailor, Butcher, etc.) as the attempt of early European states to categorise their populations and calculate likely contributions to national tax efforts (1998: Chapter 1).
8. Other policies also have an impact on the poor, of course. Regulatory policies, macroeconomic policies, and financial policies can also have important effects. Still, one of the main concerns here is to use fiscal policies to understand the impacts of decentralisation, thus the focus on revenues and expenditures.
9. The current enthusiasm for decentralisation may be new, but it is not novel. The prior apex of enthusiasm for decentralisation was as a strategy to prolong colonial rule in much of Africa (Samoff 1990: 513).
10. For an example of the zenith of decentralisation enthusiasm, see Campbell (1997). Between 1993 and 1997, fully 12 per cent of all completed World Bank projects had a decentralisation component (Litvack et al. 2000: 1).

11. See Snyder (1999) for an example of how Mexican state governments stepped in to provide regulatory frameworks where the central government abdicated its role in coffee production.
12. For an example of how decentralisation was used by the military regime in Brazil to legitimise its rule, see Sola (1991) and Samuels (2000).
13. Data from World Bank Decentralisation statistics webpage, as cited in bibliography.
14. Related to the proliferation of conceptualisations, there has also been an explosion of units of analysis in studying the concept. These include studies of individual local jurisdictions, all local jurisdictions, entire systems of national and local government, and comparisons across national systems. For a discussion, see Cohen and Peterson (1997: 12-13).
15. For a survey of the 1980s literature on the topic, see Wallis (1991). Cohen and Peterson (1996) provide an excellent overview of methodological issues on the topic.
16. Cohen and Peterson note that disciplinary differences explain some, but not all of the ambiguity. Sloppy social science and language differences also cause confusion. Specialists from France equated decentralisation with one of its subtypes, "devolution," (Prud'homme 1995); English speakers tended to settle for some variant of the Rondinelli, et al. definition (see below); and Spanish-speaking observers used "municipio" in ways that led to misunderstanding by those unfamiliar with the term.
17. According to the Oxford English dictionary, this usage has existed since the beginning of the nineteenth century.
18. On the dangers of poorly defined concepts, see Lakoff (1987).
19. The most complete discussion of concepts that become difficult is the framework offered by W.B. Gallie, who described essentially contested concepts. For an interesting discussion of measurement validity within concepts, see Collier and Adcock (1999).
20. For an analysis that examines the connection between democracy, decentralisation, and market reforms, see Fukasaku and Hausmann (1998).
21. See Collier and Adcock (1999), Collier and Mahon (1993), and Sartori (1970).
22. For a discussion of competing measures of decentralisation in a single case, see Yilmaz and Ebel (2002).
23. For a meta-theoretical review, see Crook and Sverisson (2001).
24. For a statement of the benefits of decentralisation, see Campbell (1997).
25. For a statement of the drawbacks of decentralisation, see Prud'homme (1995).
26. Leonard suggests that researchers choose a conceptual framework only after deciding the causal relationships they intend to test. 'The variety

of forms of decentralisation threatens to become unmanageable if we try to be comprehensive. To impose a limit one must specify the purpose for which the typology is being created and elaborate only those dimensions that are useful to it' (Leonard 1982: 28-29).

27. Theories of fiscal federalism begin from the assumption that fiscal interventions are necessary in the very specific cases in which government intervention improves on market operation. For example, normal market operations can produce instability (as in cases of financial panic), can misallocate resources (as in cases of monopoly or oligopoly), and can poorly distribute resources. For more detail, Stiglitz and Heertje (1989: 9-89) provides an excellent discussion.
28. Thus, a system can be fiscally decentralised without administrative decentralisation if the use of local funds is set at the central level.
29. Shah (1999) argues that fiscal decentralisation may not prejudice stabilisation, though most observers suggest that it will (DeMello 2000).
30. It is in allocation policy that most observers argue that decentralised systems hold an advantage (Tanzi 1995).
31. There are some who argue that decentralised systems will generate a more just distribution of wealth (Galasso 1999; Pauly 1973), but they are in the minority (Bardhan and Mookherjee 2000).
32. It should be noted that some applications of the categories differentiate a syndrome of characteristics. These applications mark the distinctions across categories in terms of a host of factors, and not simply in terms of different levels of autonomy. Also, some form of privatisation is often included as another category (Rondinelli 1990).
33. Both delegation and deconcentration open the potential for a principal-agent problem, created by the self-interested behaviour of the entity that receives the decentralised power and resources. Of course, in the case of deconcentration, the agent may be easier to control, as it is simply the field office of a central government hierarchy. Delegation introduces increased possibility of divergence between interests of the central government principal and the local government/semi-autonomous agent.
34. Arguments about democratic decentralisation tend to include accountability to the local population as part of its argument. 'Whilst increased participation had a positive impact on the performance of decentralized institutions, adequate resources for councils were also essential, and—as we shall see—the social and political contexts within which decentralization was undertaken also influenced outcomes. But the most critical determinant was the existence of a combination of all these factors with effective mechanisms of institutional and popular accountability. It is those mechanisms which provided—and are likely to provide more generally—the crucial link between enhanced participation and enhanced institutional performance' (Crook and Manor 1998: 21).

35. It should be noted that all three types of administrative decentralisation can be analysed using economic theories of principal-agent, moral hazard, and adverse selection techniques. Under all arrangements besides centralisation, central governments have imperfect information about non-central units and the capacity or effort they will dedicate to assigned tasks. In terms of achieving administrative goals, this imperfect information is what makes central governments nervous about ceding autonomy—they do not know for sure what the outcome will be.
36. Simplifying the syndrome of characteristics into the single dimension of autonomy becomes more complicated when we consider other aspects of decentralisation at the same time. For example, the level of autonomy becomes unclear when we compare a local government with significant resources (fiscal decentralisation) and deconcentrated authority (administrative centralisation) to a local authority with few resources (fiscal centralisation) but devolved authority (administrative decentralisation). Correct measurement of autonomy requires taking into account the interrelationship of the dimensions.
37. Linz and Stepan (2000) examine the impact of political decentralisation in federal systems.
38. For an analysis of different systems of economic interest aggregation, see Schmitter (1971; 1974; 1977).
39. Three times two gives the number of relationships. For example, changes in fiscal decentralisation can be either positively or negatively related to changes in administrative decentralisation and/or political decentralisation, and changes in administrative decentralisation can be either positively or negatively related to political decentralisation. Additional possibilities will not be examined here. The interaction could be more complex; in which decentralisation along two dimensions augments or offsets decentralisation along the third. Alternatively, decentralisation along one dimension might augment decentralisation along another, but this relationship might not work in reverse. These possibilities are more difficult to test statistically and have therefore been left out of the current exercise. More detailed comparative case study might be capable of drawing out some of the subtlety.
40. In Brazil, decentralised fiscal resources meant that local governments were *de facto* implementing tasks that were constitutionally attributed to the central level (Afonso 1996).
41. In West Bengal, decentralised administrative autonomy gave local governments control over tax bases that they then used to increase their share of resources (D. Bandyopadhyay, personal communication).
42. For an excellent review of the literature, see Campbell (1993).
43. 'Decentralization of policy-making authority has generally mobilized socially heterogeneous forces (*e.g.* regionally specific cultural groups), undercut progressive and egalitarian political forces at the national level (*e.g.* trade union movements, cross-class coalitions) and favoured local economic and political elites. In addition, institutional structures

that decentralize policy-making responsibility tend to undercut the formation of coherent national policy strategies by groups and parties; the organization of parties and groups tends to be concentrated at regional and local levels and politics tends to focus on narrow distributional issues within regional and local jurisdictions' (Swank 2002: 46-48).

44. Weingast argues a similar point (1995). Levi (1988) and Bates and Lien (1985) build on the notion of a revenue-maximising political elite, and state as "Leviathan." See Oates (1985) for an empirical test of this proposition that finds the opposite: decentralisation does not lead to smaller government.

45. The growth of the informal sector in developing countries is one reflection of the shift away from those activities that government can tax (Tendler 2002).

46. Many models of administrative competition rest on the model of a "market" in which jurisdictions compete to keep their citizens, who use voice and exit to discipline local government. Tiebout (1956) applied this model for individual citizens; Oates and Schwab (1991) do the same for firms.

47. Michels (1966) described this process of bureaucratic rigidification as the "iron law of oligarchy".

48. 'After all, there are few policy areas in which the redistributive interests of different social classes come into sharper conflict than tax policy' (Steinmo 1988: 404).

49. See Grodzins (1960: 974-78) for the US case. Also commenting on the US, Congressman Barney Frank observed, '99.9 per cent of Congress clearly prefer that the issue be decided at that level of government which will decide the issue the way they like' (Rosen 1997: 484).

50. There are some who argue that participation is only possible on a small scale, and therefore at the local level (Pateman 1970: 109; Dahl 1970: 132; and Mansbridge 1980: 293; Olson 1965: 33-36).

51. A similar application has been made to the case of environmental interests. Environmental activists seek protection from pollution, which necessarily involves externalities and spill-overs from one jurisdiction to another. If environmentalists win many local struggles but have no representation at the national level, spill-overs from a single polluter in a single jurisdiction can overturn the impact of environmental victories in many local jurisdictions (Ames 1995; Ames and Keck 1998). For an application to the issue of representing the poor, see von Braun and Grote (2000); Crook and Sverisson (2001); and Swank (2002).

52. Some argue, in fact, that the market automatically organises the interests of the rich. See Block (1977); Lindblom (1977).

53. Some argue that decentralisation increases the strength of capital with respect to the state, as local governments must compete against each other, as well as against foreign competitors. Others argue that in the

current context, national governments are equally as weak. The debate on the "structural dependence of the state" has aroused significant research, see Swank (1992: 32-54); Quinn and Shapiro (1991: 851-74); Williams and Collins (1997: 208-44), though none of it suggests that national governments are less able to discipline capital than local governments.

54. Some might even argue that the effectiveness of weapons of the rich is even higher at the local level. Coordination and collective action problems that exist at the national level may be absent at the local level, where structures of production and class interest are more homogenous.
55. Wallerstein shows that centralised and cohesive labour unions are more effective in promoting wage gains and redistributing wealth than decentralised ones (1997).
56. Of course, while the economic impact of the poor may be greater at the national level than at the local level, the economic tools available to the poor are still probably less politically significant than those available to the rich.
57. Olson (1965) emphasises the difficulty of overcoming collective action constraints. To do so once, in a single, national organisation is difficult, to do so many times in multiple jurisdictions is even harder.
58. Crook and Manor (1998: Chapter 6) conclude that accountability is the crucial variable that influences the performance of democratic decentralisation.
59. Hausmann and Stein (1995) discuss these potential problems in the context of agency and collective action problems. Agency problems occur any time a principal attempts to contract an agent to carry out a task in which monitoring effort and judging ability involves some transaction cost. Collective action problems arise any time members of a group have incentives to free-ride on the efforts of others within the group.
60. O'Donnell (1993) describes these local, authoritarian patches in Latin America as "brown areas" within new democracies.
61. Others have focused on different aspects of fiscal decentralisation. Some choose to focus on the relationship between expenditures and allocated revenues ("vertical imbalance") to get a sense for the fiscal pressure that is being put on lower (or upper) levels of government. Some pay attention to the nature of inter-governmental transfers to understand the impact on lower government behaviour (Nice 1987; Ahmad 1997). The current application is focused on the authority relations between levels of government, in which the nature of resource transfers is an indicator of administrative decentralisation.
62. See Government Finance Statistics Handbook (2000) for a description of the statistical details. Also, see Byskov (2001) for a discussion of the reliability and validity of the data.

63. There are some drawbacks to expenditures as a percentage of total expenditures, as they miss those expenditures that do not appear as cash outlays, such as credit guarantees, nor does this measurement distinguish among expenditures mandated by the central government as opposed to those that are decided wholly locally. Still, sub-national expenditures as a percentage of total expenditure focuses on the fiscal power exercised by lower governments as opposed to that exercised by central governments. Altering the indicators did not adjust the results of factor analysis. For example, measuring sub-national expenditures and revenues as a percentage of GDP also load heavily on a single dimension, though these indicators relate more to the impact of local governments on the economy.
64. There are some drawbacks to this specification, which does not distinguish for example between revenues over which lower levels of government have total control, such as block grants, and revenues that are tied to central government priorities, such as ear-marked transfers. This distinction will be taken into account below, however, in measuring the degree of administrative autonomy exercised by sub-national governments.
65. The kind of revenue is at best only a rough indicator of the amount of administrative control. Grants and loans can arrive either with conditions or without them. Though unconditional loans or grants (block grants) suggest local control, the fact that the centre can withhold them implies some limitation of local autonomy. Own-taxes are probably the most controllable form of local revenue, though even in these revenues, the centre can exert some authority by earmarking tax streams to certain expenditures.
66. Literature on federalism has paid particular attention to the way decentralisation interacts with partisan politics and elections (Grodzins 1960).
67. For a more thorough discussion of factor analytic techniques, see Kim and Mueller (1978); Long (1983); and Bollen (1989). For an application, see Brady (1990).
68. See, for example, World Bank, World Development Indicators, table 5.5.
69. Many of these studies have focused almost exclusively on developed countries. Examples include Esping-Anderson (1990); Cameron (1978).
70. The findings were robust to using other denominators, such as total revenues or current revenues. Also, the findings were robust to using the individual spending items alone as the numerator. For an examination of the impact of decentralisation on taxation, see Schneider (2002b).
71. Calculating the log transformation of GDP per capita resolves the problem of the abnormal distribution of cases, with most cases clustered at high incomes or low incomes, and few in the middle.

72. For examples of those who argue that globalisation weakens state capacity to promote pro-poor social policy, see Huber and Stephens (1992) and Evans (1997). For examples of those who argue that globalisation actually has the opposite impact, see Rodrik and Fernandez (1991) or Rodrik (1996).
73. Data from the 2000 Human Development Report.
74. Data from the 2002 World Bank, World Development Indicators.
75. The Polity IV dataset scored countries on a continuous scale from democratic to authoritarian in terms of regulation, competitiveness, and openness of executive recruitment, constraints on executives, institutions of participation, and extent of non-elite participation. For more detail, see <www.bsos.umd.edu/cidcm/inscr/polity/#data>
76. The equation for tax capacity was Yk = ?jajFjk + a(Fjk*Fjk)+ ?j bDk + uk, in which 'Y' is tax capacity, 'F' is the factor score, and 'D' are control variables. The subscript 'k' indicates the case, and the subscript 'j' indicates the factor.
77. For a prior version of the analysis of pro-poor expenditure, see Schneider (2002b).
78. The development variable, income per capita, was transformed using a logarithmic transformation, thus its coefficient can be interpreted as the impact of a per cent change in income per capita.
79. The impact of trade openness was significant and slightly positive in this final model. For every percentage increase in imports and exports as a percentage of GDP, there was a small increase in tax capacity (.0038).
80. The development variable, income per capita, was transformed using a logarithmic transformation, thus its coefficient can be interpreted as the impact of a per cent change in income per capita.
81. A more extended version of this factor analytic exercise can be found in Schneider (2002b).
82. For a more thorough discussion of factor analytic techniques, see Kim and Mueller (1978); Long (1983); or Bollen (1989). For an application, see Brady (1990).
83. Confirmatory factor analysis tests the marginal increase in variance explained by adding another dimension against the variance explained by randomly organising the data. The statistic used to show the relative amount of variance explained by the dimensions is called the eigenvalue, and eigenvalues below one suggest that there is little marginal increase from adding more dimensions (Kim and Mueller 1978: 32-37). An additional method of confirming the number of dimensions is graphical, in which the eigenvalues of each added dimension are graphed, called a scree plot. When the graph begins to flatten, *i.e.* adding dimensions is explaining little more of the data, then there is little marginal benefit to adding dimensions. It is possible to use exploratory factor analysis to discover how many dimensions exist, and simply add dimensions until

the eigenvalue drops below one or the scree plot flattens. Here there are strong hypotheses that three dimensions should exist, so confirmatory factor analysis is used.

84. The equation for each observed variable is given by: Xi = ?jibijFj + diUi

    The observed variable is 'X'; 'F' is a common factor shared by two or more variables; and 'U' is a factor unique to a given variable. The correlation between the observed variable and the shared factor is 'b', and 'd' is the correlation between the unique factor and the observed variable. The subscript i indicates the observed variable and the subscript j indicates the common factor.
85. Websites listed in the bibliography.
86. On the other hand, local elections and representative processes can be a key factor in politically decentralising an authoritarian regime. For example, in Brazil, local elections forced military leaders to consider local and regional pressures, even though the national executive was controlled through undemocratic means. See Hagopian (1996).
87. The results were robust to excluding non-democracies. Using an indicator of democracy from the Polity IV database, eleven non-democratic cases were excluded from the analysis. Confirmatory factor analysis results on the democratic cases alone produced few differences from the analysis of all cases together. Three dimensions underlay the data, and factor coefficients and factor scores changed only slightly.
88. The importance of transfers was reversed to keep the signs positive.
89. The scree plot did not show a significant change in the amount of variance explained by each dimension. Each added dimension appeared to explain about as much as the next, though the eigenvalues did drop far below one after the third dimension.
90. The solution was rotated to obtain orthogonal factors using a varimax rotation technique.
91. The factor scores are not completely straightforward to interpret, but they do provide an interval measure of the dimensions. The difference between a country that scores .1 and another that scores .2 is the same magnitude as the difference between countries that score .6 and .7. On the other hand, zero indicates that a country was simply the least decentralised among the sample; zero does not mean that local jurisdictions had no resources, autonomy, or political functions.
92. http://www1.worldbank.org/publicsector/decentralization/dataondecen.htm accessed June, 2002.
93. The only countries that moved position were Tajikistan, Trinidad and Tobago, and Mauritius, and even they only swapped places with a neighbour on the scales of the different dimension.

9

Need for Healthy Cities in Asia with a Focus on Iran: A Sociological Study

MOHAMMAD TAGHI SHEYKHI

mstshkhi@yahoo.com

Associate Professor of Sociology, Department of Social Science,
Al-Zahra University, Tehran, Iran.

ABSTRACT

The paper examines how the growth of cities and towns throughout Asia including Iran is facing significant health problems. The urban poor are particularly affected and faced with the worst problems of pollution, stress and crimes that should be put on the agenda of urban officials. Most of the world's population, and most of the large and rapidly growing cities belonging to Asia, with emerging and increasing problems and challenges, need to be tackled. In the present paper, the author tries to touch and reflect some of those so far as the Healthy Cities Standards are concerned. The paper reflects the causes and consequences of the people migrating to cities in search of better prospects in their lives, and that contributes to urbanization to become an important feature in our modern time. Under such circumstances "Healthy Cities Movement" defeats. However, under such controversial conditions, adequate planning, regulation and control of development are necessary in the cities. In some other parts of the paper the author examines the case of Iran as a rapidly urbanizing society—being faced with various social, economic and environmental problems—all of which jeopardize the safety of the cities.

Keywords: Social Change, Quality of Life, Environment, Security, Industrialization, Urbanization.

The aim of study

Healthy Cities study aims to make sure that health must be of high priority for the decision-makers, and it should be so directed as to improve the health status and environment. The study seeks to establish healthy lifestyles and a general improvement in the environment in various dimensions. The cities should be so arranged and conditioned that the inhabitants have access to the prerequisites for health [food, income and shelter], and for that purpose, the economy should also be vital and innovative. The paper aims to cover all the essential aspects of urban life in Asia in general, with special reference to the Iranian conditions. It also seeks to illustrate urban conservation and useful planning to create Healthy Cities Standards.

Introduction

Broadly speaking, social change is highly responsible for change in life patterns and outlook of cities. In this respect, the World Health Organization [WHO] has been responsible for the initiation and development of the Healthy Cities concept, and to its promotion both in the North and the South [Kenzer: 1999]. Most of the projects being implemented in this regard, have received advice from WHO. At the same time, many other individuals, institutions and networks have helped develop the basic concepts and contexts with regard to Healthy Cities. So the "Healthy Cities Movement" has also come into consideration in Asia, with high population growth rates and speedy urbanization trends. At its core, the "Healthy Cities Movement" is about the connections between urban living conditions and health, and the central ideas behind the movement are:

1. That Cities provide a good setting in which to develop action strategies to promote health, and are centres for human actions.
2. That the city has an unmatched potential for producing healthy human beings when attention is paid to the values of those living within the city.

The definition of "health" and that of the most appropriate means of ensuring good health within an urban context has been debated since the 19th Century, when many European and North American cities witnessed rapid growth, usually underpinned by industrialization. This debate was spurred by the very serious health problems linked to this rapid urbanization, since it was accompanied by inadequate provision for water supplies, sanitation, the collection of waste, pollution control and housing [Kenzer: 1999]. These debates continued, and as increasing numbers of countries in Asia also experienced rapid urban growth, but usually without adequate political commitment and institutional structure to address their health consequences, extensive problems and challenges arose so far as the Asian urban communities are concerned. Reaching the end of the 20th Century, these problems and controversies have become more complicated so far as the Healthy Cities Issue in Asia is concerned.

As a public health approach, McKeown [1999] states that the major factor in improving health in Britain as well as elsewhere in the nineteenth and twentieth centuries was not advanced medical care technology, but social, environmental and economic changes, the limitation of family size, and increase in food supplies, a healthier physical environment, and specific preventive and therapeutic measures. They all originate in Healthy Cities and influence them too.

Methodology

The method of investigation used to manipulate data and acquire knowledge in the present paper is of library type, based on the use of existing sources. Through such exploratory, descriptive and qualitative research, necessary data and facts were found. In such an appealing method, the researcher utilized the existing records, books, documents and periodicals. Through such method, data were drawn from the sources previously collected by others. The author, realizing the need and necessity of the work, proceeded to conduct it through the means possible. Through such qualitative method, factual information is made available to the society, and thereby many socio-economic problems of the cities are discovered. However, while social problems especially in urban contexts are very complex and complicated, such a possible technique is quite adequate to pursue the research. In addition to the methods mentioned, the researcher used observation method too, through visiting people and centres concerned, and on the basis of which the necessary information was elicited. To find out right and relevant information on the issue, some informants and experts on the issue were interviewed.

Theoretical perspectives

Various sociologists have tried to reflect their accounts of urbanism as an attractive and controversial way of life. Ferdinand Toennies [1855-1937], the German sociologist, used the term *Gemeinschaft* [community] to refer to a type of social organization by which people are bound together closely by kinship and tradition, and that is primarily found in villages. On the other hand, he used the term *Gesellschaft* to refer to an organization by which people stand apart from one another in pursuit of self-interest [Toennies 1963; orig. 1886].

The French sociologist Emile Durkheim agreed with much of Toennies' thinking about cities. Yet, Durkheim countered, urbanites do not lack social bonds; they simply organize social life differently than rural people do. Traditional rural life is mainly based on what Durkheim called *mechanical solidarity i.e.* social bonds based on collective conformity to tradition. Durkheim's concept of mechanical solidarity bears a striking similarity to Toennies' Gemeinschaft. He illustrated that though urbanization erodes some mechanical solidarity, it also generates a new type of bonding, which he termed *organic solidarity* equivalent to Gesellschaft *i.e.* social bonds based on specialization and interdependence [Durkheim: 1964; orig. 1895].

Another perspective indicates that the evolution of cities depends on the development of agriculture. Only when agriculture produces a surplus can people withdraw their labour from food production and gather in cities to spend time in other pursuits. *A city,* in fact, can be defined as a permanently based large number of people who do not produce their own food. Thus, more efficient agricultural techniques provide impetus to urban development. The invention of the plow during the Fourth Millennium BC, which created a widespread agricultural surplus, particularly stimulated the development of towns and cities [Curwin 1961].

When large numbers of people come together and form cities, problems are created, especially those of adequately meeting people's needs. This includes meeting their physical needs of course, such as food, shelter, and safety, but it also includes *community*; the feeling of belonging—the sense that others care what happens to you and that you can depend on the people around you. Some people find this sense of community in the city, but many do not [Henslin 1983: 434].

However, city life is ever increasing social problems, which are mainly controversial. For example, the rates of burglary, robbery, suicide, alcoholism, and rape are higher in cities in general as compared with the rural areas. The complexities of the city, its organization and ways of life, lend themselves to many contrasting analyses.

Louis Wirth, as a major member of Chicago School of urban sociology [1897-1952], defines the city in terms of large population, dense settlement, and social diversity. These traits, he argued, interact to form an impersonal, superficial and transitory way of life.

Wirth also developed the concept of *urban ecology*: the study of the link between the physical and social dimensions of cities.[1] It considers for example, why cities are located where they are. It also studies the physical design of cities, followed by the location of factories, residential rings that become more expensive with greater distance from the noise and pollution of the city's centre [Macionis 1998: 381].

Under the condition of rapid population growth, urbanization is taking place in the Third World cities[2] while in the First World cities are in decline. However, urbanization being a crucial dimension of making modern societies, it inevitably takes place without having infrastructures enough. Such a process creates various controversies, environmental problems, social and behavioural abnormalities. Such pressures, *i.e.* population increase and urbanism have qualitatively and quantitatively changed the cities, and such complexities require new levels of planning and organization [Bilton 2002: 37]. However, the changing conditions experienced as a result of increasing globalization and urbanization, require refinements to the established understanding and practice in disaster and development [Pelling 2003: 125]. That is to say, to reach Healthy Cities Standards, criteria and values should get rectified accordingly.

Healthy cities concept

The Healthy Cities concept is significant not only for stressing the critical role of all sectors in contributing to health and the importance of better coordination between them, but also for stressing the importance of "good governance."

The 1978 Alma Ata conference also endorsed the notion that health is linked to the living conditions of a population. It stated clearly that inequity and injustice are at the root of many health problems and that comprehensive social responses are needed to protect and improve health. Alma Ata also formally acknowledged the role of community participation in health, and that could be achieved within the conditions of a Healthy Cities approach. Hence, in a Healthy Cities framework, public health measures and promotion of health could be implemented.

Healthy Cities concept is found and considered both innovative and opportune. Though Healthy Cities concept often develops strong bureaucratic and administrative elements due to the emphasis on local government, yet, it is a participatory process and needs community empowerment. Healthy Cities concept is also concerned with the change in the power relations, health and illness, and with social and health rights.

Recently the writings and conference presentations of Leonard J. Duhl and Trevor Hancock have been found as important in developing the Healthy Cities concept [Duhl 1986, 1990 and Hancock 1990].

Though most of the Healthy Cities project initiatives come from projects implemented in the developed countries, and while the idea for a Healthy Cities project first became explicit in Toronto in 1984, yet, gradually many Asian countries have followed suit, and started building Healthy Cities.

Trevor Hancock [1990], one of the architects of the Healthy Cities Movement, suggests that the challenge the international community now faces in cities is no longer how to understand the links between health, environment and the economy, but how to put into practice the available elements in an integrated manner.

Asia, as a major part of the South, now has most of the world's urban population *i.e.* 38 per cent or a total 3.7 billion in mid-2002 [PRB 2002]. The expansion in its urban population has been more rapid than the expansion in its basic infrastructure and services. The urban poor often have to cope with the health hazards not only of inadequate provision of water, sanitation and health care as well as of poor quality housing, but also of the health hazards associated with industrial development.

Status of Asia

There are currently Healthy Cities projects underway in many parts of Asia including Bangladesh, Nepal, Thailand, Iran, China, Malaysia and Vietnam. Many of these countries, despite rapid industrialization in process in their various cities, have tried to preserve their rich social and cultural values as well as Healthy Cities plans, but not in all cases. Many of the findings of the surveys in some of these cities with different sectors of people indicate more demands for public transport, need for more parks, more open-space, strategic locations for shopping malls and the like. The main aims of Healthy Cities being improvements in the quality of life and a holistic perspective on health. These are in many cases underway—but there is still a long way to go.

There are at the time being many complications and controversies in many Asian cities. As Anne Haila [1998] puts it: The most salient feature in many modern Asian cities is the quality of imitating the North American corporate cities; the highest skyscrapers, the most lavish shopping malls, and the like which have eventually brought about controversies for these countries so far as their peaceful life and "Healthy Cities" expectations are concerned. In many cases, unmindful and unsuitable projects and steps towards modernization have caused crises. As found out by [Haila: 1998], in Shanghai [China], the vacancy rate of skyscraper is estimated to be 40% to 70%, and many remain vacant in Bangkok. Hence, rise and fall of the Asian economies leave ill effects on the quality of life and Healthy Cities Movement, which need renewal and specific considerations.

Determinants of healthy cities

Some major factors as population, natural increase, age structure of population, percentage of urban dwellers, gross national product, social change, national quality of life, access to medical care, sanitation, safe water accessibility, socio-economic security, health security, consumption patterns, rate of poverty, adequate housing and the like are directly or indirectly responsible for creating Healthy Cities.

Asia, with more than 60 per cent of the world's population, including more than 50 countries with multiplicity of cultures and value systems is involved with different problems so far as Healthy Cities Issue is concerned. The ever-increasing cities and urban centres in Asia where economic resources are very limited, while their populations, patterns of consumption and their life-styles are ever prone to change, are severely facing social problems and very distant and far off from Healthy Cities standards.

Population profile

Population density and pressure in Asia [60.6% of the world total], has highly affected the urban conditions in the region. The mid-2002 population of Asia was 3.7 billion [with an annual growth rate of 1.3 per cent]. Its population will double in 35 years. About one-third, or 30 per cent of the population of the region being under 15 years of age, will increase the population of the continent to 4.7 billion by 2025. Such a population structure increased the urban dwellers to 38 per cent in 2002. While many East Asian countries are progressing well so far as their population planning is concerned, many countries still lag behind, and that has much contributed to their unhealthy city conditions. However, many countries in Asia must make serious efforts so as to change their social, economic and demographic indicators, to consequently gain ground for Healthy Cities shift.

Ageing as a product of demographic evolution is also well observed in many parts of Asia with special reference to the urban areas. Many people migrating to cities at working age accompanied by their families, are currently in the process of ageing, and in many cases, it is accompanied by worsening of public health. The process of population ageing in many parts of Asia, including Iran, is facing a number of socio-economic, medical, pension, psychological and many other consequences. However, the rising expenditures and lack of additional financial support for the elderly all have created various controversial problems for these people in cities. It is noteworthy that the problems of this kind will even be worse in the years to come. Analysis of the status of the elderly persons include their main socio-economic, poverty, poor health, loneliness, and low quality of life characteristics.

At the turn of the 21st Century, scientists know that the health agenda of the elderly is important because of the dramatic demographic shift with special reference to Asia which is pushing more and more of our population into the senior bracket with new emerging problems in larger cities.

Urban health and social development[3]

The large-scale deterioration of urban environments and increasing health and social inequalities among the urban residents in Asia have led to a situation of crisis proportions in many cities of the region. The increase in poverty in the past two decades has largely been concentrated in cities with poor urban dwellers, experiencing greater deterioration in income [Ghai: 1991] than living in rural areas. In this situation, the health risks faced by the urban poor have become more acute than those in rural areas.

So for as the incidence of Healthy Cities is concerned, the Asian cities must effectively address the pressing health and social issues arising from the urban poverty and the marginalization of the urban poor, and for that, appropriate resources and technologies should be applied, and health and environment issues in the cities should be maintained. For the implementation of such action, integrated strategies should be developed in order to improve the general living conditions of various socio-economic strata.

Hence, a reorientation of theory and practice is necessary in order to urgently address the realities of the poor people's lives, and to promote health as a vital part of wider development goals. This requires operational research and intervention strategies that aim to be integrated, multi-disciplinary and participatory manner. In this context, information plays a vital role in the course of reorientation.

Healthy Cities programme in Asia is found to be multi-disciplinary and involves collaborative activities around the following interrelated components. They could play as vital determinants of Healthy Cities:

1. Strengthening strategic planning processes for urban health.
2. Undertaking participatory research in collaboration with community based organizations, municipal health departments and research institutes.
3. Developing appropriate interventions based on needs.
4. Increasing awareness about the issues both among the community and decision-makers.
5. Developing communication strategies at local level.
6. Establishing national and regional information networks to ensure that relevant information is widely shared.

One of the key objectives of the Healthy Cities network is to increase the involvement of the urban poor in the initiatives to improve both urban health and the urban environment. Many projects have therefore been developed to address the needs of the vulnerable groups identified through the situation analyses. The process will culminate in socio-economic equity among various social groups and reduction in crime rates.

To further substantiate the Healthy Cities determinants, though they are complex enough, they can be related to four sets of factors:

1. Poverty, including low income, low level of education and inadequate household food security.
2. Physical environment, including overcrowding, inadequate or non-existent shelter, pollution, traffic and exposure to infectious agents.
3. Social and cultural factors, including composition of family, cultural restriction, age, gender, race, religion, extent of mental stress, and use of violence.

4. Political, including distribution of income and assets within the city, and commitment to and practice of participatory democracy.

Megacities versus Healthy cities

The phenomenon of megacities[4]—being a new event—needs due attention so far a Healthy Cities Movement is concerned. Citizens of Mumbai, Kolkata, Beijing, Bangkok, Jakarta, Tehran and the like, all face problems of severely stressed urban infrastructure, poverty, partly political turmoil, social and cultural alienation—severely in need of a transformation into a "Healthy Cities" process. As A.A. Badshah and J.E. Perlman [1996] put it: The world's largest metropolises —the megacities—are experiencing even more economic stress and cultural alienation. As the global economy produces benefits for the elites in the mega-cities, most citizens face rapidly deteriorating urban environments. Such a scenario—the problem emerging out of megacities—could extensively be solved through planning "Healthy Cities". According to the United Nations estimates, 43 per cent [2.3 billion] of the world's population used to live in urban areas in mid-1990. With the urban population growing 2.5 faster than its rural counterpart, the level of urbanization is projected to cross 50 per cent mark in 2005. The UN projections further show that by 2025, more than three-fifths of the world's population will be living in urban areas. The urban population in that year will be approximately 5.2 billion, of whom 77 per cent will live in developing countries, in which the ratio of Asia will be quite remarkable.

The problem of increasing megacities versus "Healthy Cities" is worth considering with special reference to Asia, and the phenomenon needs adequate solutions. Another estimate declares that out of the 26 expected agglomerations/megacities to have 10 million or more inhabitants by 2010, 21 cities will be in developing countries, in which Asia will host 14 of the very large cities; 5 will be in Latin America and 2 in Africa. Therefore, we must intensify and improve the global efforts to address population, consumption, social welfare, social security and distribution trends in our cities if we are to preserve a livable future for all the humanity in general, and the Asian nations in particular.

TABLE 1: Global Population Trends [in millions]

2025	1995	Country/Region	2025	1995	Region
322	263	USA	4773	3282	Asia
541	516	Europe	1583	744	Africa
127	125	Japan	690	475	Latin America
344	288	Ex-USSR	92	66	Oceania/Other
1334	1192	Sub Total	8472	5759	World
15.7	20.6	% of World			

Source: City [1996].

Coordination and functional integration of various sectors such as government, business, academia, mass media and non-government organizations ease the movement and dynamism of megacities. If not, various dysfunctions and deviations appear in the functioning of city life. As the phenomenon is very much concerned with Asia, new initiatives must be searched towards creating "Healthy Cities" in Asia.

Environmental education and healthy cities

Environmental education[5] can play as a catalyst for sustainable development as long as Healthy Cities process is concerned. Various challenges and needs could be responded through environmental education, and hence Healthy Cities process could be better sustained. It will broadly help in resolving environmental issues. What constitutes an "environmental issue" depends on the perceptions and earlier experiences of the learner as well as the context in which education takes place. An illustration of such participatory approach to "Healthy Cities" maintenance would result in better socio-economic movements, and better and higher quality of life for the people in general in Asia.

Education for social and environmental change requires an understanding of the way people define their own situation [Lucas: 1980, Huckle: 1993]. Hence, it acts as a prerequisite of planning and creating Healthy Cities. Likewise, if the change component of environmental education is ignored for whatever reason, then educational process will inevitably fall short in helping people understand the roots of oppression, inequality and environmental deterioration on the one hand, and in empowering them to becoming agents of social change and sustainable development on the other.

As poverty reduction schemes generally play a vital role in creating Healthy Cities, Plans of Action, and hence increasing literacy rates by the Asian countries have much improved the quality of life in the region in the past two decades. In this process of development, improvement in the means of communications also has been quite influential.

Likewise, though the explosive urban growth that gave rise to the modern city was made possible by the Industrial Revolution, and the greatly improved agricultural technology it brought along to help and support the densely populated cities [Keller: 1994], yet, education took progressive steps towards changing the growing cities into Healthy Cities. Also, it is yet needed to speed on, so as to reach the objectives of Healthy Cities. Hence, education, schemes to lower poverty and other determinants must functionally be integrated to reach a desired social structure.

Iran's urban profile and challenges

Iran, with an area of 1,648,000 sq. km., 28 provinces and 889 cities [SCI 2002: 6], is under the pressure of urbanization [nearly 1 per cent growth per year. The country's estimated population of 65.6 million in mid-2002 has created a complex of social, economic and environmental problems. About 60 per cent of Iran's population falls in the age category 0-24. This leads to problems so far as housing and environmental needs are concerned.

Well-planned housing can create conditions that are hygienic and environmentally conductive for healthy and immune growth of human civilization, but it is not happening as expected and to the standards, so far as Iran is concerned. If the cities in Iran are not environmentally and structurally conditioned and reformed, many cities are prone to disasters such as the earthquake disaster of Bam [26 December 2003] that killed more than 30 thousand people, and destroyed the entire city. On the contrary, unplanned and unsuitable housing can lead to unlawful and unhealthy environment [Rao 2001: 106].

However, the major prevailing housing problems in Iran stem from high rate of migration, slums and squatters, dearth of land in cities, lack of finance and shortage of purchasing power, violation of building regulations and so on. All such issues seriously affect the Healthy Cities Standards in Iran. These experiences have shown that the management of the projects has proved to be extremely difficult in cities, especially when there is not integration enough among different sectors and institutions.

Urban conservation concept is also currently observed as a controversial issue. However, urban conservation philosophy centres round the relationship between man and his built-environment. Though urban conservation idea developed in Europe, it is rather a new thought in Iran. With rapid social and technological changes in cities in Iran through urbanization, the land use is constantly changed by additions, demolition or alteration. In this process, many precious heritage buildings, greeneries and the like are pulled down to meet the money greed of the builders. Such a trend may create a void between Iran's present and past values, leaving it lost and uninspired. Under these circumstances, urban conservation assumes significant role in city development and the creation of Healthy Cities. Thus, the social and environmental policies being inter-related, will lead to better and improved quality of life [Cahill 2002: 26]. As a result, the health of individuals is linked to the culture and values to be found within the society in which those individuals live. However, the twin processes of industrialization and urbanization which now have the entire world in their grip, will further disrupt patterns of livelihood and produce continuing problems for public health with special reference to cities.

What Iran at present requires is, to have access to new and modern city planning schemes based on empirical and organized researches, so as to be able to produce some necessary knowledge, and technical know-how in the field followed by imposition of relevant laws and regulations [Zanjani 1991: 10].

Case of Tehran

Tehran as a metropolis with a growing population of more than 8 million is highly involved with Healthy Cities Standards. The city increasingly surrounded by industrial plants and manufacturing complexes, and a high rate of in-migration, is extensively trying to keep to standards of Healthy Cities project, though it is hard enough, but every effort is made to achieve the goal. For the fulfilment of the purpose, the Tehran municipal department has made great efforts and investments to combat massive pollution, transportation complexities, shortage of greenery and squatters so as to build up Healthy Cities.

In 1991, the Tehran's twentieth municipal district [Kooy-e-Sizd eh Aban] was formally selected for a Healthy Cities project. To move further towards the development of this project, close links and collaboration were forged and implemented among all the relevant local authorities [Functional Integration] of the district and city. The city developed a public awareness campaign to encourage actions by the population towards improving health. The project itself sought both to increase health standards and improve services. To help accomplish these goals as planned, the mayor of Tehran donated a building situated in the pilot area to serve as a city health centre. The city then chose a Healthy City High Council to serve as a steering committee with representatives from the ministries of Health and Medical Education [Salmanmanesh: 1996].

What is worth mentioning is the participatory role and cooperation of the people in the project. Though the project is being extended to the other parts and districts of the city, there is a long way to go.

Proposals for healthy cities

We know that the existing Western planning theories cannot successfully be applied in the Asian context. Therefore, we must identify and adopt new approaches to the critical issues of the cities in Asia. Although we need to establish meaningful communications with others elsewhere in search of new solutions, yet we must also apply approaches appropriate to our societies. Some of the immediate approaches and proposals effective in reaching Healthy Cities or transforming and improving the cities by, may be classified as follows:

1. Poverty reduction and job creation.
2. Access to appropriate shelter.
3. Improvement in production and consumption cycles.

4. Improvement in waste recycling and re-use.
5. Improvement in transport and communications.
6. Detente and combating social exclusion.
7. Crime prevention and social justice.
8. Improvement in infrastructure, water and energy supply.
9. Protection of environment and rehabilitation.
10. Policy-making and planning.

Conclusion

Asian cities are moving fast and will be very different in the years to come as compared with today. The cities in Asia are developing at such a great pace—perhaps too fast. But they must more think of building Healthy Cities, and not only arc in a great hurry to catch up, and even to overtake the advanced economies. In this process, the super-rapid development will have many casualties such an environmental deterioration, pollution, slums and squatters.

In the meantime, we must redefine that the most important function of the Asian cities today must be to provide the best possible environment and quality of life for every one living and working there. In other words, Asian cities must be people-oriented. However, people and citizens have very complex individual demands, and to meet them, is not that easy. That will be only possible in "Healthy Cities" conditions, which will by itself guarantee the health and safety of the generations to come too.

So far as Iran is concerned, it is no surprise that increasing urbanization correlates with increasing risks. As unplanned growth in Iran is continuing, many cities are prone to physical hazards, *i.e.* many of the fastest growing cities of the country are in earthquake zone. Moreover, in urban settlements, the livelihood strategies of the poor are complex. That is, contexts are changing and uncertain; with rapid urban growth, increasing crimes and unhealthy cities are appearing. Similarly, so far as human assets are concerned, cities in Iran provide a variety of opportunities for earning income, especially in the informal sectors of the economy. However, the scenario remains complicated and unsolved in various contexts.

REFERENCES

Ageing and Health: A Global Challenge for the 21st Century, Proceedings of a WHO Symposium, 285, Kobe [Japan], 10-13 November 1998.

Badshah, Akhtar and J.E. Perlman, 1991. *Megacities and the Urban Future*, London, Zed Books.

Bilton, T. et al., 2002. *Introductory Sociology*, 4th ed., 37, London, Palgrave Macmillan.

Cahill, M., 2002. *The Environment and Social Policy*, New York, Routledge.

Census Results [1996], Statistical Centre of Iran.

City, 3-4, October 1996, Bristol, Arrowsmith.

City, 7, May 1997, Bristol, Arrowsmith.

Curwin, E.C. and Hart, 1962. *Plough and Pasture*, New York, Collier Books.

Duhl, Leonard J., 1986. "The Healthy City: Its Function and Its Future", *Health Promotion*, Vol. 1, No. 1, New York.

Durkheim, E., 1964; orig. 1895. *The Division of Labour in Society*, New York, Free Press.

Environment and Urbanization, Vol. 11, No. 1, April 1999, London, Russel Press.

Haila, Anne, 1998. "The Highest and Emptiest Skyscrapers in the World: Asian Cities and the Rise and Fall of Economies", Presentation at the 1998 ISA World Congress of Sociology, Montreal.

Hall, Nicolas *et al.*, 1996. *The Urban Opportunity*, London, Intermediate Technology Publications Ltd.

Hancock, Trevor, 1990. "Towards Healthy and Sustainable Communities: Health, Environment and Economy at the Local Level", Presentation at the 3rd Colloquium on Environmental Health, Quebec.

Henslin, J.M., *et al.*, 1983. *Social Problems*, New York, McGraw-Hill, Inc.

Huckle, J., 1991. "Education for Sustainability: Assessing Pathways to the Future", *Australian Journal of Environmental Education* (7), 49 and 69.

Keller, S., *et al.*, 1994. *Sociology*, New York, McGraw-Hill, Inc.

Kenzer, Marina, 1998, *Healthy Cities: A Guide to the Literature*, Pennsylvania, Bryn Mawr.

Local Environment, Vol. 1, No. 3, 1996, Journals Oxford Ltd.

Lucas, A.M., 1980. "The Role of Science Education in Education for Environment", *Journal of Environmental Education*, 12 [3], 3 and 23.

Macionis, J.J., 1998. *Sociology*. London, Prentice-Hall, Inc., 381.

McKeown, T., 1979. *The Role of Medicine: Dream, Mirage or Nemesis?* Second Edition, Oxford, Blackwell.

Pelling, M., 2003. *Natural Disasters and Development in a Globalizing World*, New York, Routledge.

Proceeding, *The Socio-Cultural Conference on Development and Counter-Development in Tehran*, November 2001.

Rao, M.P., 2001. *Urban Planning: Theory & Practice.* New Delhi, CBS Publishers & Distributors, 106.

Salmanmanesh, Hassan, 1996. "Tehran Success in a Suburb", *World Health*, No. 1, January-February, Geneva.

State Statistical Year Book of Iran, 2002, 6, Statistical Centre of Iran.

Toennies, F., 1963; orig. 1887, *Continuity and Society* [*Gemeinschaft and Gesellschaft*], New York, Harper and Row.

Wirth, L., "Urbanism as a Way of Life", *American Journal of Sociology*, July 1938: 1-24.

World Population Data Sheet, 2002, Population Reference Bureau, Washington DC.

Zanjani, H., 1991. *Issues and Methods of Urban Planning* [Vol. 1 (*Population*) as quoted by Hashemi, S.R., 10], Tehran, Urban Planning and Architecture Centre, Ministry of Housing and Urban Development Publications.

NOTES

1. The study of the city in terms of the social characteristics of areas or neighbourhoods, which originated in the University of Chicago in the 1920s, is a part of urban ecology. High rates of immigration into Chicago from Europe in the first two decades of the 20th Century led to rapid urban growth and change, and stimulated research into the nature of urban living and origins of social problems.
2. The cities in the countries mainly found in Asia, Africa, Latin America and the Caribbean, many having been colonies until the mid-20th Century, and today manifesting lower levels of industrialization, but increasing sub-standard urbanization, and lower general living standards as compared with the First World are known as the Third World cities. The term was first used in the early 1950s, and then taken up by the Third World political leaders engaged in independence movements against European colonialism.
3. Refers to any change that results in increased prosperity, and new and more complex forms of social structure and organization. The study of such development was a central concern of classical sociological theory [Evolutionary Theory, Social Change].
4. As estimated before, at the turn of the Third Millennium, there would be 21 megacities with population of ten million or more of these, eighteen would be in developing countries, including the most impoverished societies in the world.
5. Refers to the aspect of environment that analyzes the institutions, organizations and basics of education. It is the application of environmental theories, perspectives and research methods in the course of analysis of educational processes and practices.

10

Approaches to Urbanization in India: Theory, Policy and Challenges

KALA SEETHARAM SRIDHAR
kala@nipfp.org.in
Fellow, National Institute of Public Finance and Policy, New Delhi, India.

ABSTRACT

This paper, being conceptual in nature, explores the consequences of increased urbanization/rural-urban migration, then discusses possible approaches through which the negative consequences of urbanization can be overcome, and finally, studies the emerging trends in India's urbanization, and demonstrates how can we measure them. It discusses slums and the provision of urban infrastructure services as the negative consequences of urbanization. Further it summarizes suggestions in the literature regarding how these problems can be overcome, and compares what actually has been done in practice. It offers some prescriptions and approaches to the provision of urban infrastructure services, and slums, based on the theory. Finally, it demonstrates how the gradient approach can be used to understand the trends in suburbanization of India's cities, and what this means for policy.

JEL classification: O18, P25, R0.

Keywords: Urbanization, Suburbanization, Urban infrastructure services.

Introduction

Urbanization in India has increased significantly, consistent with the worldwide phenomenon. The share of urban population in the total population of the country grew from

11% in 1901 to 26% in 1991. In 2001, the urban share of population in the country increased to 29%. The urban population is expected to increase to about 500 million by 2021. This phenomenon has been attributed to the "attraction of city lights." Rural-urban migration in India increased from 33,441,000 in 1981 to 39,910,000 in 1991 (Census of India), showing a 19% increase over this period (2001 Census data are not yet available). As Mills and Becker (1986) find, although India is not over-urbanized compared to other countries, it is at a stage of development at which urbanization responds rapidly to economic growth.[1]

My objectives here are to explore the following:

1. What are the consequences of increased urbanization/rural-urban migration?
2. What are possible approaches through which the negative consequences of urbanization can be overcome?
3. What are the emerging trends in India's urbanization? How can we measure them?

A. Consequences of urbanization

While the urbanization phenomenon is widely accepted as being an inevitable by-product of development, there are many undesirable outcomes that have resulted in urban areas from rural-urban migration. I consider the following:

1. Slums
2. Lack of adequate urban infrastructure services

Slums are areas in which buildings are not fit for human habitation, and lack ventilation, light or sanitation facilities for various reasons (such as dilapidation or overcrowding) that are detrimental to health and safety. On average, more than one-fourth of population in the country lives in slums, varying from a maximum of nearly two-thirds slum population in Patna to about 13% in Bangalore in 1991. In a few urban areas such as Bangalore, slum population decreased to 8 per cent of population in 2001, possibly due to governmental intervention as well as NGO activity. It is, however, disturbing that proportions of slum population in 2001 in other urban areas of the country have remained the same or have worsened.

In 2001, slum population in Chennai was nearly 18 per cent of the total population, it increased in Kanpur from 10 per cent of total population in 1991 to 14 per cent in 2001 (retrieved from NIUA's website: <http://www.indiaurbaninfo.com/niua/index.htm>).

Undesirable outcomes that have also reached alarming proportions with urbanization are denial of access to safe drinking water, sanitation, and adequate waste management for a substantial portion of the country's urban households. According to India's Union Urban Development ministry, 20 per cent of the country's urban households are denied access to safe drinking water, 58 per cent do not have safe sanitation, and more than 40 per cent of garbage generated is left uncollected for want of proper waste management.[2] While the problems highlighted by India's Urban Development Ministry imply that there are probably too many immigrants into the city, the problems could well be due to the fact that migrants do not compensate for the social costs they create.

B. Approaches to urbanization

Here I focus on two approaches:

1. How to decongest urban areas;
2. How to manage urbanization through better delivery of urban infrastructure services.

Decongestion of urban areas

While it is common knowledge that slums are caused by the migration of rural population to urban areas, it is only because non-agricultural employment in India has not grown rapidly enough to absorb the labour force, that the tide of rural-urban migration has kept increasing. To reduce disparities in backwardness among areas, and disperse industrial activity in the remote areas of the country, the Government of India introduced the "growth centres" programme in June 1988. According to this programme, 71 growth centres were set up throughout the country that were allotted to the various states on the basis of a combined criteria of area, population and the extent of industrial backwardness.[3] These growth centres provide basic industrial infrastructure like power, water, telecom, and banking to enable rural areas to attract industries.

Sridhar (2003c) does not find growth centres to have a statistically significant effect on the unemployment rate of districts that contain them, using district-level unemployment data for the country. However, this study finds that wherever growth centres exist, they positively affect the number of firms locating there. This study also finds infrastructure to be an important determinant of firm location in non-urban areas. The implication is that the states and their industrial development authorities have to aggressively promote their backward areas by providing infrastructure including road/highway access, power supply, telecom and Internet infrastructure, which would not be available to firms otherwise.

The costs of doing business in the major cities of the country make it difficult for Indian companies to win the price war. In addition to prohibitive real estate costs in metro areas, firms have to incur higher logistic costs (the costs of transport) in metro areas that are avoidable in smaller cities. For instance, an average commute in Delhi or Mumbai costs 20-30 kms whereas in a smaller town this could be a maximum of 10 kms. There are several implications for industry and policy that are faced with the transition that occurs as a city grows, as I point out elsewhere (Sridhar 2001).

The first is for industry to relocate to smaller and medium towns, as the growth centres programme rightly emphasises. Operational costs (*e.g.*, rental/leasing costs) for industry are much higher in metro and urban areas. If state and local governments invest in improving the physical infrastructure in small and medium towns, it is possible that they can compete as alternative locations. Mills and Becker (1986) support this. They point out that governments can influence the growth of particular cities, even of particular size classes of cities, by investments in infrastructure and providing public services.

In smaller and medium-sized towns, where the growth centres are located, firms will also be able to get adequately trained labour force at relatively low cost. This is because the cost-of-living adjusted wage is itself lower in smaller and medium towns, holding quality constant. Industries can exploit this advantage. An *Economic Times* Special Report

(December 23, 2003) recently found that as costs rise in metros, the business process outsourcing industry will necessarily have to migrate to smaller cities to retain the labour cost arbitrage.

The other reason for industry to locate to semi-urban and rural areas (the emphasis of the growth centre programme) is that it would change their economic base. Urban theory shows that rural-urban migration occurs in search of employment. Data compiled by the National Institute of Urban Affairs (NIUA) show that more than half of men that migrated from rural to the urban areas of India in 1991 did so for the sake of employment (corresponding data for 2001 are not yet available). Relocation of industry to rural and semi-urban areas helps the rural poor and surplus labour to find alternative employment in their own areas. This acts as a check on urban migration that causes critical shortages in urban housing and prevents the creation of slums. Besides, relocation of industry also facilitates the coordination of government's poverty alleviation programmes in a better manner. So far, it has been found that recipients of various employment training programmes have not been able to find suitable employment in rural areas.

Finally, the development of smaller and medium towns might imply that they are self-contained communities, but eventually automotive ties have to develop between urban areas and their satellite towns. This implies that development of roads and highways that has been neglected for a long time in India, gets the attention it needs.

In fact, studying the impact of firms on the local communities where they have located, Sridhar (2003b) finds that 26 per cent of firms had engaged in some form of community service in areas where they had located. While it is not desirable for firms to spend a lot of resources on social service especially when they are making losses,[4] other options exist. Apart from relocating to rural areas so that the growth of slums will be reduced, more generally, businesses can engage in various kinds of activity to improve slums and their corporate social responsibility, as I point in Sridhar (2000) and Sridhar (2003a):

1. Adopt a slum in the vicinity and provide financial assistance for its rehabilitation.
2. Construct cheap housing in the periphery of the firm premises. This is important in cities like Mumbai. Dharavi residents were recently provided low-cost housing in New Mumbai (Vashi), but workers refused to take it because of the commuting that was involved to their place of work.
3. Supply infrastructure to the houses.
4. Adopt a block or district for improvements.
5. Co-ordinate awareness talks and discussions to disseminate need to do something about slums.
6. Provide training to slum dwellers so that they can take up gainful employment.

Provision of urban infrastructure services

Over and above the issue of slums, one outcome with too many city immigrants could be that the change in the total cost of providing infrastructure services resulting from migration (the marginal cost), would be *higher* than the user prices actually charged. As Williamson (1988) points out, there has been no attempt to assess the quantitative relevance of this question. Further, there are no estimates of marginal costs for urban infrastructure services in India. However, this is crucial for efficient allocation of resources and for answering the rural-urban migration question. In fact, Mills and Becker (1986) put forth the hypothesis that it is large infrastructure investments financed by taxes levied elsewhere that stimulate migration and consequently city size. Further, they point out that excessive expansion (migration) of large cities is especially a problem in countries where governments spend excessively on local government services financed by taxes levied elsewhere. This, however, is not a problem in the Indian context since local governments have little autonomy or resources to spend excessively on anything.

For us to be able to say whether or not we have to close India's cities to in-migration, we need to assess the marginal cost (the change in the total cost of service resulting from unit change in demand) of providing urban infrastructure services. Further, to answer the question of closing the cities to in-migration, there is a need to study how the estimated normative user prices compare in relation to those actually charged in various Indian cities. If current user prices charged are lower than marginal costs, there may not be too many immigrants. If not, then there may well be too many immigrants.

There is a reason why marginal, not average costs, should be the basis of pricing. Take the example of water supply. A city usually develops its least expensive water sources first, but it then becomes increasingly expensive to produce an additional unit of water as demand grows with increasing migration into the urban area. In such an instance, using the average cost of today would lead to an underestimation of the cost of water production in the future.

While in theory, costs should be the basis of pricing, in India, after independence, the public sector was assigned the primary responsibility for the provision of these 'public goods,' that subsidized these services because of their essential nature. However, with a decade of economic liberalization in India, it is appropriate that the private sector should participate in the provision of these services. For that to happen, there is a need to make these projects viable for the private sector, which calls for market-based mechanisms in the provision of these services. This is also the only way in which reforms can percolate to urban policy and infrastructure services.

C. Suburbanization of India

Suburbanization is the process where the percentage of population in the suburbs rises.[5] Given the importance of land costs in the cost of living in cities,[6] suburbanization of population, households and firms in the metro areas of India have been slowly, but certainly occurring. For instance, in 1981, only 10 and 24 per cent of Delhi and Chennai's populations were suburban, but in 1991, suburban populations in these metros had increased to 11 and 29 per cent respectively.[7]

It is plausible to believe that the suburbanization of employment has started occurring in the metro areas of India primarily because of two phenomena that have bid up the price of land:

1. *The rapid growth of Information Technology (IT) sector:* The IT sector consisting of software and IT-enabled services sectors (back-office operations, Business Process Outsourcing (BPO), call-centres, payroll, medical transcription to mention a few) in India has fuelled the demand for land to house these various facilities.
2. *Revolution in the retail services sector:* Due to increased disposable incomes and increased purchasing power of consumers, large department stores, spacious malls and brand stores in metropolitan and smaller cities have become characteristic of the retail scenario in India. According to international property consultant C.B. Richard Ellis, the success of retailing in India in the new millennium depends on three factors: availability of retail space, supply chain parameters and infrastructure such as highways and rail network needed for development of out of town shopping malls.

Hence firms have started locating in the suburbs and periphery of cities to avoid land costs of the CBD.[8] For instance, office rentals in the CBD of Mumbai range from Rs. 75-110 per square foot per month compared to Rs. 70-85 in suburbs such as Bandra/Kurla. In terms of capital values, the differences between central city and the suburbs are even more. In the National Capital Region, for instance, CBD prime area costs Rs. 8,213 per square foot whereas in the Gurgaon prime area, capital value is only Rs. 3,664 per square foot. When we take residential land, the story regarding rental values and capital costs, is similar. (See Tables 1 and 2)

The suburbanization of metropolitan areas in a large country like the United States has drawn a lot of attention of the researchers (Mills and Price 1984; Mills 1992; Margo 1992; Mieszkowski and Mills 1993). However, for a large sub-continent like India that contains a large number of cities and towns, suburbanization has drawn very little attention of the literature. Only one study by the Census of India (Jain 1993) studies the emerging trend in the suburbanization of India over 1971-81. The study does not analyze suburbanization as much as it analyzes changes in the composition of Standard

TABLE 1: Office Rentals and Capital Values in Selected Metro Areas

Metro Area	CBD Rental (Rs./Sqft/Month)	Suburb Rental (Rs./Sqft/Month)	CBD Capital Value (Rs./Sqft)	Suburban Capital Value (Rs./Sqft)
NCR	20	37	8,213	3,664
Mumbai*	75-110	70-85	10,000-12,000	6,000-7,000
Bangalore**	42	26	4,000	2,700
Average	**52**	**47**	**7,738**	**4,288**

Source: Compiled from *Economic Times* Realty Bites, December 28, 2003.

* Suburb is defined as Bandra Kurla.

** CBD is defined as MG Road.

TABLE 2: Residential Rentals and Capital Values in Selected Metro Areas

Metro Area	CBD Rental (Rs/Month)	Suburb Rental (Rs/Month)	CBD Capital Value (Rs/Sqft)	Suburban Capital Value (Rs/Sqft)
NCR*	100,000-175,000	25,000-35,000	7,000-10,000	2,400-3,200
Mumbai**	60,000-125,000	45,000-100,000	7,000-15,000	6,500-10,000
Bangalore***	40,000-100,000	25,000-80,000	2,200-3,800	1,800-2,600
Average	**1,00,000**	**51,667**	**7,500**	**4,417**

Source: Compiled from *Economic Times* Realty Bites, December 28, 2003.

* For NCR, CBD is defined as Shanti Niketan, Westend and Vasant Vihar. Suburbs for NCR are defined as consisting of Gurgaon.

** For Mumbai, CBD is defined as consisting of South Cuff Parade, Churchgate and Colaba. Bandra and Juhu are defined as suburbs.

*** CBD is defined as Richmond Lavelle Road, suburbs are defined as Cunningham Road/Brunton Road (off MG Road) and Indiranagar.

Urban Areas. It also does not perform any more systematic analyses than calculating trends.

A systematic understanding, however, is really needed, and an estimation of the extent of population and employment suburbanisation that have definitely taken place in the urban areas of the country, similar to phenomena occurring in the other countries. Standard urban economic theory shows that increases in income and population have the effect of increasing suburbanization. In the standard urban model, employment is concentrated in the CBD and the locational choice of households is modeled solely on access to the employment centre. Currently we are in darkness with respect to these phenomena in Indian cities.

In urban economic theory, the density gradient is used as a measure of population, household, or employment suburbanization. The gradient shows how population (or household or employment) density (number of persons/HHs/jobs per square km) changes with distance from the CBD. Suburbanization is the process that occurs when the absolute value of the gradient falls.

There are two ways of measuring the gradient. We can either *estimate* or *calculate* it. Data that are required to *estimate* density gradients are population density (per square km) for census wards and their distances from the city centre. If we were to have the luxury of such disaggregated data, the gradient is the coefficient in a regression of density of various pockets (in India's case, census wards, in the U.S. case, census tracts or block groups), on their distances from the city centre, as in the following equation:

$$D(r) = D_0 e^{-br}$$

where D (r) is density r kms from the centre, e is the base of the natural logarithm, b and D_0 are constants to be estimated from the data, if they are available at such a disaggregated level. In this approach, as may be clear, this regression is required for every city. I have checked with the Census of India, and found that data on land area are not available for census wards in India, although population data are available.

Since, as we can see, estimation of gradients is a very data intensive process, we can *calculate* rather than estimate the gradient, through Mills' two-point gradient technique, based on data for just two points in the city, CBD and urban area. For calculating the gradient, from the theoretical exponential density function in equation [1], we may derive the ratio of L_C to L. If we have data on L_C (population of the central city), R_C (radius of the central city), L (population of the entire metro area), and R (radius of the entire metro area), we may calculate the gradient.

The calculation of density gradients for Indian cities has not been attempted in any earlier study. Data on population, households, employment and land area, of India's cities and their agglomerations, are available yet only for 1981 and

1991. The 2001 Census has not yet released corresponding data. Population, household, and employment gradients for Indian cities would indicate the extent of, and trends in their suburbanization. This would enable us to further understand the determinants of suburbanization in the Indian context.

This analysis could have implications for policies (such as rent control) that restrict the supply of land in the CBD of Indian cities, and other problems in Indian central cities that persuades firms and households to move away from the core city to the suburbs. May be, we need to start a "back to the central city movement," as American cities have started doing, and revitalize our inner cities as good places to live and do business.

REFERENCES

Jain, M.K., 1993. "Emerging Trend of Suburbanisation in India, 1971-81: An Analysis of Data on Standard Urban Areas," *Census of India Occasional Paper No. 2* of 1993.

Margo, R., 1992. "Explaining the Postwar Suburbanization of Population in the United States: The Role of Income." *Journal of Urban Economics.* 31: 301-10.

Mieszkowski, Peter and Edwin Mills, 1993. "The Causes of Metropolitan Suburbanization." *Journal of Economic Perspectives.* 7 (3): 135-47.

Mills, Edwin and Charles M. Becker, 1986. *Studies in Indian Urban Development,* OUP: New York.

Mills, Edwin, 1992. "The Measurement and Determinants of Suburbanization." *Journal of Urban Economics.* 32: 377-87.

—— and R. Price, 1984. "Metropolitan Suburbanization and Central City Problems." *Journal of Urban Economics.* 15: 1-17.

Sridhar, Kala S. 2003a. "A Market-based Approach to Communal Tensions," *Economic and Political Weekly* 38 (3) January 18, 2003: 181-82.

——, 2003b. "Firm Location Decisions and Impact on Local Economies," *Economic and Political Weekly* 38 (39) September 27, 2003: 4121-30.

——, 2003c. "Growth Centres in India: Impact on Firm Location and Employment," *NIPFP Working Paper* 4/2004.

——, 2001. "Synergies of urban employment strategies," *The Business Line,* October 8, 2001.

——, 2000. "Tackling growth of city slums," *The Economic Times,* August 6, 2000.

Williamson, J.G., 1988. Migration and Urbanization, in *Handbook of Development Economics,* Volume I, edited by Hollis Chenery and T.N. Srinivasan. Amsterdam: North Holland.

NOTES

1. We may expect urbanization to follow economic growth because with increased economic growth, increased agricultural productivity leads to smaller share of labour force involved in production, and induces rural to urban migration.
2. These data are for urban areas in the country. It is possible that analogous, if not worse, problems exist in the rural areas regarding which reliable data are not available. However, if urbanization is an inevitable occurrence, it is important to address these infrastructure problems in the urban areas. If such problems cannot be addressed in the urban areas, it would be much more difficult to address them in the rural areas.
3. Currently the criteria for selection of growth centres are as follows (these criteria are described in circular No. 14/23/88-DBA-I issued by the Ministry of Industry, Government of India, dated December 8, 1988):

   I. Growth centres shall not be located:

      1. Within 50 kms of the boundary of 7 cities in the country with a population above 25 lakhs;
      2. Within 30 kms of the 2 cities with a population between 15-25 lakhs; and
      3. Within 15 kms from the boundary of the 12 cities in the country with a population between 7.5-15 lakhs.

   II. The growth centres should be located close to District/Sub-Divisional/Block/Taluk Headquarters or Developing Urban Centres.

   III. Growth centres shall have access to basic facilities—proximity to railheads, national or state highways, water supply, power, telecommunications, and educational and health facilities. If such facilities are not readily available, it should be ensured that they are developed with priority and commitment.
4. Various theories of Corporate Social Responsibility (CSR) suggest that firms can be expected to engage in such activity only when it increases demand for their goods and services, and when the cost of supplying the CSR good or service is lower (McWilliams and Siegel 2001). Evidence from India's corporate sector suggests that only large firms, and profitable ones engage in such activity.
5. Note here that we hold population of the urban area constant, since we are looking at *percentage living in the suburbs.*
6. According to the standard monocentric urban model in which everyone commutes to the CBD for work, total living costs consist of land and transport costs. In equilibrium, total living costs are assumed to be the same everywhere in the city. Since employment is concentrated at the CBD, for those that live in the suburbs and commute to work, transport

costs are high, but land (and housing) costs are low (it is easy to conceive cities that have multiple employment centres. However, as long as employment density in the CBD is greater than it is in the suburbs, the monocentric urban model still holds good). But no commuting is involved for residents that live in the CBD (since they probably can walk to work or commute for short periods). Hence their transport costs are (close to) zero. However, their land costs are high. It is therefore efficient for central city residents and/or businesses to economise on the use of land in the CBD and build multi-storeyed complexes using relatively more capital and less land.

7. These figures are calculated based on 1981 and 1991 Census data for the municipal corporation and urban agglomeration (UA). The percentage of population suburban has been calculated as:

   (Population living in the UA—Population in the municipal corporation)/ Population living in the UA.

8. It is well-known that when firms move to suburbia, households follow, since people follow jobs. This is true even if it is an unresolved issue in the literature, whether people follow jobs or jobs follow people (skills).

11

A Comparison of European and Asian ICT Clusters and Their Promotion Policies

MEINE PIETER VAN DIJK AND WILLEM VAN WINDEN

mpvandijk@few.eur.nl

Economic Faculty and European Institute for Comparative Urban Research [EURICUR], Erasmus University, Rotterdam, The Netherlands.

1. Introduction

Many cities invest heavily in the information and communication technology (ICT) sector, developing existing and attracting new ICT enterprises. Many governments are attracted by the buoyant success of Silicon Valley, a well-known concentration of ICT activities. The subject of this chapter is the factors influencing the development the ICT sector in four cities: The Hague and Helsinki in Europe and Bangalore and Nanjing in Asia. We describe the development of the cluster, analyse the policies the cities pursued to strengthen their local ICT clusters, and finally attempt to identify important differences between the ICT clusters in these different cities.

Section 2 reviews the relevant literature on (ICT) clustering and urban development, and elaborates on the methodology used. Section 3 contains a brief description of the ICT cluster in The Hague and Helsinki and describes the urban policies, which these cities pursue to strengthen their ICT clusters. In section 4 we do the same for Bangalore and Nanjing. Subsequently in section 5, the clusters are compared on the relevant dimensions derived from the literature. In section 6 we draw some conclusions and identify issues for further research.

2. ICT sector growth in urban regions: some notions from theory

OECD (2001) makes a distinction between ICT manufacturing and services. Manufacturing must be intended to fulfil the function of information processing and communication including transmission and display; ICT service industries must be intended to enable the function of information processing and communication by electronic means. This comprises the wholesale of ICT products, telecommunications services, and consultancy services. Another much-used distinction in the ICT sector is that between hardware, software and content. Hardware is the physical equipment (PCs, servers, cables, etc.), software are all kind of computer programmes and systems that run on the hardware, and content is the information that is processed and generated by the technology.

A combination of the value chain and the knowledge intensity approach is useful for our purpose, which is to describe analyse local and regional ICT cluster and cluster policies in Europe and Asia. Each of the functions in the value chain has specific locational needs. R&D functions in ICT are dependent on high-quality technological labour; (standard) manufacturing is probably more sensitive to costs differences, and will locate where sufficient cheap labour is available; Sales and marketing functions need proximity to the market. A number of studies have appeared on the location behaviour of innovative industries, but also on the opportunities and constraints for cities to develop their ICT industries. A strong spatial clustering of innovative industries has been observed in most countries. To explain this, some authors stress the importance of inter-firm co-operation and regional knowledge transfer (Boekholt, 1994; Malmberg et al., 1996; Lazonick, 1992; Cooke, 1995).

A very relevant issue is the role of large, transnational companies (TNCs). They play a pivotal role in the way local innovative networks relate to global networks. Malmberg et al. (1996) and Van den Berg, Braun and Van Winden (2001) stress that if a TNC is rooted and integrated ("fledged") in the region and engaging in regional networks, it can act as an important disseminator of new knowledge, information and innovation from abroad into the region. This is particularly relevant for research and development (R&D) activities. Finally, Porter (1998) stresses the importance of large and critical local demand as condition for cluster development and trigger for innovations. This demand may be important for ICT clusters as well: there is some evidence that ICT-firms tend to locate near their main customers, in regions with high concentrations of financial and business services (Roost, 1998).

All the cities studied are centres of ICT industries. A number of factors determine the development of an ICT cluster. High tech services as information- and communication-based industry are almost always reliant on a network of universities and urban labour markets. A high quality of life is also important. All cities have a policy to develop their ICT cluster. At the same time, these cities are very different in their economic structure and their position in their national urban systems. The following research questions were formulated:

1. What is the role of (local) demand in the urban cluster's development?
2. What is the role of large firms in urban ICT cluster development?
3. What is the role of R&D and the educational infrastructure?
4. What is the importance of quality of life for ICT development?

3. The ICT clusters in The Hague and Helsinki

The Hague is the third largest city of the Netherlands (445,000 inhabitants). It is the seat of the Dutch national government and hosts virtually all the national ministries, as well as foreign embassies and other diplomatic functions. The city's ambition is to become a strong ICT/telecom city, which forms part of its general strategy to develop more (international) private business. The Hague counts several headquarters of telephone service providers. It is only since the second half of the 1990s that the cities' ICT sector began to grow. The fastest growth was achieved recently with the arrival of the mobile communications service providers: Ben (320 staff) and Dutchtone (550 staff), new entrants in the since 1998 liberalised Dutch telecom market. For these foreign owned companies The Hague was attractive because of the nearness of political decision makers (several ministries, and the telecom regulation body, the OPTA), which is relevant for the telecom sector. In the slipstream of these telecom providers, The Hague attracted technical equipment firms such as Alcatel, Siemens and Nokia, mainly functioning as sales outlets and customer services centres, but without R&D facilities. Other well-known players are Amazon.com, the American e-bookstore and Mapquest, a leader in interactive geographic information systems. These companies wanted to locate in The Netherlands anyway, but choose the city of The Hague for its international atmosphere and the availability of (ICT) staff. ICT educational facilities in the region are the Haagse Hogeschool (2,600 students in the field of ICT), and the nearby Delft Technical University (1,850 students).

Along the highway to The Hague, branches of ICT consultancy companies are located (such as CMG) and the cluster counts some small and young firms active in software development, all kind of internet business, e-commerce companies and so on. The adjacent cities of Delft and Zoetermeer also host a lot of ICT activity.

With a population of 532,000 Helsinki is by far the largest city in Finland. The region's economy is strongly dominated by services; some 80% of employment falls into that category. Manufacturing is much less important in this city to Finland's average. Finland is very advanced when it comes to the production and application of state-of-the-art telecommunication services and new media services. It has the highest penetration rate of mobile telephones in the world, exceeding 50% in 1998, and Internet and new media services are also relatively widespread. The main reason for the high penetration rates of new communication devices are, the low prices. However, the success of Finnish telecom service and equipment producers can be traced back to the early liberalisation of the Finnish telecom market.

Helsinki is the principal ICT cluster in Finland. One very dominant player is Nokia. This firm is famous for its development and production of mobile telephones. With a global market share of 21%, it is a true world leader in the field. Nokia has grown tremendously during the last few years. The firm employs 7,000 people in Helsinki, 22,000 in Finland, and 42,000 worldwide. There are very many smaller firms in the Helsinki region active in ICT. Many of them have some links to Nokia, as suppliers of parts, components, software or other services. Other customers of these firms are buying new media services mainly for the purpose of corporate communication, internal communication and advertising. Besides, foreign equipment manufacturers have establishments in Helsinki. An example is Ericsson, the Swedish competitor of Nokia, which employs over 1,000 people in the Helsinki region. Another important category of players in the cluster are the providers of telecom services, such as telephone companies of different kind and size, internet providers and others. The research and education infrastructure is well developed, with a technical university, a university of art and design, a general university and several polytechnics (details: Van Winden, 2003).

4. Bangalore and Nanjing

With over 925 software companies employing over 80,000 ICT professionals. Bangalore is the undisputed ICT Capital of India (*The Hindu*, 28-2-2002). According to the same article in 2000-2001, every week, at least one company with 100% foreign equity participation has set up shop in this city. Apart from ICT majors like Infosys, Wipro, Tata Consultancy Services and Microland, the world's leading ICT companies like GE, Texas Instruments, CISCO, Digital, IBM, HP, Compaq, Motorola, Lucent Technologies, Microsoft, Sun Micro Systems, Oracle, Novell and several others have made Bangalore their home.

Already in the Second World War India's first aircraft factory was founded in Bangalore and hence the city had one of the most technologically advanced industries and a well-trained workforce in India (Srinivas, 1998). Bangalore is now known as a centre for outsourcing the development of software, a practice that came up in the 1970s. The improvement of satellite communications has been a catalyst to this outsourcing. Presently about two-third of Indian software exports goes to the United States (US) and in total more than 500,000 people are working in the ICT sector in the country. The real growth in Bangalore came in the 1980s, with for example a compound annual growth of production of almost 30 per cent between 1987 and 1991 (Renu, 2000). Indian software expanded almost twice as fast as the world leading software industry (the US) in the same period. New activities are developing in particular what is called business process outsourcing industries, ranging from call centres to managing back-office tasks. Many ICT companies selected Bangalore for setting up a plant because of the availability of cheap specialized labour and because this was the first state to develop its own ICT policy.

Local government is very active in Bangalore and developed for example its own ICT policy and looks for public-private partnerships for infrastructure development. It provided for example policy related incentives, for example ICT companies settling in Bangalore usually get a number of tax incentives. The companies would also benefit from the large number of education and training institutes in the city. Plus the State government is actively promoting Bangalore as the capital of software in India and abroad. The Bangalore municipal government started to formulate positive economic policies, also with respect to small and medium ICT enterprises in the city.

In the case of Bangalore local demand is not so important. The role of large firms is important, but these were not necessarily foreign large firms. R&D was present and has been developed, although it is not the key to understanding the success of Bangalore. Finally the factor quality of life certainly contributed to making Bangalore an attractive city for a knowledge intensive industry (details: Van Dijk 2003b).

China's main cities have developed 'electronic roads'; the term used for places where computer related shops are concentrated. The best-known ones are in Beijing, Shanghai and Shenzhen. Our study is based on a sample of 50 ICT enterprises on Zhujiang electronic road in Nanjing, which is the capital city of Jiangsu province (Van Dijk, 2003a). The city counts more than 5 million inhabitants. It is an important business centre in the eastern part of China. Already in 1989 the municipality decided to start an electronic road. The enterprises occupying plots along Zhujiang road were notified that this street would be reserved for ICT companies and that they would have to move if ICT is not their core business. Alternative locations were offered and empty plots and buildings were allocated to ICT firms.

In due course over 1000 enterprises (925 in 1999) found a place on Zhujiang road or along neighbouring streets. Local government reinforced this concentration process by reserving a number of buildings known as 'enterprise buildings' for ICT companies. Usually some common services are offered, such as accountancy and cleaning. About two-third of the enterprises in the cluster are private enterprises, a 46 per cent increase over 1998, or a doubling of the number compared to 1997. This is strongly related to the promotion efforts of the local government, notably of the Xuanwu district authorities. This is the district where the electronic road is located. The total industrial product of the firms clustered along Zhujiang electronic road was about 321 million US dollar in 1998 and grew 40 per cent in 1999. The nature of the firms actually concentrated in the Zhujiang road is very mixed. One can find the regular sellers of specific soft and hardware, but also specialised firms providing hospital information systems, software for system integration (including installation and adaptation) or companies repairing monitors or other parts of a computer system. ICT consultancy firms can be found side by side with firms recycling old computers. Many of the companies on Zhujiang road are mainly selling hard or software.

The advantages and disadvantages of a cluster of ICT enterprises mentioned are nearness, exchange of ideas, providing choice to customers, positive policies by local government and supporting services in the business buildings. The major factors determining the competitiveness of this network of enterprises negatively seem to be the location of Nanjing away from the coast and the lack of an enterprise culture in the city. It is also difficult to find good people in Nanjing and the impact of the universities and specialised research institutes is also not as positive in this case as they seem to be in the other Chinese cities. Compared with similar concentrations of ICT firms in Beijing, Shanghai and Shenzhen Nanjing is not considered very competitive. This lack of competitiveness is a problem according to a large number of the people interviewed. Underlying problems are the problem to hire good personnel at the current wage rate and many employees consider Beijing, Shenzhen or Shanghai more attractive cities to work in.

5. Comparable factors for the four ICT clusters

The research and development (R&D) infrastructure and the educational system (defined as universities and polytechnics) are an important part of most ICT clusters. They serve as a source for staff for the urban ICT industry; as generator of new knowledge (although this role should not be overestimated); and produce new start-up firms. All the cities in this investigation stress the quality (and quantity) of their universities in their promotion activities to attract foreign ICT firms. ICT companies attach heavy weight to his infrastructure in their location decisions.

We have mentioned the importance of specialised labour markets for ICT firms. Labour shortages and rapid business expansion make that there is a great and increasing global competition for ICT talent. This group of professionals also tends to show a high job rotation. However, job-hopping is also one of the positive knowledge spillovers of a cluster. Linked to the presence of specialised labour markets is the quality of life in the cities, a point that will be discussed after this one.

The quality of life in the urban region—availability of comfortable housing, metropolitan ambiance, cultural conditions, green spaces, but also climate etc.— is an important condition to attract (or retain) staff to the city and thus for developing a cluster. Mitchell (1999) states that in the end the "pleasant places" on earth will be the main ICT centres might be somewhat extreme, but there is much truth in it. Most policymakers in the cities studied realise the importance of quality of life as general condition for knowledge-intensive activities such as the ICT sector.

6. Special and city-specific factors

We now like to point to some factors, which are also important for the development of urban ICT clusters, but are very specific for each of the four cities studied. We start with the importance of specific products produced, then look at the role of different demand conditions and of large firms and finally point to the importance of different policies pursued in each of the four cities.

In The Hague the ICT companies are mostly telecom companies. In Helsinki Nokia is dominating the scene producing telephones. Bangalore has the advantage that most of its inhabitants have learned the English language. In Nanjing the rapid economic growth in China and in particular in most Southern cities like Nanjing generates an enormous demand for ICT. Consumers continued to increase their demand for ICT with more than seven per cent per year in this populous city and provincial capital.

Although the specific products have some influence on the eventual development of the ICT clusters they are not so crucial as is sometimes suggested. In fact as long as there is a good subcontracting system and if complementary services are available ICT companies can develop everywhere. In line with Porter's argument in his work on clusters and competitive advantage (Porter, 1998), we found indications that the development direction of an ICT cluster is strongly related to the economic structure in the urban region. The most "heavy" users of ICT are corporate headquarters, financial institutions and the media industry (Saxenian, 1994; Hall, 1998). Particularly the rapid development of on-line banking and new media (on-line publishing, web-TV and radio) and entertainment services provide a mixing of the ICT sector and the banking and media sectors.

The presence in the urban area of a dominant strong ICT firm may have a strong positive effect on the cluster's development in a number of respects. First, it may give the hosting city an internationally known "ICT-image". Second, it provides for a pool of qualified labour, which makes the city attractive for competitors that may "buy" staff; third, especially if the firm has an open culture, it serves as important client for other ICT-related firms (suppliers). As they are active in international partnerships, they have access to global source of knowledge and technology, some of which is transferred in the local economy. Also, often a large firm spin-offs in terms of new companies that are started up by its staff.

All four cities benefit of the rapid general growth of the ICT sector, and actively seek to expand it with various policies. All four cities run programmes to enhance ICT adoption by firms in their city. In this way, they not only seek to improve the competitiveness of "old economy" firms (mostly SME), but also indirectly stimulate the ICT sector. Some ICT related policies cannot be influenced directly by urban policymakers but they depend on higher levels of government. Policies differ for the European and the Asian cluster. In Europe urban managers can formulate the following cluster-specific policies: starters policies, infrastructure policies, ICT adoption policies, inward investment policies and the development of business locations for new-economy activities. In Asia the advantages are usually tax incentives, the availability of cheap and serviced land and sometimes of links with existing research and development centres.

In the European cities the municipality financially supports start-up support in many ways, but the actual exploitation of the support policies is left to a specialised organisation: in Helsinki, support is given by public-private companies (Culminatum in Helsinki). The Hague runs for example projects to help SME make the shift to the information economy, by offering them free advice in the form of consultancy days. In The Hague, the Chamber of Commerce offers "starters packages" with general information, and the Polytechnic helps its own students with ICT-start-ups.

In India and China the policies focused on creating an enterprise friendly environment and on attracting foreign capital. They did use the locally available knowledge resources. The Bangalore municipal government started for example to formulate positive economic policies, also with respect to small and medium ICT enterprises in the city. Local government is also very active and developed for example its own ICT policy. It also looks for public-private partnerships for infrastructure development.

The cities studied all seek to expand their local ICT sector with marketing efforts directed towards foreign ICT companies. In Nanjing the municipal investment agency has designated ICT as spearhead sector. It offers US and Canada based firms general information on the region, and supports them to find a good location, and staff and tax reduction and subsidy possibilities. The organisation works on a regional basis. In Nanjing different policies are pursued at different levels of government to promote the city as an ICT city. The city has several policies to attract investment in the ICT sector.

7. Not significant factors for success of ICT clusters

We studied four very specific cases, which does not really allow a firm conclusion about the importance of the place in the urban hierarchy. The impression is that this factor does not significantly contribute to the success of the ICT sector in the cities studied.

Helsinki is the capital and the only real big city in Finland. That may have contributed to the development of this ICT cluster. However, it is certainly not enough to explain its success. The Hague is the administrative capital of the Netherlands, but certainly not the summit of a geographical hierarchy. It is rather one city in the Randstad well connected to a number of other relatively big cities.

Bangalore is only a state capital and the first concentration of technology industries in India, but not one of the most important cities in India. It rather happened to be the first technology centre in India. Finally, Nanjing is a provincial capital and an administrative city, but not one of the most important cities in China as far the competitiveness of the ICT sector is concerned. The conclusion is that the importance of the place in the urban hierarchy is difficult to prove. It seems every city has a chance and other factors are more important.

The economic cycle of boom and bust is important in the urban economy. However, it tends to hit different sectors at different moments of time and hence can hardly be a variable explaining the success of the four ICT clusters. In Bangalore the year 2001 was the first recession the ICT sector. Bangalore has weathered the recession quite well and even achieved some growth in their production (*Financial Times*, 6-2-2002).

8. Conclusions

The growth of the ICT sector is high, but the way different cities benefit differs widely. The clusters in our four case cities differ in character in many respects. An average cluster is diversified, with a varied mix of ICT business. With some exceptions, most firms in the studied clusters serve regional markets, as service providers or sale outlets.

Bangalore mainly depends on international markets and the Helsinki ICT cluster is more internationally oriented, dominated by the global player Nokia, but also telecom service providers (such as Sonera) and small firms are increasingly international. Many firms are active in R&D. The cluster in The Hague has a very different nature: it lacks a strong R&D base, but mainly consists of administrative headquarters of telecom operators that are active in the Dutch market. Nanjing has the most clear regional function.

Different trajectories of ICT sector development in cities may be traced back to national circumstances and chance factors. In Helsinki, for instance, early market liberalisation was an important trigger for the development of its cluster. The same can be said of Nokia's lucky shift towards mobile communications in the 1980s. In The Hague, the location of KPN, the former telecom monopolist, proved to be the engine of the cluster development in the late 1990s. In Bangalore the early investments in the aeroplane industry paid off, while Nanjing serves an important market in Southeast China.

It may also be concluded that for the future, a high quality of the urban living environment will be more than ever a precondition for ICT cluster development: because of the increased mobility (and scarcity) of ICT professionals cities need to be attractive to attract and retain talent, the basic resource of the ICT sector. This means that investments in, for example, the environment and cultural provisions, may have a high return on the long haul, as proven for example by Bangalore and Nanjing.

What more can cities do to strengthen their ICT cluster? A first thing could be to exploit local knowledge resources embedded in universities by stimulating industry-university co-operation. Furthermore, rather than attracting just any type of ICT-companies cities should make well-considered efforts to attract ICT-companies that fit their economic structure. Another frequent mistake is to focus one-sidedly on the construction of ICT-infrastructure and facilities, in the belief that once the infrastructure is there, economic activities will follow as a matter of course.

There is a risk that optimistic growth expectations lead to ill-considered policies. Salomon (1998) saw many regions make mistaken efforts to become another Silicon Valley by attracting high-tech industry without understanding the ingredients of real success. An example from the 1980s and early 1990s is the investment by many cities in teleports, assuming that in the 21st century these teleports would have economic relevancy comparable to airports and seaports. However, the one-sided emphasis on providing the infrastructure and technology and the lack of integration and economic judgment have caused many a teleport project to fall through.

A more promising strategy is the co-ordinated investment in infrastructure, technology and human capital. That is the strategy pursued by Singapore (Warf, 1995; Corey, 1991). That city-state has, in close co-operation with the private sector, invested on a massive scale in ICT-infrastructure as well as in people and training courses. The efforts were directed not only to stimulating ICT as an independent growth sector, but also, explicitly and consistently, to making capital of ICTs potential for enhancing the existing strong points of the economy: the trade function, the port and the financial sector. Integrality is yet another strong point: much money is invested not only in infrastructure but also in education, on the assumption that the presence of human capital can tip the scales in investment decisions.

To conduct an ICT-policy oriented towards starting entrepreneurs is another way for towns to strengthen the local ICT-sector. The local government can act as provider of generic support, such as (cheap) accommodation and venture capital, but also as purchaser of the products of new companies, or as broker and connecting factor between starters and both the existing private sector and the knowledge institutions.

It can be concluded that public-private co-operation is a prerequisite to develop effective and efficient cluster-policies. "Interactive policymaking" is needed in the marketing of the cluster, in attracting new firms, in helping start-ups and in all other aspects of cluster policies, to make optimum use of the knowledge and resources of the existing actors in the cluster. This also implies that civil servants involved in cluster policies need to be well educated and have sufficient "feeling" with the cluster.

REFERENCES

Aydalot, P. and Keeble, D., 1988. High technology industry and Innovative environments in Europe: An overview. In: Aydalot, P. and Keeble, D. (eds.), *High technology industry and Innovative environments: The European experience*, 1-21. Routledge, London.

Berg, L. van den, Braun E., and Winden W. van, 2001. Growth clusters in European cities: An integral approach, Urban Studies. 38-1, 185-205.

Boekholt, P., 1994. *Methodology to identify regional clusters of firms and their needs*, Paper for Sprint-RITTS Workshop, Luxemburg.

Corey, K., 1991. The role of information technology in the planning and development of Singapore, in: Brunn, S., Leinbach, T. (eds.), *Collapsing space and time: geographic aspects of communications and information*, Harper Collins, New York, 217-31.

Cooke, P., 1995. Regions, clusters and innovation networks, in Cooke, P. (ed.) (1995), *The rise of the Rustbelt*, UCL, London.

Dijk, M .P. van, 2003a. Is Nanjing. Is the concentration of ICT enterprises in Nanjing an innovative cluster? In: T. Brenner and D. Fornahl (eds., 2003), Clusters and innovations. Cheltenham: Edward Elgar.

——, 2003b. Government policies with respect to an information technology cluster in Bangalore India. In: *European Journal of Development Research*, Vol. 15, No. 2, 93-109.

Hall, P., 1998. *Cities in civilization*, Pantheon Books, New York.

Lazonick, W., 1992. *Industry clusters versus global webs*, dep. of economics, Columbia University, New York.

Malmberg, A., Sölvell O. and Zander I., 1996. Spatial clustering, local accumulation of knowledge and firm competitiveness, *Geografiska Annaler* 78b (1992-2).

Mitchell, W.J., 1999. *E-Topia: Urban Life, Jim—But Not As We Know It*, MIT, Boston.

OECD, 2001. OECD productivity manual: A guide to the measurement of industry-level and aggregate productivity growth. Paris.

Porter, M.E., 1998. Clusters and the new Economic of Competition, *Harvard Business Review*, No. 6, November/December.

Putnam, R.D., 1993. *Making democracy work: civic traditions in Modern Italy*, Princeton University Press, Princeton.

Renu, R., 2000. Autonomous IT firms in Bangalore city: Location rationale. Ahmedabad: Thesis for the postgraduate diploma in planning at the School of Planning.

Roost, F., 1998. Recreating the city as entertainment centre: The media industry's role in transforming Potzdamer Platz and Times Square, *Journal of Urban Technology*, vol. 5.

Salomon, I., 1998. *Telecommunications, cities and technological opportunism*, Regional Science Association.

Saxenian, A., 1994. *Regional Advantage: Culture and competition in Silicon Valley and Route 128*, Cambridge MA: Harvard University Press.

Srinivas, S., 1998. The information technology industry in Bangalore, A case of Urban competitiveness. London: DPU Working Paper No. 89, April.

Warf, B., 1995. Telecommunications and the changing geography of knowledge transmission in the late 20th century, *Urban Studies*, vol. 32(2), 361-78.

Winden, W. van, 2003. Essays on urban ICT policies. Rotterdam: Tinbergen Institute.

12

State-Level Financial Institutions and the Development of Urban Infrastructure: Case Studies from Karnataka and Gujarat

MEINE PIETER VAN DIJK
m.vandijk@unesco-ihe.org
IHS Professor of Urban Management in Emerging Economies at Erasmus University in Rotterdam, The Netherlands.

There is a clear need for investment in urban development in India, given its population growth and increasing urbanization. The 74th constitutional amendment promotes decentralisation and suggests strengthening and establishing State Level Financial Institutions (SLFIs). A number of State level Infrastructure Development Corporations have been created in India since 1992.[1] Their mandate is to provide financial assistance (loans and advances) to urban local bodies (ULBs) for financing infrastructure and services. They were often used to channel Central Government grant money to municipalities. Later also (HUDCO) loans were channelled through them. Private or semi-public institutions that have indicated that they are willing to finance urban infrastructure are IL&FS and ICICI.[2] Traditionally infrastructure finance organizations would be set up as government organizations. An important alternative would be to involve the private sector more.

Local government bodies should eventually gain access to capital markets. This requires improved municipal accounting and other reforms, which will be discussed briefly. Improving the accounting standards of all Indian local governments and developing uniform financial reporting standards will take years, however. Before discussing some issues related to the creation or upgrading of a State Level Financial Institutions we will first deal with the arguments to create one and the roles and attributes it should have. Subsequently the difference between a bond bank and direct issuing bonds by local governments will mentioned briefly. Karnataka's has a SLFI (KUIDFC), which could function as a bond bank. However, in Gujarat a SLFI should be created because at present no institution plays the role of an intermediary financial institution, issuing bonds on behalf of local governments.[3] Ahmedabad issued bonds itself in line with the FIRE approach, which is based on the approach chosen in the United States.

An alternative mechanism for financing urban infrastructure

The India Infrastructure Report has suggested certain steps for bringing in the vibrancy and depth in the debt market. The development of domestic debt markets requires an efficient and liquid market for government debt, which provides the foundation for a broader market for corporate debt. It also requires the development of institutions engaged in mobilizing long-term savings, especially insurance and pensions funds. Another alternative would be to go for credit enhancement through partial credit risk guarantees of the type now being offered by multilateral development banks. Further, it is necessary to continue to tap funds for international lending agencies and utilize these resources as seed capital for leveraging funds from the market through the creation of national level financial intermediaries.

What are the arguments to create a SLFI and what roles and attributes should it have? Different states in India have different institutions and hence may require a different set of actions. A SLFI should have the Project Development (P), the Project Management (M) and the Project finance function (F). The question is then: can these roles be combined? The optimal SLFI design may include a network of institutions covering the range of requisite roles. The best role-competency fit maximizes efficiency and available means. A number of issues should not be overlooked, however, and will be discussed briefly:

1. The need to create new institutions? To what extent do we want to create a new or rather use an existing institution?
2. What are the necessary financial and administrative reforms?
3. Should it be a private or a public institution?

A SLFI is necessary to improve the ability of local governments to access finance for urban infrastructure. It would link cities with the capital market. The key question concerning such SLFI is: can they be sustainable? Yes, if taken in the meaning of self-supporting. Another question is whether this should be provided through the government sector, or the private sector? We have distinguished five types of SLFIs, based on their main activities and the financing modalities provided. They range from acting as a single window system for the government to performing the role of a full-fledged financial institution. The different roles that can be adopted by the SLFI are described below in more detail.[4]

Five types of SLFI

1. *Single window system or clearinghouse*

Sometimes no special institution is created to passes on money to municipalities in the state, either from the state or central government. In such case loan funds for local authorities operate directly under the ministry concerned. This is the case in many previously British and French colonies and also in Indonesia. The funds are usually revolving funds capitalized from government budgets, occasionally with foreign aid supplements. In India, Andhra Pradesh Urban Finance and Infrastructure Development Corporation (APUFIDC) is an example of this type of SLFI, just like the Gujarat Municipal Finance Board (GMFB). It was created to channel Government grant money and loans from financial institutions like HUDCO to the ULBs for financing infrastructure and services.

2. *Project Preparation unit and linking with a potential financier*

In India we have examples of organization like Project Development Corporation of Rajasthan (PDCOR) type organizations: combining project preparation and seeking potential financiers. This type of organizations may be able to help structure projects in such a way that they become financeable. This requires taking care to meet the complex risks involved and also satisfying the complex risk mitigation requirements of different types of investors. At this stage these type of SLFI are experimenting with 'take-out-financing', which may be relevant in the present context.

3. *Municipal development fund*

A Municipal Development Fund (MDF) is an autonomous institution for the promotion of municipal infrastructure developed in a number of countries, including India (in particular in Tamil Nadu and West Bengal). Municipal development funds have the basic purpose of channeling more investment to urban infrastructure through municipal government and of strengthening the capacity of these institutions in the process. Municipal development funds also provide financing and contribute to institutional development by enhancing the financial and technical capacity of municipal governments.

To make a MDF successful they also need to adhere to the basic principles of sustainable finance. If the interest rates are too high to finance for example social projects, the money provided by the MDF should be blended with softer loans or grants (matching grants) as in the case of Brazil and Ecuador. National government also has a role to play. Local urban bodies are presently ill equipped for this kind of work, while the need for urban infrastructure is huge.

4. *Facilitating infrastructure financing through debt instruments*

A more mature financial institution can issue bonds to finance urban infrastructure such as bridges, toll roads, mass-transport systems. In that case it would not be the municipalities issuing, but some organization would do it for them, to pass on the money in the forms of loans for bankable infrastructure projects. This is the US Bond Bank, or the Dutch BNG model.

5. *Full repertoire of financial functions*

Such a financial institution would have different sources to finance its activities, work with the private sector and use a large number of financial instruments to serve one or several sectors of the economy. SLFIs can create a future market working in this more commercial way because they get to know the good ULBs and their repayment capacity. These would be the first ones in the future to benefits from the loans to be provided by them.

Key requisites of a SLFI

Key requisites of a SLFI are professional management and committed permanent staff with career opportunities. At present a lot of staff members are on deputation in different government organizations, which is not always the best formula to get motivated staff. A recruitment strategy should focus on highly professional staff which could be offered a compensation plan with market to market and performance linked increments.

A greater market orientation is desired in this sector and would lead to a more rigorous project appraisal procedure and selection process. State owned SLFIs would require operational independence and mandatory performance requirements. The advantage would be a close relationship with and better insights in the local governments, which would be the ultimate customers. It is important to balance state support with private sector development. In this sector the chances of developing lean cohesive professional organizations is much bigger.

A SLFI will not just finance infrastructure projects using traditional financial instruments, but could also get involved in developing projects in a commercial format, creating special purpose vehicles (SPVs) and selling the participation off at a later stage. They should certainly also play a role in the project clearance procedures and could copy the speedy procedures of the GIDB. The organization would have a multiplicity of tasks. The challenge will be to optimize the mix of government and private sector competencies by identifying win-win situations.

The future financial resources of a SLFI could come from very different sources, such as returns on equity and on the revolving fund activities, from arrangers fees and consulting fees, from technical assistance for multilateral financial institutions and from project management, or from selling stakes in SPVs.

Thus, there is a multitude of financial instruments and options for financing urban development. The emerging need is to evolve an efficient market mechanism wherein an appropriate institutional framework can effect intermediation between "surplus spenders" and "deficit spenders" in the economy and channels the funds into the infrastructure sector supplemented by an investor-friendly regulatory environment.

The private sector can be involved in many different ways in these SLFIs. It could start by nominating a representative of a private sector institution on the board of the SLFI. Subsequently joint projects can be undertaken. Finally, the private sector could become minority or eventually majority shareholder in the SLFI.

Intermediation: The FIRE versus the bond bank approach

Municipal bond markets are a growing market in developing countries. USAID (1996) intended to help Indian cities to prepare projects in such a way that bonds can be issued at the American capital market, using a partial USAID guarantee. In principle water supply, sewerage, roads, land development, education and health facilities could be financed under the Financial Institutions Reform and Expansion Project (FIRE, 1996). The formula is that each city would issue bonds itself. If the SLFI issues bonds it would not be the individual municipalities issuing, but a state level organization would do it for them and this is called the bond bank model. A more mature financial institution can issue bonds itself to finance urban infrastructure.

KUIDFC facts and opportunities

The Karnataka Urban Infrastructure Development Finance Corporation (KUIDFC) is since 1993 a 100 per cent government shareholding company with a wide mandate. Project development is usually subcontracted to private consultants and KUIDFC focuses on project management for the Central or State government, the ADB and the World Bank. Some financing of infrastructure in cities in the state from its own sources is taking place. However, the project management activities are not considered a means to the end of becoming a full-fledged financial institution. KUIDFC is doing its present tasks well and may be somewhat reluctant to pursue the project finance role much further. However, there are excellent opportunities for KUIDFC in this field. Given its wide mandate and its excellent relations with the State government KUIDFC could use its project management experience as stepping stones for a more important role, eventually becoming a mature SLFI. It has already knowledge of local governments, knowing how they financed and executed infrastructure projects. They have already a small revolving fund, which will develop rapidly in the next years and could be used to test the water and KUIDFC could easily get a credit rating and start issuing bonds.

State-level experience in Gujarat

There are important differences per state in India as far as legislation and existing institutions is concerned. An institution similar to KUIDFC does not exist in Gujarat for example. In this state the Gujarat Municipal Finance Board (GMFB) exists since 1979 and disburses primarily Central and State level grants and loans. It also helps local governments with their accounting and has substantial unutilized scheme funds. The Gujarat Infrastructure Development Board (GIDB) is the state institution to facilitate investments in advanced infrastructure such as ports, electricity and major roads. It is a high level nodal agency, falling directly under the Chief Minister of the state.

Project development and project financing activities are best suited to the private sector. This sector is better able to package and pool important projects, while the government could take the necessary policy reform initiatives. Government can also influence local governments to adopt the necessary reforms and to undertake the project preparation activities. Its role should be enabling, deploying strategies to ensure confluence of the financial institutions needs with the local government offerings.

Infrastructure development in Gujarat is hindered by limited borrowing capacities rather than limited fund availability. It can also be noted that restrictive municipal laws need amendment to allow private sector participation and capital. Finally, there is a lack of contract documentation for evolving project vehicles with private sector participation. There are a number of challenges concerning infrastructure in the state and the sector seems to be ripe with opportunities.

There is a certain sector preparedness in Gujarat. In this state the biggest city, Ahmedabad, has already gained experience with obtaining a credit rating and issuing bonds. Several toll roads have been built and private financial institutions are eager to get involved in infrastructure. The State government has prepared and launched an Infrastructure 2000 Plan, which gives a vision and a strategy. The state was the first one in the country to draft a BOT law and has experience with giving concessions to the private sector. Inherent is the entrepreneurial spirit, which can be proven by the number of private consultants and specialized NGOs in this field. A combination of roles by involving different institutions may be the best solution in the case of Gujarat. It would boil down to creating a SLFI network with for example GMFB as the capacity building institution and the private sector taking care of the project development and the project finance functions.

Necessary reforms at the Local Government level

Decentralisation requires more local revenues. However, the need for financial reform at the municipal level should be mentioned if municipalities want to qualify for loans to finance their infrastructure. Decentralisation is the trend (Van Dijk, 2000a), but the financial means need to be available at lower levels of government to carry out the tasks assigned to them are often lacking. In Andhra Pradesh the assessment of the financial capabilities of the municipalities led to important suggestions concerning the necessary reforms in the financial practices of municipalities (APUSP, 1998). A number of reforms at the municipal level are necessary to qualify for support in the framework of an urban infrastructure project in Andhra Pradesh (Van Dijk, 2000a). In general user fees directly related to the service provided are to be preferred over general taxes. To achieve repayment people need to perceive a relation between their payment and the service concerned. In the same way real repayment is better than repayment through deduction from future loans or grants. It requires the authority to raise and increase taxes and often necessitates a reform of municipal finances. Good governance requires a good basic accounting system and financial reporting. Local governments need budgets and to prepare them they need to take decisions where they want to go.

Good accounting increases transparency. Hence the population, the councillors, the donors and the ADB all want to see better accounting. That is exactly the reason why so many initiatives have already been taken. TCS (2000) has detailed the procedures for Karnataka. The Institute of Chartered Accountants of India (ICAI) plays a crucial role. Local governments need accounts that give the information financial institutions need. These problems can be solved however if an appropriate accounting system is designed. Detailed guidelines and have gone around. The assumption is that people will pay for water and other services if they know they will get the services and that they will get good quality services.

Conclusions: The major issues concerning infrastructure development

To what extent do we want to create a new or use an existing institution for financing urban infrastructure? The ADB lends money for infrastructure, but it wants to develop the intermediary institutions. Such financing institutions can become important actors because one creates structures, which receive responsibilities that the government no longer has. These institutions can pursue their own objectives and go their own way, which may not exactly be what the government had in mind when they created these institutions. This makes urban management again more complicated if only because the government has to negotiate for the conditions for financing infrastructure, which may be a tough game of identifying and allocating risks.

The question is whether each Indian state should try to create in the government sector the infrastructure project preparation, project management and financing capacity. The government sector remains bureaucratic and often does not think in financial terms. Often politicians influence the decisions and the government cannot afford to hire the necessary financial experts, because it cannot pay the salaries necessary to attract specialists. For that reason the private sector should be used more.

The Indian government creates and has created similar institutions, which will eventually compete with the private sector, unless privatisation is envisaged as we have recommended. In many states the lack of project preparation capacity is the real issue. If enough good urban infrastructure projects would be prepared, and real 'cost recovery' would be introduced, financing through the private sector, and through international capital flows would come forward, in particular in the present situation where the rate of interest is relatively high and state governments often provide guarantees for repayment of the loans or bonds. A situation that should not be continued once real commercial infrastructure projects are prepared as is happening in Rajasthan for example.

An important issue is what is the role of the private sector in infrastructure development? It is good to stimulate people to set up companies for infrastructure development in the private sector. We gradually became convinced that governments could not do a number of the things it did in the past. This certainly applies for complicated and expensive infrastructure, which also needs to be maintained afterwards. The government does not have the money, but should also not be involved heavily in infrastructure development, but rather create the conditions for private sector involvement. At the same time it may be necessary to strengthen and leverage certain existing government organisations, in particular if they monitor the process of private sector involvement.

The conclusion about private sector involvement in other infrastructure activities (telecommunication for example) is that the development of new technologies, combined with unbundling and more competition has led to much lower prices for consumers. The government would still play an important role as the supervisor, who would see to it that prices remain affordable, in particular for the poor and that the quality of the services remains at a certain level.

India will have to choose between the European and the US system of issuing bonds, although the country is big enough to try both! Because of the 74th Constitutional amendment local government and higher levels of government have become equal partners. To make that real, local governments need to have the financial information to allow them to be an equal partner. We suggest to use 'user charges', local taxes, inter-governmental income transfers and possible contributions of the private sector.

REFERENCES

APUSP (1999): *Project document.* New Delhi: DFID.

Dijk, M.P. van (2000a): *Summer in the city, Inaugural address.* Rotterdam: EUR/HIS.

Dijk, M.P. van (2000b): *Urban infrastructure development in India, incorporating the environmental considerations.* Rotterdam: Erasmus University, lecture.

Dijk, M.P. and N.G. Schulte Nordholt (1994): *Privatisation experiences in Africa and Asia.* Amsterdam: SISWO.

FIRE (1996): *Municipal bond market for urban infrastructure.* New Delhi: FIRE project, 1-23.

Roth, G. (1989): *The private provision of public services in developing countries.* Washington: IBRD-EDI.

Sinha, S. (1995): Return to equity, financial structure and risk contracting in infrastructure projects. In: *Vikalpa,* Vol. 20, No. 4, 11-21.

TCS-IHS (2000): *Final report in the framework of the ADB project Strengthening urban infrastructure.* New Delhi/Rotterdam.

UNCHS (1993): *Public/private partnerships in enabling shelter strategies.* Nairobi: Habitat.

USAID (1996): *Using the bond market for urban development.* New Delhi: FIRE Programme.

World Bank (1994): *World development report on Infrastructure.* New York: Oxford.

NOTES

1. A number of states have created urban infrastructure financing corporations or trust funds. In Tamil Nadu this fund has been created with support from the World Bank and functions at 'arm length' of the state government. In other states this is not yet the case.
2. IFCI also issued bonds, which would be used mostly for infrastructure.
3. A distinction should be made between the General obligation bonds, carrying full faith and credit of the issuing government and Revenue bonds, which rely on specified sources of revenues from facilities and services which are financed out of the bond proceeds and are usually issued by specific service or functional authorities. The latter (revenue bonds) require user charges to generate the necessary cash flow to service the bond.
4. A specialized financing institution can also securitize any cash flow from loans provided from a pool of successfully operating infrastructure projects. This would help to make available new capital to finance additional infrastructure projects submitted by municipalities. A well functioning MDF could and would do so to increase the flow of funds it can invest in infrastructure.

Contributors

Prasenjit Maiti [1971-] <pmaiti@vsnl.com> is presently associated with the Kolkata Environmental Improvement Project [as Member, Resettlement Implementation Working Group] <http://www.kolkatamunicipalcorporation.com/keip.html> funded by the Asian Development Bank and implemented by the Kolkata Municipal Corporation in association with the Government of West Bengal. Dr Maiti worked as Research Associate at the Council for Development Studies [Calcutta] on a UNIFEM project and was consultant to Shelter Promotion Council [India] where he worked on an urban development project funded by the Ministry of Science and Technology, Government of India [2003]. Maiti was on secondment as a Doctoral Fellow at the Institute of Federalism, University of Fribourg, Switzerland [1999] while employed as a Lecturer in Political Science, University of Burdwan, India [1995-2002]. He was promoted to Senior Lectureship after his Ph.D. [University of Burdwan, 2001] was awarded. Maiti taught Tourism Administration at Burdwan University and served as a resource person at distant education and teachers' training programmes sponsored by the University, Grants Commission [New Delhi]. He now serves as an academic counsellor to the Netaji Subhas Open University [Kolkata]. Maiti's maiden publication based on his doctoral research ["Problems of Governance in India since Independence: The Bengal Success Story" (New Delhi: Vedams, 2002)] developed from a German Research Council project on "Governance in India" [1997-98] coordinated by the Department of Political Science, South Asia Institute, University of Heidelberg, Germany. He was invited to the International Conference on Federalism 2002 organized by the Swiss Government at the University of St Gallen. Maiti served as reviewer [2001] for *Policing: An International Journal of Police Strategies & Management* [College of

Education, Division of Criminal Justice, University of Cincinnati, USA]. He is also referee for *Environment & Development Economics* [University of York, Heslington, York, UK] published by the Cambridge University Press and *Crime Prevention & Community Safety: An International Journal* [Perpetuity Press, Leicester, UK]. Maiti is Life Member of the Indian Political Science Association, West Bengal Political Science Association, Council for Political Studies [Kolkata] and the Indian Institute of Public Administration [New Delhi].

M.R. Biju <mrbijueditor@yahoo.com> is Editor, *South Asian Journal of Socio-Political Studies* <www.sajospsjournal.com> and Faculty Member, Post Graduate & Research Department of Political Science, Sree Narayana College, University of Kerala, India. Dr Biju started his career as Research Associate at the Institute of Social Sciences, New Delhi in a research project on the *Present Status and Future Prospects of Panchayati Raj in India.* After the completion of this project he joined the Department of Political Science at Sree Narayana College, Cherthala as Lecturer [1994]. He was transferred to the Post-Graduate and Research Department of Political Science at Sree Narayana College, Kollam [affiliated to the University of Kerala] in 1998. Dr Biju presently guides doctoral scholars of the University of Kerala and pursues postdoctoral research on the Politics and Administration of Urban Local Governance in India. He has written five books and nearly fifty research papers till date in edited volumes and journals such as the *Economic and Political Weekly, Mainstream, Indian Journal of Political Science, Indian Journal of Political Studies, Journal of Political Studies, Journal of the Institute for the Study of Developing Areas, Social Science Review* and *Southern Economist.* Some of his papers have been abstracted in the International Political Science Abstracts published from Paris. His areas of research interest include decentralization, democracy, electoral politics, foreign policy, environmental issues and hospitality management.

Carlos R. Hernández-Velasco [1968-] <0205896H@student.gla.ac.uk> is presently enrolled in a Ph.D. programme at the Department of Urban Studies, University of Glasgow <www.gla.ac.uk/departments/urbanstudies/index.html> [Scotland, United Kingdom]. Hernández-Velasco earned a Master of Architecture degree (focused on *Low-cost Housing in Developing Countries*) at McGill University, Canada (1998-2000). He worked as Assessor at the Urban Planning and Informal Settlements Offices at the Social Development Ministry in Aguascalientes, Mexico (2001-2003). He was invited by Masa Noguchi (McGill University) to participate in the implementation of a revolutionary concept called *Mass Custom Home®* by which clients may participate in the design of their own homes through this system. Hernández-Velasco has been teaching at the Cuauhtemoc University (2000-) and the Autonomous University at Aguascalientes (1994-1995) in Mexico. He also recently won a competition for a design of "Low-cost Housing for the Disable" launched by the Association of Architects at Aguascalientes, Mexico. This was the first ever contest of this sort in the country. Hernández-Velasco has delivered the conference "Low-cost Housing for the Disable" (2003) in Aguascalientes and "Mass Custom Home" (2001) in the 5th Congress of Latin American Architecture, Puerto Vallarta, Mexico.

Pragya Jaswal <pragyaj@teri.res.in> took her Master's Degree in Economics from the Delhi School of Economics [India] and subsequently worked on the policy trends in the automobile and oil industry. Her special focus has been on the environmental regulatory regime in the automobile industry and the use of market based instruments in the transport sector. Pragya worked on developing and suggesting strategies for promoting sustainable and environment friendly transport system in India. She has also been involved extensively in carrying out economic and econometric analysis in the transport sector, including demand estimation, fuel cost and price analyses. Pragya has a number of publications to her credit. She is presently working with The Energy and Resources Institute <www.teriin.org> [New Delhi] as a Research Associate in the Urban Governance and Infrastructure Area.

Kaushik Deb <kdeb@teri.res.in> is an applied economist. He has undertaken research assignments in a variety of energy and resource sectors, focusing on policy interventions in the transport sector. In particular, Deb has developed policy interventions in the transport sector to correct market failures in the overall context of liberalization of the Indian economy. He has worked closely with several government departments and policy makers in India, advising them on the design and impact of deregulation of public transport and strategies to reduce transport sector emissions. His efforts have concentrated on the need for, and the design of, privatization strategies for the transport sector. Deb has several publications to his credit, including four in refereed journals, and one book with Dr Shyamal Kumar Sarkar IAS, ex-Senior Fellow at The Energy and Resources Institute [New Delhi] and Member Secretary, West Bengal Pollution Control Board. As Area Convener of the Urban Governance and Infrastructure Area in TERI <www.teriin.org> Deb provides research direction and guidance, and develops research programmes in the transport sector.

Andrew Kirby <andrew.kirby@asu.edu> is Professor of Social and Behavioral Sciences at Arizona State University in Phoenix. He received his Ph.D. in Geography from Newcastle University and has been a faculty member at the University of Reading, England, the University of Colorado, and the University of Arizona. He has held visiting appointments at the Institute for Urban and Regional Development at the University of California, Berkeley, and at the Centre for Advanced Studies at Stanford University. He has also been a faculty associate at the National Centre for Atmospheric Research in Boulder, and recently a Residential Scholar in the ASU Centre for Urban Inquiry. His research on urban change and development has appeared in journals such as *Urban Geography*, *Urban Studies*, *Urban Affairs Quarterly*, and the *Journal of Social Issues*. His most recent books were *Pentagon and the Cities* (Sage, 1992) and *Power/Resistance* (Indiana University Press, 1993), and he has also published edited collections *Globalization and its Outcomes* (2004), *The Spaces of Hate*

(2003), *Geographies of Power* (2002), *Geopolitical Traditions* (2000) and *The Urban Growth Machine* (1999). He is currently working with two multidisciplinary teams, one on a National Science Foundation supported project dealing with neighborhood change in Phoenix, the other a critical examination of the human dimensions of homeland security post September 11. A board member for a number of international journals, he has been Editor for the Elsevier journal *Cities: An International Journal of Urban Policy and Planning* since 1995.

Ronaldo Munck [1951-] is Professor of Political Sociology at the University of Liverpool <R.P.Munck@liv.ac.uk> and Director of the Globalisation and Social Exclusion Unit <www.gseu.org.uk> in the United Kingdom. Munck was born in Argentina and received his Ph.D. from the University of Essex [UK] in 1977. He is a leading international expert on labour and development issues, having recently published *Globalisation and Labour: The New Great Transformation* [Delhi: Madhyan Books, 2002] to critical acclaim. Over the years Munck has published on Latin American politics, development theory and the contemporary relevance of Marx [*Marx @ 2000: Late Marxist Perspectives*, London: Zed Books, 2000]. He was recently asked to edit a special issue of the *Annals of the American Academy of Political and Social Science* on globalisation and democracy and to edit a series Transforming Globalisation for the progressive US publisher Kumarian Press. Munck has worked in Latin America, South Africa and Ireland before coming to Liverpool. In that city he has helped generate progressive community oriented research on urban development that resulted in the volume *Reinventing the City? Liverpool in Comparative Perspective* (Liverpool: Liverpool University Press, 2003). Ongoing local research projects are examining the issues of waste management and sustainable urban growth as well as the broader issue of social exclusion in the era of globalisation that are the focus of the GSEU committed to bringing together local research and global political issues and concerns.

Ruth Melville <ruth1@liv.ac.uk> is Research Director at the Department of Sociology, Social Policy and Social Work Studies in the University of Liverpool [England, United Kingdom]. Her principal methodological interests lie in the utilization of social science research in empowerment and change and adaptation of action research as well as ethnographic techniques to involve research participants in all stages of the research process. Ruth's specific research areas include community participation in regeneration and application of international development models and global perspectives to social exclusion in the UK. She is also committed to developing practical projects that encourage people to take a global view of their own realities, particularly focusing on traditionally excluded groups and areas in regeneration.

Hans Schenk <schenk1937@planet.nl> is presently associated with the Amsterdam Research Institute for Global Issues and Development Studies [AGIDS] <www2.fmg.uva.nl/agids> University of Amsterdam, The Netherlands. Dr Schenk specializes in urban planning, geography and sociology issues as well as urban issues in South, South-East and East Asia. His research projects include Housing and Urban Development in Hanoi and The Changing Role of the State in Urban Fringe Development in Asia.

Aaron Schneider [1971-] <a.schneider@ids.ac.uk> is presently associated with the Institute of Development Studies at the University of Sussex <www.ids.ac.uk> in the United Kingdom. Schneider completed his Ph.D. in Political Science at the University of California at Berkeley [USA] in 2001. His research interests include questions of political economy and the causes of and links between power and wealth. Schneider is presently engaged in questions of federalism, decentralisation, party systems, public finance, fiscal adjustment and budgeting. He is currently Director of the M.Phil. Programme in Development Studies and Convener of the Politics and Political Economy of Development, Social Science Research Methods and Theories of Development.

Mohammad Taghi Sheykhi <mtshykhi@yahoo.com> did his Ph.D. in sociology [gold medallist]. Dr Sheykhi is at present

Associate Professor of Sociology at the Social Science Department at Al-Zahra University in Tehran [Iran]. He is the author of 15 books in various fields of sociology, including urban sociology. Dr Sheykhi has carried out extensive research work in sociology, and written more than 15 papers in international journals. He has participated in international congresses and conferences to present his papers.

Kala Seetharam Sridhar <kala@nipfp.org.in> is currently Fellow at the National Institute of Public Finance and Policy in New Delhi [India]. She received her Ph.D. in Public Policy & Management from the Ohio State University at Columbus, Ohio [USA] in 1998 after having obtained an M.A. in Economics from the University of Mysore [India] in 1989. She also did an M.S. in Urban & Regional Planning from the University of Iowa, Iowa City [USA]. Dr Sridhar was Research Economist at the National Association of Home Builders in Washington DC [November 1998—May 1999]. She was Assistant Professor at the Indian Institute of Management, Lucknow during September 1999—May 2003 and later Associate Professor [June 2003]. Dr Sridhar has been at NIPFP since September 2003. Her research interests are in the areas of urban economics and policy, infrastructure and developmental issues. She has published her research in international journals including *Applied Economics, Journal of Regional Analysis and Policy, Review of Regional Studies, Urban Affairs Review* and *Economic Development Quarterly*. She also contributes regularly to leading business newspapers in India such as *Economic Times, Business Standard* and the *Hindu Business Line* with views on current policy issues. Dr Sridhar has received several academic awards, including the *Doctoral Dissertation Research Grant* from the US Department of Housing and Urban Development (HUD) in 1997 for her proposed Ph.D. dissertation. She was one of three finalists in the Eighth Annual Competition for the *Charles M. Tiebout Prize in Regional Science* sponsored by the Western Regional Science Association (WRSA) for her paper "Tax Costs and Employment Benefits of Enterprise Zones" [1994] which she was invited to present at Tucson, Arizona. Dr Sridhar was nominated by the University of Iowa for the *American Institute of Certified Planners (AICP) Outstanding Student Award* in 1992. She received the *Sir Hugh Daly Memorial Gold Medal* as well as the *Sir M. Kantheraje Urs Gold Medal* at the University of Mysore at the postgraduate level [1989].

Meine Pieter van Dijk <m.vandijk@unesco-ihe.org> obtained his Ph.D. in Economics from the Free University at Amsterdam in The Netherlands. He is Professor of Water Services Management at the UNESCO-IHE Institute for Water Education in Delft and Visiting Professor of Urban Management in Emerging Economies at the Erasmus University in Rotterdam [EUR]. Dr van Dijk is member of CERES [a research school] and the European Institute for Comparative Urban Research [Euricur]. He worked in developing countries since 1973, especially on the role of small enterprises in urban development and urban finance issues. Dr van Dijk also worked as a consultant for NGOs, the Asian Development Bank, the Inter-American Development Bank, the World Bank, different bilateral donors and UN Agencies. His recent books were co-edited with M. Noordhoek and E. Wegelin [*Governing Cities: New Institutional Forms in Developing Countries and Transitional Economies* (London: ITDG, 2002)] and H. Sandee [*Innovation and Small Enterprises in the Third World* (Cheltenham: Edward Elgar, 2002)]. Dr van Dijk's earlier works included *Local Economies in Turmoil* [London: Macmillan, 2000], *Government and Non-Government Interventions in Rural India* [New Delhi: Manohar, 2000] and *Developing Female Entrepreneurs in Zimbabwe* [Maastricht: Shaker, 2000]. His other books dealt with the informal sector in Ouagadougou and Dakar, small and medium enterprise development, industrialization, NGOs and the problems of the Sahel.

Willem van Winden [1971-] works as a senior researcher at the European Institute for Comparative Urban Research [EURICUR] and the Department of Regional, Port and Transport Economics, Erasmus University [Rotterdam, The Netherlands]. He has been involved in a number of international projects on comparative urban studies in the field of urban innovation and technology policy. Willem van Winden conducted several studies on the impact of ICTs on urban economic development, social inclusion in cities and urban governance, and published a number of books and articles in international journals in the field of urban and regional studies.